WILD THINGS
DON'T SWIM

WILD HORSES
DON'T SWIM

MICHAEL KEENAN

BANTAM BOOKS
SYDNEY • AUCKLAND • TORONTO • NEW YORK • LONDON

WILD HORSES DON'T SWIM
A BANTAM BOOK

First published in Australia and New Zealand in 2000 by Bantam

National Library of Australia
Cataloguing-in-Publication Entry

Keenan, Michael, 1943–   .
    Wild horses don't swim.

    Bibliography
    ISBN 1 86325 183 9.

    1. Keenan, Michael, 1943–   . 2. Adventure and adventurers –
    Australia – Biography. 3. Wilderness areas – Western
    Australia – Kimberley. 4. Fitzroy River Region (W.A.) –
    Description and travel. 5. Kimberley (W.A.) – Description
    and travel. I. Title.

919.414

Transworld Publishers,
a division of Random House Australia Pty Ltd
20 Alfred Street, Milsons Point, NSW 2061

Random House New Zealand Limited
18 Poland Road, Glenfield, Auckland

Transworld Publishers,
61-63 Uxbridge Road, Ealing, London W5 5SA
A division of The Random House Group Ltd

Random House Inc
1540 Broadway, New York, New York 10036

Edited by Jude McGee
Cover design by Liz Seymour
Cover and author photograph by Sal Keenan

Typeset by Midland Typesetters, Maryborough, Victoria
Printed and bound by Griffin Press, Netley, South Australia

10 9 8 7 6 5 4 3 2 1

I dedicate the book to my wife Sal, who courageously followed me step for step. In a remote gorge I silently put the rope on her and began a vertical cliff ascent, not knowing whether she would follow, or could — she did, with the camera strapped to her back.

Contents

Acknowledgments   ix

Maps   xiii

Foreword   xv

1. Mornington Station   1

2. Village on an Untamed River   22

3. Land of the Red Chief   44

4. A Handful of Wild Horses   66

5. The Saltwater Lady   97

6. Bunuba Land   124

7. Fragile   153

8. Wild Horses Don't Swim   175

9. The Tenacity of a Woman   191

10. Willa Cather's Inspiration   210

11. Desert Time Bomb   230

Epilogue   259

Author's Notes   265

Acknowledgments

Telstra made the expedition possible. So remote was this area in the Kimberley any serious injury would have been life threatening without a satellite phone. Telstra also later loaned a satellite telephone to Peter Brooking unconditionally and for an indefinite period. The first safari, in May 2000, could not have left Derby without it. The possibility of a serious accident 300 kilometres east of Derby with no access to communications is unthinkable. I believe this was a genuine act of Reconciliation on the part of Telstra and it should be acknowledged.

Konica donated all the films used during the expedition. Thanks to the quality of their films we have a wonderful cover and picture section.

Qantas assisted with discounts and waived overweight charges when the packsaddles and all the sundry equipment hit the scales at the Sydney airport.

Michael Cur of Mornington Station assisted with invaluable advice from start to finish and donated meat when we were right out of tucker. Michael owns and operates the most successful wilderness tourist camp in the west Kimberley. Old Mornington Bush Camp can be contacted on 1800 631 946.

Joe Ross from Fitzroy Crossing provided the inspiration. He has never wavered from his conviction that the Fitzroy River can be saved. He gave me many contacts.

Pat Lowe and her husband Jimmy Pike's love of the land prompted me to inquire more and more about the complex ecology of the Kimberley. Pat wrote *The Boab Tree* and her research for that book provided fuel for an interesting hypothesis.

Maria Mann was always a stalwart support. She assisted me with research and her enthusiasm for Broome and the environment was an inspiration.

Reverend Glenice Gill and her husband Don provided a second home in Broome, at the Uniting Church Bed and Breakfast. Glenice provided something that is very elusive when I am away from home – a desk to write on.

John Clegg, an archaeologist based at the University of Sydney, gave me a lot of assistance with my inquiries on prehistoric Australian rock art. Some of his conclusions may have triggered 'laser beams', as I call them in the book, but he always listened and was never afraid to give an opinion.

John McDonagh from Gunnedah was a living 'history book' when it came to the Liverpool Plains, where he was born. My only regret was this book didn't have room for his fascinating accounts of the pioneer days.

Mick Horne, who was recovering from a black snake bite when I wrote my notes walking along the banks of the Mooki, captured for me the sadness on the Liverpool Plains at the turn of the century, yet his enthusiasm and his extraordinary art gave me hope for the future.

Hesperian Press I would like to give a special thanks to, for kindly allowing me to publish an extract from *Northern Patrol* and a handful of quotes from Frank Hann's diaries, *Do Not Yield to Despair*.

Peter Brooking provided the horses and the bush skills. Pat Hurst, a well known identity from Fitzroy Crossing, a veteran stockman and a successful gold prospector at the turn of the millennium, said to me one day: 'I doubt if it can be done. If the speargrass and jagged rock doesn't beat you, the running bands of cliff will.' Peter Brooking did do it. Pathfinder and treasured friend, Peter is a man rare in the world today. He is mentor to so many young men he wouldn't know the count himself. Today (May 2000) he operates Millie Windie Pack-horse Safaris and can be contacted by telephone (08) 9191 1358 or fax (08) 9193 1596.

Sam Lovell – without Sam's briefing we would not have been able to cross the Lady Forrest and Precipice ranges. Every day we would rein in somewhere and Peter would say, 'Now, Sam said to look for . . .'.

George Brooking told the campfire stories and shared with us life on the stations in the days of the 'Kings in Grass Castles'.

Rob's knowledge of the wild fruits transformed the gorges into a lush supermarket. When Rob leaves to go bush at Millie Windie he doesn't even take a packet of flour.

Harold, Buddha, Lenny, Rachelle and **Priscilla** added a unique character to the expedition. To cross the mountains we had to part company and we missed them. When we met up again on the Adcock River the girls' laughter once again infected our moods, and Harold and Buddha covered our campfire coals with fish.

John Sinclair, the storekeeper from the village of Iminji, provided valuable local knowledge, including Aboriginal place names.

Murray and **Barbara Pipe** own and operate Topless Rentals. They always had a 4wd for me and never asked where I was going. I have a feeling they never wanted to know in order to sleep well at night.

Last but definitely not least, **Greg Kater** guided me through the morass of geological landforms in the King Leopold Ranges. He made me very thankful I was searching for ancient art and not compiling a geological thesis.

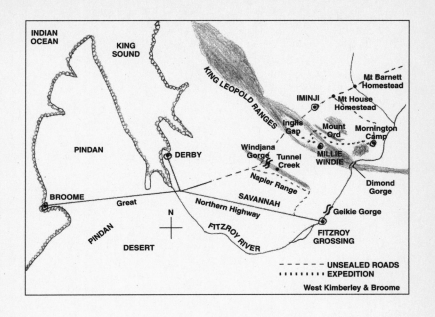

INDIAN OCEAN

KING SOUND

KING LEOPOLD RANGES

Mt Barnett Homestead

IMINJI

Mt House Homestead

Inglis Gap

Mount Ord

Mornington Camp

PINDAN

DERBY

Windjana Gorge

Tunnel Creek

MILLIE WINDIE

Napier Range

Dimond Gorge

BROOME

Great

SAVANNAH

Northern Highway

Geikie Gorge

N

FITZROY RIVER

PINDAN

DESERT

FITZROY CROSSING

- - - - - UNSEALED ROADS
· · · · · · · · EXPEDITION

West Kimberley & Broome

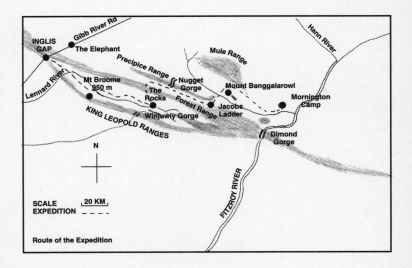

INGLIS GAP

Gibb River Rd

Hann River

The Elephant

Precipice Range

Mule Range

Lennard River

Mt Broome 950 m

The Rocks

Nugget Gorge

Mount Banggalarowl

Mornington Camp

Forest Range

Jacobs Ladder

KING LEOPOLD RANGES

Winjuwiy Gorge

Dimond Gorge

N

FITZROY RIVER

SCALE
EXPEDITION

20 KM

- - - -

Route of the Expedition

Foreword

Lennard valley, May 2000

I always woke to a piccaninny dawn. The long silent fingers of darkness receded slowly out of the Lennard valley and onto the slopes of the arid range. Each wakening was to a different sound, like the lead instrument on the next melancholy song. Sometimes it was the murmur and gurgle of the river or the scrape of the tea billy on rock and crack of dry twigs as the flames shot up from the strike of a match. Sometimes it was a horse snorting, and if I drowsed on between sleep and the rigours of the impending day, the long mournful howl of a wild dog would entice me to lift my head from the lump of clothes I used for a pillow and look through the mosquito net to the high spine of the King Leopold Ranges.

A year had passed since our first expedition into the King Leopolds and now I was back. The Bunuba men out tailing the horses had become my friends. Of Irish descent myself, I felt a kinship with their mythology and superstitions. More than that, I felt privileged to be in the homeland of Jandemarra, a legendary hero to the Aborigines. The warrior and his little band had taken refuge in the King Leopolds during the tragic years of resistance in the 1890s. Most fell to a bullet, some were hung and others died in jail. But they didn't die in vain. Jan-demarra's spirit lived on right across the Leopolds from Walcott Inlet to Halls Creek. The fight to save the King Leo-polds, one of the world's last great wildernesses, proved it.

The health of an ecosystem like the Leopolds is measured by the quality of its river, and if the river no longer flows according to the seasons the whole ecosystem will deteriorate or even die. When the corporate players in cotton irrigation announced a plan to dam the Fitzroy River at Dimond Gorge in the heart of the Leopolds, the battle lines were drawn. The dam proponents declared they would create the food bowl for south-east Asia. They argued it was a crime against humanity to let so much monsoon flood water reach the Indian Ocean. The dam opponents claimed one of the world's most fragile ecosystems would be lost forever. There was more at stake than the free flow of a river, they implored. Emptying more fresh water into the ocean than Africa's Zambezi, the mighty Fitzroy pushed a muddy tide of organic matter through the Buccaneer Archipelago – locally named the sea of a thousand islands – every wet. The consequences of severely reducing this seasonal influx were incalculable. What was known was that the Archi-pelago was one of the most unique and pristine marine envi-ronments in the world. No less sobering was the thought of the toxins that would leach and drain towards the ocean from the irrigation of the Pindan (arid old-growth forest) east and south-east of Broome. These toxins, residues from nitrogenous fertilisers and pesticides, would pollute the vast tidal mudflats between Broome and Port Hedland, where tens of thousands of migratory birds feed.

For me, however, the issue extended even beyond marine ecosystems and migratory birds from the Artic tundra. I grew up in a land of sweeping plains and sparkling rivers. For thirty years I rode at the bush amateur picnic races from Orange in New South Wales to Roma in Queensland. I saw a whole culture fade away in my own lifetime. In 1999 I lived in a land where I no longer belonged. Technology and progress had altered the landscape almost as drastically as the first pioneers had. I saw the west Kimberley sliding towards the same insidious economic malaise.

Wild Horse Don't Swim is a simple story to begin with, about a man and a woman wanting to do their bit to help save a river, which in turn would preserve the whole region. We decided to explore what alternatives the King Leopolds offered for economic development. We would search too, for something that had great value – an endangered mammal, stands of rare flora or something of extraordinary aesthetic value. The more we probed the more entrenched became our commitment. We met a multitude of people from linguists to horse breakers, from custodians of the sacred sites to Aboriginal artists, from hard-nosed tour operators to whitewater adventurers. In one way or another all stood to lose from a drastically reshaped west Kimberley, but the big losers from a dam on the Fitzroy were the traditional owners of the land. Like a scratchy old record rescued from the tip, it was the old colonial story all over again.

The packhorse expedition over the three ranges, the King Leopolds, Lady Forrest and Precipice, was not a picture postcard ride. My Aboriginal friends guided us through to a wilderness in peril, a brutalised land where the new custodians shook their heads in defiance and showed a set of ivory that would spark fear in a Spanish bullfighter. It was a land my Bunuba friends wanted back. It was a land where whitemen had failed. In 1999 it was a land the big corporations wanted.

My story is about a wild land and simple people. It is about the quality of our lives verse economic rationalism.

Michael Keenan, 2000

CHAPTER 1

Mornington Station

June 1998

It looked like a normal gravel road, a gunmetal grey in the harsh light fired by a Kimberley sun. Snaking through the stunted box trees, it disappeared over low ridges under coarse grasses, and then far in the distance it emerged again to reassure the driver. We would arrive at the camp with a couple of hours of daylight in hand.

The first tyre blew near the northern spur of Mount House. The 600-million-year-old mesa had been a landmark for the northern patrols here in the West Kimberleys, in Western Australia. Right up until World War II only packhorse expeditions ventured north of the King Leopold ranges.

When the second tyre blew Mount House still dominated the landscape. Bewildered, I shifted some luggage to find the tyre levers. This time it was not a simple matter of putting a spare wheel on – I had to remove the blown tyre from the rim. My wife, Sal, and son Nicholas watched with trusting confidence as I commenced a job that would take a roadside tyre specialist just one and half minutes.

The modern world hadn't only overtaken Australian cities in the past thirty years. The farming regions of New South Wales had also succumbed. My nearest little town, Binnaway, was closer in time to my house than Sydney University was to

the G.P.O. When I got a puncture in the truck, the plough or
the car, I took the tyre to town and my off-farm mechanic
changed it in the time it took me to buy the paper. So now,
as the heat bore down (for in the slate rock country there was
no such thing as winter) I realised I hadn't changed a tyre on
a rim since the mid-sixties. More sobering still, tyres designed
for four-wheel-drive vehicles were impervious to little levers
and forgotten knowledge.

Nicholas and I tried until our shirts were soaked in sweat.
Nick, my third boy, was a strong, lean young man, and when
his strength failed to pop the shredded tyre off the rim I realised we were in trouble. I had forgotten the knack. I looked at
Sal and there were tears in her eyes. To her the Kimberley was
like that part of Africa yet to be explored, and I caught her
looking fearfully into a landscape that had altered yet again.
Gone were the Darwin box trees and snappy gums. The
country had flattened out, arid and waterless under scrub vegetation I later identified as being predominantly prickly acacia
and Chinese lantern, also known as prickly bush.

'We can't shift if off the rim,' I finally admitted, straightening
and dropping the useless levers into the dust. 'You need the
big gear for these tyres.'

Nicholas was pale and speechless.

Sal spoke with a quavering voice. 'How many cars a week do
you think?'

'Oh come on,' I said feebly, trying to make light of it. 'Four
a day at least.' I walked slowly across the road in front of the
car. The fresh tracks suggested a better rate than four.

We waited. Every minute registered in the brain, like the
prick of a needle. To bolster confidence I refused to unload
and set up camp, but I couldn't stop Sal tying her plastic bags
over the leaves of some unlikely acacia for droplets of water.
The bags had been part of her very private preparations. Over
the years my treasured image of Sal had never altered. In my

dreams too it never changed. She was wearing a full-length frock with the hem covering her knees, just her delicate calves and ankles exposed. It was an image that never fitted into the outback. She was fearful of it and brave to be here in the first place. I winced secretly when I saw her with those plastic bags. At Derby I had unloaded water to make room for jerry cans of fuel. With reasonable roads, maps and it supposedly being the middle of winter, I had thought two gallons would be ample. It wasn't.

A spiral of dust drifted above the western horizon. The source of it was two angels in the form of hefty prison officers from Broome. On the way to some uninhabited gorge near the infamous Tableland track, they carried more tools than I had back on the farm. With an air of good grace and a few jokes, they slammed the new tyre on the rim. In addition they pumped up the other three tyres, explaining freshly graded roads in the slate country left broken stone points like daggers. For the first week scores of tyres were shredded, then the road packed down and returned to normal. We had simply arrived at the wrong time – two days after the grader.

With a bottle of Lehmann shiraz from Sal as a present, they left us feeling no more secure, without a spare and now aware of the dangers in the road. On the map it was another fifty kilometres to Mornington Station. The only way to go was slow, slow, slowly. Better to take five hours if necessary. At ten kilometres an hour a tyre would have to roll onto a steel spike to blow.

The road deteriorated to a track. There had been a turn-off and following the map I didn't see how I could go wrong. But late afternoon always accentuated gathering doubts and when we spotted another spiral of dust we stopped. This time the vehicle was coming towards us.

'We're okay,' I said quickly to the scowling black face. The Aboriginal driver was in a hurry. 'Just want to check with you. We on the right track to Mornington?'

He nodded and would have left without uttering a word if Nicholas hadn't got out and asked him where to find water if we had another puncture.

To my surprise the driver got out of his car. Late middle age, a paunch, there was a confident feel about the man. 'Water all along that range,' he said in a deep guttural tone, expansively waving his arm.

Nicholas looked out towards the distant range in the south, now a pale pink mounted upon the shaded blue of the savanna foreground. The sun was an hour from setting. 'Be dead before I got there,' he said gamely.

'No, no,' the driver rasped. 'Plenty water this side of old Glenroy for drinking. I thought you askin about big water. They flood all this country. Big dam comin.'

Some corporation or the government must have been planning to construct a huge dam. From where we stood the country didn't inspire any opposition. I thought no more of it and introduced Sal, Nicholas and myself. He said his name was Wallace. There were four others in the land cruiser, but he didn't introduce them.

'You going to the Derby Cup on Saturday?' I asked. Wallace seemed like an interesting character. That rugged face had seen a lot. I wanted to have a drink with him.

'Yeah, we go to races.' For the first time he smiled.

'We'll have a drink there,' I said enthusiastically.

He nodded and smiled again, just a little. In his eyes there was a glint of incredulity. I didn't understand then.

We had left Derby that morning. Despite being about to enter the new millennium in eighteen months' time, Derby, in Western Australia's far north-west, still seemed like a frontier town. I had momentarily forgotten where we were, in our luxury hotel room that morning, and thought the three hundred and sixty kilometres to Mornington Station would be an easy drive. It must have been the effect of the luxurious surroundings. As a family we always tried to avoid expensive accommodation – farmers don't have that sort of money any more. In fact, if you were a New South Wales farmer in 1998 you were lucky to get out the front gate to go anywhere, let alone the Kimberley. So Derby had sounded like a place to be avoided for people on my budget. They said the blacks were bad. Thieved everything from the roofracks. To be safe you had to stay in a compound. So we did. The boab trees and the three-metre-high protection fence around the rear of the hotel created an image of a bankrupt east African country.

The plan was to go to old Mornington Camp and get aboard a tour to a gorge that looked stunning in the brochure. It was called Dimond Gorge and the Fitzroy River flowed through it. We intended to camp three nights and on the second day try our hand at one of the fishing holes. After that it was back to Derby via the famous Windjana Gorge.

Despite some of the rumours about Derby, I was looking forward to the Cup race day. Way out here in Australia's far-flung frontier I was seeking a bit of nostalgia. For thirty years I had ridden as an amateur jockey in north-western New South Wales.

I had been launched as a rider by my father, a man who was deeply ambiguous about Aborigines. The worst denunciation of a place that he could deliver – be it a hospital or a hotel – was 'It's not fit for blacks.' Yet underneath there was a warmness; he often had horses with Aboriginal trainers. My father introduced me to a colour on the Australian racetrack now gone forever. On race day black and white communicated, often as though no barrier ever existed. At the New South Wales town of Gilgandra on the Castlereagh River I recalled a horse called Border Ghost. I didn't know who owned the gelding, but that horse must have won ten races on the tight-turning Gilgandra track, and when his grey surged to the front the old wooden grandstand would nearly collapse under the weight of cheering black people. That old track by the Castle-reagh buzzed with an atmosphere that would have sent famous poet Banjo Paterson scrambling for his pad.

Those black trainers were good, too. Not since I dismounted the last horse I rode for an Aboriginal trainer had I observed such guile. I remembered one day being legged aboard the favourite in the feature race of the day. The big black trainer had a wild look – the horse was even money. Couldn't pay the rent on those odds, he grumbled. I trotted around to the barrier, but there was a delay. Presently the stipendiary steward's car left the enclosure at high acceleration. The steward slammed shut the door of the car, marched up to me and accused me of being 'dead' on the favourite. Told me to win or else. I broke from the barrier three in front and was never headed. Back in the enclo-sure was a grin like a busted watermelon waiting for me. The trainer had got four to one by abusing the steward from the thick of the crowd for giving him the top handicap weight and claiming he had no choice but to pull the horse up. The bookies fell for it and the crowd shied off the horse. He was only fined one hundred dollars and he'd laid a thousand. Yes – I would meet them all at Derby, I thought, like old times.

As the car lurched and swayed, the darkness focusing our eyes on a rocky track in the headlights, the thought of going to the Derby races elevated my spirits. I knew by the silence that Sal and Nick had other things on their minds. Locked in four-wheel drive, the wheels spun in washed-out creeks. Passing through old Glenroy Station the lights picked up the aban-doned homestead and some feral-looking cattle that were camped in the remains of the garden. Another hour and the tall grass and thickening timber threatened to consume the track itself. Branches scraped over our roofrack and leaves rustled along the windows. Still, we had come out here for adventure. Routine living can get so comfortable.

Ostensibly it was to be a camping holiday. Sal and I had

driven across the continent via Longreach in Queensland and Katherine in the Northern Territory. Nick could only get a week off from his job in Sydney and had flown to Broome to meet us. He was excited about seeing the Kimberley. The region conjured up images of Australia's last frontier. For Sal and me it was a little more. In 1983 we had flown up to inspect Drysdale Station in the northern tableland country of the Kimberley. At the time, we were wondering what the potential might be for a tourist operation. We'd had some tourism experience already, having run a packhorse tourism outfit in the Warrumbungle mountains. Using my highland farm as a base, I used to take up to eight people on horseback to a high camp in the mountains, where we stayed overnight and hobbled out the horses. Features of the ride were Aboriginal cave sites and stunning views. In due course properties changed hands and access became difficult and in 1983 we were looking to move on to another project.

The trip, however, had been ill-fated from the beginning. I got food poisoning in Darwin, the agent's plane was delayed at Kununurra for repairs, and while we waited I made some inquiries. White ants had reduced the station improvements to near rubble and none of the cattle had been yarded for eight years. The agent apologised. He hadn't been out there and we were the first requesting an inspection. He very sportingly suggested we accompany him to Jubilee Station in the west Kimberley, on the Fitzroy River, knowing we didn't have anywhere near the finance for this renowned cattle station.

Our first experience of the west Kimberley raw frontier was at the station aerodrome. The manager greeted us with a drawn revolver. I had wished I had seen the snake first! Disturbed on the runway by the plane, a king brown had made an escape bid in the wrong direction. That this bloke had managed to shoot it with a revolver was impressive, but we were more interested in why he had a revolver slung from his waist in the first place. It was surprises like these that made the Australian outback so colourful. Almost everybody was a 'character' – distinguishable at once in a crowd.

We had stayed two nights on Jubilee Station. The agent had referred to it as the 'island'. The river forked into two large channels. The huge flood plain in between offered some of the best bullock-fattening country in Australia.

Returning from the 'island' we'd stopped at the channel crossing, stretched our legs and drank out of the river.

'You'll be back,' the manager had said to me. He never smiled. He was totally devoid of any humour.

'What do you mean?'

'You've just drunk the water. Legend has it if you drink from the Fitzroy you will return and die here.'

It was sobering stuff, especially when a humourless man related it. And now here we were – 5000 kilometres from home, heading for the Fitzroy. It was Aboriginal legend, of course. In tribal days they didn't have to leave the watershed of their beloved Fitzroy.

Around nine o'clock we saw the flicker of a light ahead. It came and went, like someone walking through the forest with a lantern. Soon the light was steady, and as we drew closer we saw a floodlit shed. Another minute or two and we could see people seated and hear that old familiar noise of the outback night – the power generator.

Dave, the manager of the camp, welcomed us and explained the camping arrangements. We decided to leave the tent until later and join some of the guests at the longest dining table the three of us had seen. We were thirsty and old Mornington Camp had a bar.

Thinking the nights might be cold, I had brought the big canvas tent. Putting up a tent in the dark is difficult enough. After a couple of drinks this one proved nearly impossible. But after ten minutes of fumbling and a bit of grumbling, the tent was up, rubber mattresses and sleeping bags inside, and Sal had a fire alight. There was never any wood at camping sites, so I had brought my own in discarded wheat bag sacks, enough yellowbox sticks for twenty cooking fires.

In the bush, tent up and fire alight is drinks time. We even had little fold-up seats. Sal had bought them at Roma in Queensland, some years before, when we were forced to move our cattle north onto feed and camp with them. She always said a good red wine should never be drunk standing, or you drank it too fast, and on that occasion the red wine was our only comfort. I knew Nick preferred a beer to a Barossa shiraz, and had thought a dry week wouldn't do him any harm. But when we saw the bar and a few young blokes about, I wasn't very hopeful.

Two hours after normal dinner time I cooked some steak on the tripod griller and Sal pulled a salad from somewhere and buttered some bread. It wasn't long before we snuffed the kerosene lanterns. Not sleepy, Nick wandered over to the bar but soon the cold air settling down on Annies Creek hunted him out of the bar and into a sleeping bag beside Sal and me.

None of us was too eager to stir early next morning. The fire-lighting paper was in the grass, wet from dew. I could have pulled pieces of bark from the trees and found dry leaves tucked under exposed roots along the creek bank. Instead, we pulled on our thickest jumpers and walked over to headquarters for breakfast.

In every sense old Mornington was a wilderness camp. The charm was the wild itself. You couldn't see far through the timber and you knew that beyond the last tree within vision was a wild land. Headquarters resembled an old hay shed, with an iron roof and cement floor. At the southern end the shed was closed in and a partition partly closed off a pantry room and cold storage area. The kitchen was open air with plenty of working space. A large urn provided hot water and there was a portagas stove.

We were last up and last for breakfast. The tour operators along the creek were packing up the breakfast items and would leave any minute for one of the gorges. Some young backpackers were eager to get started too, but it looked like they would burn every newspaper collected since they arrived on Australian soil before they got a breakfast fire going. Yet they were unruffled and I admired their sense of adventure. During my time in the Kimberley I was to see very few young Australians venturing into their country's most beautiful corner.

We sat down to bacon and eggs at the long table. Dave, who would be our guide to Dimond Gorge, was on deck and casually informed us the 'Troop Carrier' was departing for the gorge at eight-thirty.

Also seated at the long table were two middle-aged couples and a couple of young men. We would all ride together in the Troop Carrier. I got talking to a retired farmer and Sal to his wife. Nick had already met the young blokes the night before.

Dave announced it was important we left on time. There was a scatter for cameras and Nick and I helped Dave carry the canoe paddles from the pantry. The Troop Carrier turned out to be a battered old Toyota and its appearance told a story or two about the track even before we'd all climbed in.

And we thought the track into the camp was rough! We discovered there was a lot to learn about the landform of the King Leopolds and adjacent ranges. Sometimes we moved slower than an old man could walk and all of us gripped whatever we could lay our hands on. Away from the low-lying camp and onto the first elevated ridge, we gazed out upon vast undulations of wooded savanna flanked by red ranges to the east and south. In the sharp morning light the cliffs stood clear against the blue, as though painted by an artist not yet skilled at rendering diffuse light. As we crawled south the ranges began to close around us. In the vertical fissures and pocket gorges the fan palms broke the red the way glaciers broke the distant blue of mountains in other lands. In awe, we looked out onto green glaciers on red mountains.

Two hours later we stopped in a dry watercourse walled in by steep rocky slopes, except for the access valley. Behind us loomed the impressive cliffs of Fitzroy Bluff. Where was the river? I was later told that two engineers on holidays had returned to camp and asked where the river was. It never occurred to them the water in the wet had to run and it would gravitate to the lowest point.

Taking a paddle each, we walked along a strange rock floor, marble-like and a blood-red colour. At times it was tortuous and rounded, like the fresh gore of a large animal's intestines. It was caused by annual raging white water, laced with sand. In flood this river obviously carried millions of tonnes of sand.

A hundred and fifty metres downstream the canoes were beached on a strip of white sand. Before us lay a great stretch of water to a narrow rock channel. We all knew without asking that what we had come to see was through there. Nicholas, sensing the mystery, was first afloat and paddled off. An ex-oarsman, he sent the fibreglass canoe skimming along as though there was a silent outboard attached. He was through the gap before anyone else had launched.

Then he was back, arms waving and his voice echoing. 'Take a look at this,' he yelled. Seconds later he was gone again.

Sal skipped into a canoe and I got a scolding for fumbling around like an old man. 'As the sayin goes,' my old blackfella mate used to croon, 'the fruit doesn't fall far from the tree.' Sal was medium to tall, not as dark as her son, but she had given him her lovely long legs and arms. Remove the sophistication enforced upon all of us in middle age and they had identical temperaments. My jockey genes had only passed through to one son – James, our eldest. James and I were not all that small. It was just that Richard, Nicholas and Tom had grown into big men, and they dwarfed us.

We all followed, probably a little quicker than we might have planned. The expectation silenced everyone. All of us unskilled, I heard the splash of missed strokes, and high up in the red cliffs I heard the call of a strange bird. Not just any bird cry, it seemed ancient, from a world long gone. Through the bottleneck we glided into perhaps the world's most ancient natural waterway. Everyone breasted their oars and the canoes half turned in a gentle breeze. Nicholas had beached his canoe on a shelf and was standing tall on a rock projection.

People often said it was wrong to compare. I didn't know how else you took a line. This wasn't the river canyons of Utah, in the United States, three thousand feet below the plateau rim, exposing seams of colour in the rock from verdant to white. It was nothing like that. Because when I reached down with my hand for a palmful of water to drink I knew the Fitzroy River here was unique. Months before I had bent to do the same in Utah's Green River. Luckily my guide saw me. I had forgotten.

'Drink that and you'll be sick over the raft for the next five days,' he had said sharply.

Unlike Green River, the Fitzroy River would enter the twenty-first century still pristine. The world's last great river was still flowing freely to the sea. Some small rivers still did – the Franklin for example – but they were streams compared to the Fitzroy. In the wet this mighty river had the second largest flow in the world, greater than Africa's Zambezi and second only to the Amazon. A meter at Willare Bridge, near the mouth, recorded 31,000 cubic metres per second. The debris carried far out to sea through King Sound provided the food base for the teeming millions of fish of the Buccaneer Archipelago and surrounding waters, the greatest diversity of marine life anywhere in the world. The Archipelago remained unspoiled.

The canoes split up. Dimond Gorge was nearly large enough

to be described as a small harbour. For two kilometres a 20,000-tonne vessel could sail at full throttle. All of a sudden there was so much to do, in so little time. The retired farmer was a tanned, fit looking fellow, and with his wife sitting demurely up front he set off for the rapids at the far end. We were well into the dry season, and the river flow had ceased. The dry jumbles of rocks were rapids in name only. Sal and I didn't go. It was Dave who told us what to expect if we went all the way. We opted instead for the waterfall, which turned out to be a mere trickle. The other couple came with us. We chatted on occasions and compared notes on our observations, but the aesthetic grandeur was overpowering. There was little to be said, for we all had the same profound feelings about the gorge.

Nicholas paddled the entire gorge, clockwise. The other two young men didn't go far: they hauled their canoe out at the top end near the bottleneck and spent the two hours swimming and sunbaking. If it were not for hunger sharpened by the exertion of paddling, I think Dave would have been left on his own until mid-afternoon. Not that he would have minded. When we did reassemble he put his billies back into the coals and made the tea. It was a bring-your-own-lunch arrangement.

The dry watercourse had heated up while we were away in the canoes and thoughtfully Dave lit the fire in the shade of a river gum. The smooth boulders were hard seats, but with a mug of hot billy tea in hand no one complained.

'I hope you got all the camera shots you wanted.' Skilfully capturing the mood for impact, Dave dropped a bombshell. 'Because it's all going under water. Where we stand now will be forty metres deep.' He paused for a moment, taking in the stunned expressions, like a spokesman for a jury might after delivering a verdict contrary to the one anticipated. 'The concrete dam wall will fill the gorge through which you have all just paddled. Water will back up for one hundred kilometres and cover more than 100,000 hectares. They reckon cotton growers from back east are turning the heat on and the state government's behind em all the way. She's the biggest irrigation project up here since the Ord.'

In the east Kimberley the Ord river dam project had been completed in the early 1960s. For decades it had seemed to be thwarted with insurmountable problems and only in recent years had produce from the irrigated lower flood plains substantially lifted the local economy.

Everyone had the same stunned expression. The bloke who walked to the little waterfall with Sal and I threw his tea out; tiny wisps of steam lifted from rock shaded from the sun. A youthful face for a man old enough to have white hair, he suddenly looked gaunt. The retired farmer stared between his legs to the rock and began to wobble one of his boots, with the heel acting as pivot. His wife said, 'Oh heavens,' and glumly stared ahead, not seeing.

The two young men were motionless, leaning forward with elbows on knees and lips parted, as though they hadn't heard. Nick had taken his sandwiches and a fishing line back to where the canoes were beached. The other woman – the wife of the snow-haired man said, 'What bastards!' She had been jovial and bright throughout the morning, and I'd thought she might step better on a dance floor than the rounded cornices of Diamond.

Sal responded sharper than all of us. 'What wicked news,' she said. 'I am just devastated. I never thought I'd stand before a bulldozer, but I will to stop this.'

Back at the camp Nick and I dragged in some logs from the bush for a campfire. I was determined not to let the news spoil our stay at Mornington.

'I never thought I'd become an environmental activist,' I said to Sal as I stacked the logs. I was feeling edgy and busting for a drink. 'I'll fight them all the way to the bulldozers.'

'Dave said he's going to chain himself to a tree when the dam starts filling,' Sal said, not joking.

'Too late then. We have to beat them before they load the cement.'

'I don't believe they'll do it,' Sal said, busy in her little camp kitchen. 'There'll be a bigger fight over this than the Franklin and they managed to save that.'

'They wanted the Franklin dam to generate power. It's more politically sensitive than cotton.'

'Why is that do you think?'

'Because governments want power to kickstart industry. When governments want something everybody looks. When private industry wants something we run in and buy shares.' I didn't know whether I was right or not, but it sounded good.

With the camp in order the three of us strolled the one hundred metres to headquarters and the bar. We all needed a couple of drinks before dinner. On the way we passed the English backpackers. I loved hearing English women speak. Their accents reminded me of little old ladies, quaint and almost apologetic for speaking at all.

'How did you get on today?' I asked in passing.

'Oh wonderful,' the fair-haired girl replied. 'Had a splendid swim and we saw a crocodile.'

'Think you might have done better than us,' I said and meant it. She hadn't had her day dampened.

Mornington owner Michael Cur had a disarming manner and a quick calculating eye. Over a period of more than thirty years hundreds of stockmen had taken orders from him. In mustering camps the bland-mannered factory worker would rarely be sighted. Raw individuals, veteran loners and boss haters – those were the ingredients for an Australian outback cattle camp. You led like a general or got left behind to wash the enamel plates. On Mornington Michael was the general.

I ordered Emu Bitters for the three of us and following a bit of small chat the dam issue came up.

'I'm taking a couple on a scenic flight in the morning,' Michael said. 'Room for you too. For fifty bucks I can show you exactly how far the water will spread.'

I hated flying low over rugged terrain, but this was an offer I couldn't decline.

'I hate the things,' I said to Sal and Nick.

'You won't get me in it,' Nick said soberly with a look of finality that weakened my confidence further. I was glad Michael was ferreting at the bottom of the fridge in an attempt to satisfy someone's order for a soft drink.

'He's a top bush pilot,' I said. 'Does scenic flights every day. I just haven't been up in the little ones for a long time.'

'You can't think of not going,' Sal said. 'It will be much clearer in your mind once you've seen it all from the air.'

The can empty, I felt better. If Sal and I were serious about fighting the dam, Michael's knowledge was the very first weapon. Besides, I liked the frank approach the man adopted towards everyone and I felt everything he said was thought provoking. Even about his business he was open, honest and interesting. Low cattle prices, absence of suitable staff and crippling transport costs had forced tourism upon him. The rough edges on the learning curve now rounded off, he had begun to like it and saw it expanding into a business more profitable than the cattle enterprise ever was.

One drink led to another and before long I realised I might fall into the campfire cooking the steak if I didn't leave. Alcohol exaggerated the mental images and for most of us alcohol-induced writing is a failure. However, some authors and even famous playwrights had been known to write their best lines following a stimulating evening, fired up with alcohol. Drinking coffee for the sobering effect later in the

evening, and with a campfire smell and smoke in the eyes, I
wrote a few lines myself: 'The Battle-painted Warrior'.

Above the still waters, long sweeping ledges
strike jagged scars on red rock,
and like impetuous strokes from an artist's brush
the pale trunks of several bloodwoods cling
precariously like a lover's prayer.
Yet standing straight and alone and with blackened bark,
a wild mango fits the warrior,
and across his chest the thin lateral branches of mountain
    bloodwood
mirror the battle paint of white ochre.
Such is the spell of Dimond Gorge.

With a dry mouth I went to the waiting four-wheel-drive at
six-thirty next morning. There were three others, but I wasn't
interested in them. I wanted to get it over and done with.
Michael drove us out to the airstrip and without preamble we
threaded our way into the plane through the cockpit. I took
the other pilot seat, having in mind to tell Michael where I
didn't want to go. There was no doubt he had a flight plan
and he moved me to the back seat.

Soon after take off we rapidly gained one thousand feet on
the altimeter, which I could observe between the front seats.
Levelling out, Michael tracked the long valley through to
Dimond Gorge, and nearing the Lady Forrest Range he lifted
another five hundred feet, and level with the gorge's southern
entrance he banked across a gaping precipice and let the plane
gravitate gradually into the canyon. The distance above the
water was still respectable and I wondered what he meant when
he half turned and mumbled something about a closer look at
the river. Over the bottleneck we glided and I waited for the
thrust of the engine to take us up. Instead we went down and
Michael opened the throttle.

I had always said that jockeys were hooked on adrenaline or our nerves would never have stood the precarious perch on a horse's wither travelling close to seventy kilometres an hour. But I never felt I was staring death in the face. Till now – we were flying with the angels and the devils were sprinting along the river's edge. At one hundred and sixty kilometres an hour we buzzed the wild river at water level and Michael weaved to miss outspreading branches of the big native plums. Seconds only it took, but when he pulled the stick my heart was racing and my mind spinning. Recovering quickly, I looked down again at the red landscape and saw a canyon so long it cut through the rock and tree studded plateau like a gash of dark dried blood on a fresh carcass in the sun. For miles, vertical cliffs rose from the water. That meant rock shelters. I already knew there was a lot of Aboriginal rock art in the Kimberleys, a region famous for an ancient rock-art style known as Bradshaw art. The art was named after Captain Joseph Bradshaw, who had visited the Kimberley region and discovered the painting in the late 1800s. At the time he described the paintings as having an Egyptian character.

Dated recently as 1500 years old, with some contentious dates up to 17,000 years old, the origins of the Bradshaw artists remained a mystery. Some archaeologists were quite certain the art was from a cultural period overtaken by the most recent cultural period, represented by the Wandjina figures. Others were less sure. The art was so distinctive and so different it did suggest that a race of mystery people had lived in the far north-west, who had left no more clues to their existence than their rock art.

Discovering the spread of Bradshaw art across the Kimberleys was still on in earnest by archaeologists. It was hoped some hidden gallery, somewhere, would disclose some evidence of where these people came from. The canyon below was encouraging, I thought.

Banking into the west Michael began to explain where the water would spread. On the north-western horizon Mount House was no more that a thin blue line.

'Right up past Mount House,' he said, raising his voice above the engine. 'A hundred kilometres long. Two hundred and eighty thousand acres under water.'

Looking down I saw some horses. I pointed them out, then was instantly sorry I'd opened my mouth. Down we went again and we must have nearly flown up their arses. I didn't say anything again.

Back at the camp I poured a whisky and left the money on the bar. Nick had made friends with a man old enough to be his grandfather, and he and his wife invited all of us to go fishing with them in one of the Fitzroy holes. That was the wonderful thing about Mornington Camp. Everybody mingled.

I couldn't go fishing. It was Thursday – the day the Derby mail plane did its weekly drop and on board would be my new spare tyre.

I might as well have gone for all the use I was. Michael ended up putting the tyre on the hub. He was a master of many trades.

On Friday we left for Windjana Gorge, where the Lennard River slices right through the Napier Range. By road it was about 250 kilometres from Dimond Gorge in a westerly direction.

The track out seemed as good as my road to the mailbox. So much is a state of mind. On our way in we were pushing through those unexplored jungles of Africa and now it was any time-worn farm track.

At Windjana Gorge we were totally unprepared for the beauty of ancient seabed reefs that form a canyon nearly two hundred metres deep. Freshwater crocodiles basked on the sand everywhere, absorbing the winter sun. We encountered several groups of walkers on the bush track and I was struck by the effect this place had on everyone. People spoke quietly, almost whispering, as though they were being guided through a medieval cathedral and were duty bound to a form of reverence.

Reluctantly we dragged ourselves away. It would take two days to thoroughly inspect Windjana Gorge.

In Derby we booked into the hotel, and I bought a race book. Last race on the program was for Aboriginal riders – a stockmen's race. I couldn't wait. It was going to be like the good old days! I dragged Sal and Nick up to the racecourse for the pre-races lunch. They were both good sports about it, but given the choice they would have been sitting on Cable Beach at Broome. I paid for the three of us at the course entrance and went looking for the bar. It only sold soft drink. If I wanted alcohol I had to pay to go through another gate, which seemed quite expensive compared to what we were used to paying to enter New South Wales country tracks.

I realised at once what it was. The race committee had to look after their patrons and curtail the availability of alcohol to some sections of the community. It was probably a responsible decision, reflecting the reality of alcohol abuse and the likely consequences. Looking carefully around there was barely an Aboriginal in sight. At Gilgandra they had disappeared: the ones I had known in the great days of the pastoral industry were probably dead and the younger generation had left. But here in Derby there were more black people than white. Something was wrong – terribly wrong. The community was divided, just like the river towns in far western New South Wales. It was very sad to realise this division was now Australia wide.

It was an excellent day's racing and I backed three winners. I wished I had a horse there myself. I missed riding. I didn't go to the races much anymore, knowing the racing saddles were not in the boot and my name would never again be raised on the semaphore board. Plagued by injury, I had ridden in my last race in 1995.

Nick flew home from Broome and Sal and I went on to Darwin to see our youngest son, Tom, who had a job in the racing industry at Fannie Bay. A week later we returned home to freezing weather and sodden paddocks. On the way home Sal and I talked at length about the fate of the Fitzroy. Neither of us had ever been part of an environmental cause before. I often sounded off about Kakadu mines and development projects like Hinchinbrook on the Great Barrier Reef, but I hadn't done anything. We both made a commitment to fight this one.

2 Village on an Untamed River

October 1998

Four months later I booked myself onto a flight to Broome. Over and over, Sal and I had talked about the dam and what could be done. I had the notion that if I could assemble a packhorse expedition across the King Leopold Ranges following the wet (the northern monsoon was between December and March) I could search for ancient art and encourage the local Aboriginal people to get into packhorse tourism. I felt success on either project might inspire the people of Western Australia to apply the brakes on their government to stop the dam. They might convey to the government that they wanted a free-flowing river and that the west Kimberley community should be given time to elevate the region to a significant tourist destination. In the face of mining, the Kakadu tourist industry had already been affected, which may have proved to be a great shame, for all mines had a finite life span, whereas tourism may endure for the life of a civilisation. In the west Kimberley the mounting threats were even more dire. Once massive irrigation projects sprawled across the landscape and irrespective of the nature of water application, people would know large quantities of fertiliser and some pesticides were entering the soil. Any form of intensive land development was repugnant to tourists bent on fun holidays in the sun, wilderness camping, trekking and exploring. Dam the Fitzroy, commence massive irrigation projects and the tourist industry, sadly, would flounder. Lost would be an enormous opportunity. Marine biologists were warning that the Great Barrier Reef could be dead by the year 2020 – to lose the natural wonder of the Fitzroy would be just as catastrophic.

Of course, my dream was full of idealism. If you had Irish genes in your blood you were never happier than when there was a fight. For decades my father had employed a drover on the stock routes and when there was conflict with other drovers over feed he became larger than life. My uncle reminisced over the war until he died. He fought the Germans, the British (when they interrupted his sojourns with an Arab girlfriend), and the Japanese behind the lines in northern New Guinea. 'Get yourself in shape Mike,' he had said to me one day in 1965. 'Your turn's coming. See the world and have the time of your life.' Well, perhaps this was my turn at last.

I had undertaken a lot of research and had followed up some contacts before I left. From the Australian Heritage Commission I received a summary on geology, vegetation and government proposals in regard to national parks and registered rock art sites. They were most helpful, faxing me twenty-five pages of material. Tracking through various government departments I was given the name of a whitewater enthusiast from Fitzroy Crossing – Joe Ross. Rumoured to have a better knowledge of the Fitzroy River than anyone alive, he seemed the logical first contact. Joe had agreed to meet me.

With two days to go I had one loose end: the rock art itself. I needed to talk to an archaeologist – an expert on the subject. I had contacts at the University of New England, but it was out of my way. I telephoned the faculty at the Sydney University and John Clegg, head of the department, offered to put a little time aside. It was the day before my flight to Broome. I arrived in a taxi from the airport.

With my shoulders pinned back under the weight of a huge backpack and an overnight bag in one hand and a briefcase in the other I entered the old quadrangle and climbed a narrow staircase to John Clegg's office. Clegg had a kindly disposition and I felt at once I could talk to him on the same level. I explained as briefly as possible the mission I had set myself.

'I am not much of an idealist,' he said quietly, watching me closely. 'How does a western districts farmer get embroiled in this?'

'It's simple,' I said. 'I love Broome. I hope to retire there one day. But I won't go there if it's to become another cotton-growing district.'

We chatted for a few minutes and when we got to the topic of the Bradshaw art he said he had never worked in the Kimberleys and he thought the style of the Kimberley Bradshaw dynamic figures had been fully documented. I explained I was aware of that in the King Edward River region, but that my informants claimed the style had never been documented along the Fitzroy River system, three hundred kilometres due south.

'Suppose you find the art. What do you hope to achieve?'

I liked his directness. It forced me to analyse what I was doing. 'World Heritage listing of the King Leopolds and adjacent ranges.'

'State governments don't have to recognise heritage listings.' There was a flatness in his tone that was unnerving.

'What if it involves the Commonwealth government?'

'I think the state government would have to put the case in the first instance, and in the second, the Commonwealth government might be reluctant, particularly if the area's rich in minerals.' He paused and poured boiled water from a jug into a coffee plunger. 'But despite all the hurdles I am going to give a little encouragement. I have just returned from the Coa valley, in northern Portugal. At a place called Foz Coa, archaeologists in 1994 discovered petroglyphs that resemble Palaeolithic cave art. The finds sparked considerable concern in archaeological circles as there was a plan to construct a dam, flood the valley and provide water for a multi-million-dollar French–Portuguese hydroelectric scheme. By 1995 the issue had become so politically volatile the Portuguese government lost the election and the valley along with the petroglyphs has been saved.'

I wasn't sure that a proposed dam would have quite the same effect in Western Australia but I was grateful for that bit of news. The Portuguese experience surely proved attitudes were changing. Perhaps the people of Western Australia would decide the Fitzroy issue if we could put the case.

I always relaxed a little with a mug of coffee. The archaeological world is one of invisible laser beams, set to trap the ignorant and unwary. It's a science but widely exposed to speculation and romanticism and the custodians are forever watchful, on guard. With John Clegg I raised the matter of site recording and triggered one of the beams. He frowned and seemed troubled. When he spoke his demeanour had altered considerably. It appeared the Australian Heritage Commission would not be very pleased with me. There were protocols to observe. There was the question of qualifications.

There was no need to record any of the sites anyway. For my purposes, I required photographic evidence. I also had the exclusive option of never disclosing the geographic location of a site to anyone. The great lure of archaeology was the intrigue and the very nature of the mystery could be extremely destructive. In 1983 Mary Leakey reported in an article in *National Geographic* that the Tanzanian rock art sites she and her husband had recorded in 1951 were defaced beyond recognition. In 1987 archaeologist Henri Lhote also reported in the same magazine that the famous Tassili paintings in Algeria were being removed with chain saws. In the Warrumbungle

Mountains, in New South Wales, I had observed deliberate defacing for fear of a sacred site claim. We had sadly entered an era where ancient rock art may have become the new 'buried treasure' for some of society's pirates.

John concluded the discussion with some very interesting dates. A French archaeologist, Francois Bordes, had reported stone tools in association with the bones of an extinct elephant at Flores, which is on the Australian side of the Wallace line in Indonesia. He had assigned a date in excess of 200,000 years. John went on to tell me an Australian archaeologist had proposed Homo erectus got to Flores in crude boats or crossed on the backs of elephants. Elephants could swim continuously for four days. It seemed a wild call and John gave no indication either way. Archaeology was a science of agonising speculation and it was a tortuous road to credibility.

The success in Portugal occupied my thoughts for most of the long flight to Broome. Maybe the pendulum was at last swinging towards sanity, and the human race was slowly and painfully beginning to realise a clean green planet was not simply the key to survival, it was our only hope. In Australia, perhaps the west Kimberley would become the frontline for a whole new approach to the fundamentals of existence in a world lost and directionless under the yoke of profit-driven technology.

I arrived in Broome about midnight the next day and spent an uncomfortable seven hours in a tiny backpackers' room full of people on a hot night. I got a taxi out as soon as possible and spent a long day going from one coffee shop to another, waiting for the bus to Fitzroy Crossing. It was at the bus terminal that I experienced another taste of the racist polarisation in northern Western Australia.

I had arrived early, burdened with luggage and planning to read for a while. Alone, too, was an elderly Aboriginal man. Out of politeness I asked him how he was and we got talking. He was returning to Fitzroy Crossing following medical treatment. Eager to talk it emerged he was a veteran of the up-river cattle stations. Feeling hungry myself I asked him if he would like a hamburger. It was obvious he couldn't undertake the long walk back to Chinatown and he had no food. I was only gone half an hour and he minded my luggage. When I returned a lot of people had arrived, as departure time was drawing near. With the old man were now two younger men in their thirties. I gave him the hamburger and greeted the young men. They stared at me, hostile, and the hamburger was snatched away from the old man. They harangued him in their language and I watched him cringe.

In 1967 the Commonwealth government had passed legislation to enforce the equal payment of wages to Aboriginal men employed on Australia's top end cattle stations, which included the Kimberley. Although well intended, the outcome was disastrous. For Aboriginal people the stations were more than locations of employment – they were homes to all the dispossessed tribes. It was station life or one of the missions. The camps were little more than refugee sites, but the people remained in touch with the land and were not exposed to alcohol. When the equal wages decision was announced most of the people were moved off the cattle stations, with no regard to where their next home would be. The little village of Fitzroy Crossing became a refugee camp for more than 4000 people. The living conditions were dreadful.

Exposed now to alcohol, without employment or prospects, the community at Fitzroy Crossing rapidly degenerated. The town became infamous throughout Australia for litter. It was said beer cans and bottles lay a metre deep on the road leading to the river hotel. White society looked upon the town in contempt and many laughed about it. For a long period of time neither the state nor the federal government did much to assist the top end Aborigines, who were lost and in despair following this second wave of forced removal.

When the overnight bus from Broome pulled off the highway for this little town I knew nothing about it. I had heard about the beer cans, that was all. It was one-thirty in the morning and when I stepped off the air-conditioned bus it was into a dark oven. Everyone felt it. People stumbled around looking for luggage, the task made more difficult by the sudden exposure to the heat. We were four hundred kilometres east of Broome and nearly 2000 kilometres from Darwin to the north-east. I felt sorry for those going to Darwin, for they would sleep fitfully through the early hours, travel all next day and then half the following night.

I waited for a while, watching dark-skinned people file into several vehicles. I had been the only white person to disembark the bus. There was to be a vehicle to meet me. I had arranged that in Broome. It dawned on me after a few minutes it was up to me to find the vehicle. 'You looking for me?' I asked a white bloke seated in a landcruiser.

'I'm not sittin here to enjoy what's left of the moon,' he said gruffly. I noticed his head almost touched the roof of his vehicle, so I swallowed the words on the tip of my tongue. 'Throw yer stuff in the back,' he added.

'And welcome to Fitzroy Crossing,' I muttered, but at the rear of the vehicle.

I got in and we drove down the main street. It was wide, no shops, no trees, just houses.

'Seen Joe Ross about?' I hate silence.

'I'm his father. What do yer want him for?'

I didn't respond immediately. I couldn't believe it. 'I'm a writer. I want horses for an expedition into the Leopolds.'

'Yer too late. It's too bloody hot now for horses.' He paused and shifted his hat forward onto his brow. 'Joe doesn't touch the bastards, anyway. He's a canoe man.'

'I don't want them until next autumn. I've come up to make arrangements. Joe knows who's got them.'

'How many yer after?'

I shrugged. 'Twenty or thirty.'

'Shit!' He adjusted his hat again, this time pushing it back. The word seemed to hang in the vehicle and with each second I felt more stupid. Then he began to talk, as though I wasn't there. 'The people I pick up off that bloody bus from Broome.' He paused and must have reflected on what he said. 'Never mind me. I meet that bus every night. But seriously, I don't know about any horses around here. The cattle industry's stuffed.'

Peter Ross was his name and when we arrived at the backpackers' he helped me carry my gear in and showed me the dormitory layout. He owned the business and ran it with a manager. It was one of the few original buildings left in the village. It used to be the post office.

The old timber floor creaked with every step and I wondered what separated couples would do, because no one could sneak around this place – not even an ex-jockey. My dormitory, the male one, was a big improvement on the previous night in Broome. It had a bedroom feel about it and there was plenty of room to spread my gear out – I needed enough room for about three people.

Several hours later I got into some work clothes and had a peep through the window. The white glare had already gathered on the grey box plains, which lay under a thick mat of old grass, burnt tinder dry from six months' exposure to the sun. Within minutes my clothes felt sticky. I was keen to orientate myself and I headed directly for the river. There was a bit of flood debris to step through and the crumpled cane grass obscured the ground in places. Reared like a bushie, my 'checking out' procedure was routine from childhood. I rolled old logs to see what insects were about and if I spotted an old sheet of iron I loved to see what was living underneath. Once I had to run for my life, having disturbed a two-metre-long mulga snake with a nest. They could move fast.

But the only life here on the riverbank was grasshoppers. The sun had sucked dry any sign of moisture and the grasshoppers were feeding on the sap of some grass that grew near the water. Like all rivers subject to the wet season the Fitzroy had a high bank, a narrow terrace of silt and river trees below and a final steep drop into the water. The water stretched for more than one hundred metres to a sandy beach, equally as wide. There was no flow in the river. Upstream the channel of water tapered off to sandbars and downstream there were ribbons of narrow water passages, followed by a broad expanse filling the river from bank to bank. Above the low banks on either side majestic river eucalypts walled in the great watercourse, obscuring any glimpse of the hot dry savanna beyond.

Underneath one of the big red gums I found a tiny patch of short grass still not burnt brown by the pre-monsoon heat. My initial gaze across the water had missed the Aboriginal woman, who was standing hip deep in the water holding a fishing line. Across the wide sandbar and into the shade I saw another adult and some children.

Stripping off to my underpants and using protruding roots like a bush ladder I climbed down to the water and dived in. It was pleasantly cool and refreshing, washing away the sleepless hours of the bus trip. Slowly I swam across to the Aboriginal woman and asked her what she was fishing for.

'Get them catty with meat, cut em up for bait and yer catch the bream.' She didn't take her eyes off the water. It wasn't sport fishing. The kids waiting in the shade were probably hers and fresh fish for lunch depended on her skill. I swam away, knowing my presence would scare off the fish. When I got out the heat swooped on me, like a bath towel fresh from the drier. If I had to live here the river would be essential to survival. It was Sunday and I wondered vaguely if anything in the village would be open. Back at the guesthouse the manager, Rod, said there was a roadhouse with a few groceries. It was about six kilometres away.

I had only walked a kilometre when I saw a horse standing over a crudely made iron trough. It was a gelding and he looked terrible. Other horses stood away, tucked up and hollow as well. I left the road, climbed over the fence and discovered the trough was full of water. The gelding hadn't moved. He just stood there, like a propped up carcass.

Horses are like people in some respects. Happiness is reflected in their skin and the way they look at you. These horses were sad. The paddock was covered in grass, knee deep. I broke off a handful and crunched it up in my palm and gently blew the husk away. Most of the seed and awn had penetrated the outer layer of skin and stood out like miniature quills. This was a variety of the dreaded spear grass. It was unusual to find it on river plains. The land must have been severely over-stocked in the bad days, wiping out the good fattening grasses, bull Flinders and Mitchell. Spear grass had to be burnt every two or three years for stock to survive on it.

Back on the road an Aboriginal woman soon picked me up. She dropped me off at the roadhouse where I purchased a few basic items and was about to start walking back when I spotted the Englishman. He gave me a lift back.

Later in the day the temperature was a shade under forty-four degrees Celsius. On the tablelands at home the mercury had never been seen above thirty-eight. There was no escape, and I joined a bloke about ten years older than me out on the back lawn under a bauhinia tree. We sat in old wooden chairs. His name was Pat Hurst. He was a white man who had spent most of his life in the Kimberley.

'It's mule country,' he said. Quietly spoken he had a slightly shrunken frame under weathered skin. Like so many of the older bushmen he was humble about his knowledge of the country, gleaned and stored from decades in the saddle.

'There'll be no mules,' I said, feeling despondent at the prospect of facing rough terrain without them. Mules got their strength and hardy feet from the genes of the donkey. Donkeys were at home in the mountains, but horses evolved on the great plains of Eurasia and on the evolution time clock had not had time to readapt to the hard surfaces inherent to mountain ranges. In the King Leopolds they would not be very suitable.

Only a year before Sal and I had tacked onto a mule ride into Arizona's Grand Canyon. The group leader had given a long lecture and his final words were, 'If you are scared of heights for God's sake pull out now.' No one did. We mounted, fifteen of us, and with a combination of excitement, fear and awe we went single file over the rim into the world's deepest canyon. At each switchback the mules' front legs went to the trail's edge before turning. They were taught to do that so that their rumps didn't thump into the rock wall, and at that instant the riders peered down the shoulder into a void of space and rock all the way to the distant ribbon of the Colorado River. Every mule negotiated the 3500-feet descent without a single stumble and on the return journey we all marvelled at the strength of those wonderful animals. They carried us back up the canyon wall as though we were no more than gnomes on their backs. In the Leopolds they would barely raise a sweat.

'You'll need to feed the horses up a bit,' Pat said earnestly. 'Put some guts into em.' He paused and looked away into the thick green foliage, bordering the river. He was retired and did odd jobs for the guesthouse. 'Where're you headin out from?'

'I don't know until I see Joe.' Joe Ross was still away.

'Be Leopold Downs or Millie Windie, I reckon,' Pat said.

'Hard country is it?' The heat was bearing down like an invisible weight.

'If the spinifex up in the limestone doesn't stop you the cliffs will,' Pat said wryly. If there had been a trace of a smile I would have felt a little easier. He saw the look on my face. 'The old blokes will remember the stock trails. What you don't want is a great big wet this summer.'

'What about the main spine of the range?'

'If yer headin north to the Adcock River country you gotta cross three ranges from memory. The Leopold Range is the most southerly. The whole area's a tangle of rock.' He paused again and leaned forward, elbows on his knees and eyes to the ground. 'No one been in there for years. Pidgin and his warriors used to regroup in there. The gins would gather the food and nurse their wounds.'

Pidgin was the name given by the whites to Jandamarra, a black warrior alive in the 1890s who had been the only Aboriginal fighter to effectively coordinate his warriors to use guns in defence of their territory.

The heat peaked and dropped off a tiny bit while we yarned. About four o'clock Pat said he was going to have a rest. Everybody did at this time of day. The tourists in the guesthouse had been on their backs for a couple of hours. It was a nice old home, raised a metre or more above the ground to allow air circulation, and with two living rooms and a verandah the guests could keep to themselves if they wanted to.

It was tempting to have a sleep and escape the heat for a while, but my time here was short. I was thinking about the river again when Rod, the guesthouse manager, eased his way down the wooden stairs to the lawn. He was struggling to wake up.

'That's the worst of afternoon sleeps,' I said.

'It's night livin this time a year,' he said and gave me a hangdog look.

'Is there a river track down to the pub from here?' I asked. 'I want to meet as many of the locals as I can while I'm here.'

Rod sat in the chair vacated by Pat. He had a slightly bemused expression. 'You'll run into em down there,' he said at last. 'I'm havin a barbecue later. Better see if you can make it back.'

'I'm not planning to get drunk down there.'

Rod was one of those people who have the knack of saying a lot without opening their mouth. 'It's pre-monsoon time. We all swelter and drink.'

It was a pleasant walk through the white river gums, Leichhardt pines and rain trees. A breeze had sprung up from the south-west, dropping the temperature a degree or two. All along the way the bare-eyed cockatoos squabbled and shrieked, an endless racket, and I left the track and pushed through the cane grass to the river's edge to get a better look at them. It seemed their noise was in response to the presence of humans – a number of people were swimming and more still sat on the beach under makeshift shelters. Clearly, the river was the lifeblood for this community and if ever they were to lose the river they would fade away and the country would contract to a dried-up lake girthed by the skeletons of dead trees.

Fifteen to twenty people were spread along the bar and around the tables at the Crossing Inn. I fancied a rum. It opened the pores of the skin in the heat, which was why rum had always been so popular in Queensland. Unfortunately it only took a few nips to open up the brain 'pores' as well. I settled for a beer.

Spotting an aged black man with white hair sitting on his own I sat down opposite him at the table. He said his name was Butcher and he painted traditional art for a living. I had difficulty understanding his accent and two women sat down and interpreted for me. They told me he had a gallery in the village. Soon the whole table was full, and at first-hand I began to hear some of the stories I had read about. I listened to the women for a long time and was glad to shout them a couple of drinks. One older woman seemed badly scarred from the child-snatching era. The authorities would simply arrive and seize the 'mixed-blood' children. The scene would be a child screaming in hysterical fear and the mother sobbing her heart out. Some women died prematurely, heartbroken. It was federal government policy at the time in Australia.

Two or three decades earlier Native Americans were subjected to similar treatment, but the children were united with their families for holidays and allowed to return home upon completion of education. In Australia, these children were separated from their families forever, growing up not knowing where their parents were or, if they had been taken young enough, *who* they were. In consideration of political problems in Australia at the turn of the century the comparison to Native Americans' experience was important because America didn't have a stolen generation. Furthermore, the political criteria that endorsed the forced removal of children from their parents struck fear into the indigenous society and eroded self-esteem. Perhaps the policy did more to damage Aboriginal culture than we could ever evaluate and may have gone part of the way to explain why American Indian culture appeared to be in better shape in the year 2000.

I couldn't wait for the barbecue. I had drunk a few beers by this stage and needed to eat something. No one was in the hotel restaurant and with the sun still up I wasn't confident I'd get a meal. Luckily the hotel manager wanted his dinner early too, and the kitchen took our orders.

'Seems early,' I said to him. 'Dinner before dark.'

'I gotta grab a feed now before the mob move in.' He had Chinese features and was one of the strongest and most robust men I had ever seen.

'Don't seem to be many about.' I paused, taking in the strength and fierce appearance of the man. Perhaps only a man like this could manage a pub in such a volatile environment. With his hair neatly tied back in a pigtail he could have been a warrior from the Boxer Rebellion, in the days of the imperial kingdom.

'When do they come in?' I asked. 'The mob.'

He shot me a warning look. He didn't want to talk to me and I didn't blame him. Fitzroy Crossing was deeply scarred by racism. Only three years before a white gunman had opened fire on some local Aboriginal families swimming in the river and sitting around barbecue fires. In the dark the bullets were fired at random and only vehicles were hit, but the shooting caused hysterical panic. For months afterwards the village lay surrounded by a wall of fear and distrust. In the eyes of many I would be just another white man and a stranger. More suspicious still I was mixing with the community. Idealistic humanitarian stirrers had proved destructive to Aboriginal society. In the mind of the man sitting opposite I was probably just another do-gooder.

'They buy it by the carton and drink outside,' he said shortly.

'Drink through the night,' I persisted, more a comment than a question.

He didn't respond and we ate our meal in silence. I had fish; so delicately served I could have been in a Broome restaurant. Before I left the table I asked him for a carton of stubbies. I wanted them for the barbecue.

He looked at me again, trying to fathom me out. He'd finished his meal and was about to leave. 'You camped somewhere?' he asked. It was not aggressive. I felt he was about to give me some advice.

'The guesthouse.' I knew everyone called it the backpackers', but such a nice old home deserved better.

'That's where you want to do the drinking. Stay here and they'll get it off you.'

When he arrived with the carton I knew I had to get cracking and ring for a taxi. There was no telephone book.

I was thinking about how I might get the number when the oldest of the women I had been talking to before dinner appeared. 'My friends want to meet you,' she said graciously. 'We got a nice spot around the corner and down on the river. We got lots to tell you. They never met a writer before.'

The sweat was trickling down my sides again and the telephone information service hadn't found a taxi number. I seemed to be floating on alcohol and heat. I followed her, wondering what else to do. I couldn't carry the beer a mile. I let her steer me away, thinking I'd only be a few minutes.

They were all women, mostly young. In the gathering gloom, when angular and hard features are softened, they looked demure, all squatted on the dead grass. Aboriginal people could tuck their legs away and sit upright for hours. It seemed to be impolite to stand. Through the trees and into the gloom, there appeared to be another group. I could hear voices.

The older woman introduced me to each person individually and suggested they would all like a stubbie. What could I say! The old conservative side of my culturally modified nature urged me to be very rude and walk off. Yet I knew I was beginning to break through to this sad community and underlying the realisation was the sedating effect of alcohol. I asked them where their men were and one said that, away from the bar, the women and men kept apart. It was the old order of things and nothing more was said about it. When I asked what they did all day it was the river. The river was their whole life.

I drank a stubbie with them, which probably wasn't wise, for it clouded my mind almost instantly. The heat had me nearly beat. To go from the cool tablelands of New South Wales to the heat of the Fitzroy River basin would take weeks of physical adjustment. With the light fading, the beer gone and presence of the women closer, I slowly got to my feet and announced I was going to have a quick swim in the river and then head back to the guesthouse. In my muddled thinking I thought the river was a quick, sudden exit. They wouldn't want a swim and it would cool me down. Without a swim I wasn't sure I could make it back.

There was a well-worn foot track to the river, about the width of a street away. The cockies were still squawking in the river trees, their final ruckus before settling for the night. The water was still, mirror still, and when a fish broke the surface the plop of its body re-entering the water could be heard above the noisy birds.

Reared inland, I knew all about the hazards of river swimming. Hidden snags were usually blamed, but I thought most adult drownings were a combination of alcohol and the low buoyancy of fresh water. So I was a little hesitant when I peeled off my clothes. Not so the women. Soundlessly in their bare feet, many had followed me down. Their clothes were off faster than a crack skinner could extract a rabbit's fur and amid giggles and shrieks they leapt into the water.

When I was a little boy a nun told me I would have to die before I saw paradise. I am sure she had a different vision of paradise or heaven to me, but swimming in a pristine river with several naked women was the ultimate heaven could provide. My inhibitions were deeply entrenched, however, and one of the women observed I was about to enter the water in my black underpants. She splashed me lightly and more laughter burst from the river. It stirred a sense of loin-tightening unease. Like me she was on an alcohol high, totally fixed on the present, the future smothered and of no consequence. 'Wet undies under dry pants no good,' she said in a husky voice. More laughter from the river.

She was very beautiful, with a mystic and uninhibited desirability about her. She stood knee-deep in the water, facing me totally unashamed, and with the faint illumination of the first stars on the water I could see the shape of her breasts. With an effort that cut deeper than a stockman's whip on exposed skin, I turned away and launched myself into the river in a long shallow dive. I swam until I knew I was the furthest out. The water felt tepid and the warm still air hanging over the river felt like a mosquito net on a hot February night in Sydney. In the dark it was impossible not to think of crocodiles. Everyone always said, 'Further downstream.' I'd never asked, I suddenly realised, how far downstream.

I swam back to the bank and got dressed quickly. The woman was right – wet undies under dry pants is an uncomfortable sensation. I muttered something about having to meet people and took off. I had a clear head now and ran along the river track feeling like a young man. The stars were ablaze and the track was clearly defined.

At the guesthouse they had all eaten and were about to walk up to one of the Bunuba communities to hear the band Fitzroy Express. They had a case of beer to take and I threw in a few dollars. Everyone was in great spirits and the twenty-minute walk bothered no one.

We were welcomed by several people from the community and taken over to the concert venue, which was a big slab of cement under an iron roof. There were some long wooden stools spread around the perimeter. The structure had power connected and a couple of small rooms attached on the river side.

The band was warming up when we arrived. The drummer was almost imprisoned behind an array of drums and I was quietly told he had exceptional skill. They all looked very professional and when the guitars of the Fitzroy Express hit the night air that cold slab of cement was soon alive with dancers born to rhythm. The songs were sad, poignant and cut deep – 'Come on all you Bunuba people, stand up for what's yours.'

I looked at them all, fifty or more assembled, some dancing, and I saw them as though for the first time – peaceful, gentle people horribly abused for more than a century. They were more like the people God said we should be. They forgave and spared. Before I could dwell longer a black hand reached down and I was on the dance floor, swinging: 'The white cockatoos, silhouetted against the rainstorm, see the lightning flash and hear the thunder roll.' My wet undies under dry pants soon dried.

The melancholy songs, the dancing and the beer all combined to wipe out any trace of time and I woke to see the cockatoos silhouetted before my eyes, not against a rainstorm but a fiery red dawn. After months in the cold tablelands far away, it was good to sleep under the stars on a bed of old dry grass. I had a headache and could smell the beer on my breath, but it wasn't a wasted night. I had learnt a lot about the community that night. Their spirit, their talents and their willingness to let go of the past. I had always said old ghosts only faded away when the living let go. Sometimes, however, the old ghosts should not be vanquished until the true horrors of the past had been exposed. Only then could people learn from history and pledge never to let it happen again. Under postcolonial rule these people were persecuted with a degree of brutality at least equal to the worst in Ireland under British rule. Yet this closely knit Bunuba community, where some of the older people had witnessed harrowing scenes only four and five decades earlier, received us warmly in their midst.

Joe Ross had arrived back from Canberra and I managed to contact him after breakfast. After waking in the grass I had wandered down to the river for a swim. It straightened me up a bit. When I began the six-kilometre walk to Joe's office the punishment began.

Pigmented with the dark genes of his Bunuba mother, Joe Ross was striking, tall with a powerful physique. Joe and I had discussed the Bradshaw art on two occasions over the telephone. He was enthusiastic about the search and he set up a portable project blackboard.

'How exactly do you want me to help you with this project?' Joe asked. He sat on a steel frame chair in front of the blackboard.

'The only access into most of the King Leopolds is by horse-back,' I said. 'I need horses.'

'How many?'

'Twenty odd. If I had six packhorses I could take a dozen riders.'

He looked at me for a few moments, long and hard. There may have been a trace of humour. He was no fool. This was a big horse-based project and would take a lot of organisation.

'All right I'll help you,' Joe said warmly. 'I'd like the Elders to go and every spare horse for the boys.' He wanted the boys to see the old initiation sites and the art that displayed the Dreamtime mysteries.

'Women too?' I queried, feeling uneasy. In the dark days of the cattle barons, Aboriginal stockwomen had been the back-bone of the industry. Light in the saddle and skilful, white boss stockmen had snapped them up at every opportunity. J. W. Bleakley, who was Chief Protector of Aborigines in Queensland from 1914 to 1942, had claimed Aboriginal women were the real pioneers of the outback. He stated white men could not have carried on without them.

'None ride any more.' A clouded look came over his face. In Aboriginal culture throughout Australia the women dealt with the practical matters of day-to-day living.

'I'll teach them,' I said evenly.

'Two,' he said succinctly, then quickly changed the subject. 'I've been talking to the Elders and they think a fortnight is all the horses will stand. In the old days a lot of mules were used. All the packs went on mules as their feet stood up to the rock.'

I didn't think we could undertake a comprehensive search and art examination in that time. 'It's a huge area,' I said. I

wanted to get right up into the King Leopold Range, but I
had no knowledge of the country. Dimond Gorge was a mere
speck on the map and most of Mornington Station was north
of the Leopolds. I was anxious for Joe to come up with sug-
gestions on where we might start.

'We'll arrange for the horses to be assembled at Millie
Windie. It's Bunuba country, right in the heart of the
Leopolds.'

Joe went on. 'There's not much time. Outsiders are waking
up to the tourist potential here. If we're not up and running
soon someone will start before us.'

'What about the dam? What will happen if the dam project
is accepted?'

'I think we'll stop it,' Joe said forcefully. 'If we fail it's the
end of the road for the Bunuba. About a third of our homeland under water, galleries and sacred sites lost. The only
tourism will be the big-boat concept – white operators power
boating around trying to find a slimy-looking crocodile.'

Joe wasn't one to dwell upon negatives and he turned to a
cabinet with wide, narrow draws. The maps were stored
unfolded, devoid of the creases that can make map reading
difficult. There was only room on his desk for one at a time
and together we pored over the first one – Mount House, with
Millie Windie marked near the southern edge of the map. To
the north was the Adcock River country.

'Three parallel ranges here,' Joe said, using a ruler to indicate. 'You have to trek over them to get to the Adcock.'

'Where are the principal galleries?'

'They'll show you,' Joe said, then added, 'The ones they
know about. Trying to run the river I saw one that no one
knows anything about. Old people say it was the Dreamtime
people.'

'Run the river?' I queried. 'I'm told it's treacherous in the
wet.'

Joe became animated. White water was his passion. 'It's wild, all right, but no one's had a go with the big rubber boats yet. I reckon a good team can run the river. Next wet we're going to have another go.'

The heat was on track to its daily oven blast when we walked outside. The people were impervious to it. Children played as they did everywhere and old women chatted up and down the street. Three dogs created from a vast gene pool picked up my white smell and checked me out. It was a thorough smell-up and I refrained from putting my hand down for a pat. In Hall's Creek packs of dogs had killed and partially eaten two drunks. The story had been on the ABC news. When I got back to the guesthouse I was going to have a sleep and keep away from the grog.

Joe stopped near the guesthouse and we shook hands. 'See you back here next year,' he said. 'We might get another tourist venture up and running.' Joe and his father were involved with the boat trips at Geikie Gorge.

CHAPTER 3

Land of the Red Chief

I left Fitzroy Crossing on the midnight bus. The heat was extreme and I had no further business there. Back in Broome I was able to continue vital research for the task ahead. Geographically Broome is on the outer western edge of the Kimberley, but it is the principal town and capital of Australia's far north-west. Research for the mission I had in mind would encompass more than libraries, museums and departments. The most valuable informants were contacts, and during my few days in Broome I met people with diverse interests and careers, from linguists to whitewater adventurers.

I was invited to do an interview on A.B.C. radio. We talked about packhorse tourism in the King Leopolds and I declared I would be back to write a book about the adventures I felt certain would spring from the expedition. The dam issue was raised and I said I thought it would amount to an opportunity lost for Broome. Once Broome became a big cotton centre, tourists would shy away. I couldn't think of an example where tourism and cotton successfully coexisted. I went on to say desert tourism in America's south-west was a multi-million dollar industry and that it was possible to manage an influx of tourists on a seasonal basis and maintain high environmental standards.

After five days in Broome I took three connecting flights to

Dubbo, my home city in western New South Wales. Sal and I lived one hundred kilometres north-east of the city, but we did our shopping and most of our business there.

Sal met me at the airport. We'd be heading straight home, she informed me as I loaded my luggage into the car, for the heifers on their first calf were having birth difficulties and she was sick of midwife duties.

A few days later I was seated at our long dining table. In front of me was a pile of books and scattered across the table lay numerous manila folders. Sal had let me take over her dining room. She was a good sport like that, because most women would have made me stay in my office. Sal realised the office had no outlook and it was important for me to see out into the garden, where the bird life was probably equal to anything in Australia. Galahs, magpies, willie wagtails, yellow-faced honeyeaters, the grey strike-thrush – if you listened hard the ping-pong chirp of the wrens floated up from the lawn.

'You're worried aren't you?' Sal said, removing the coffee that had long gone cold.

I admitted it. 'No one yet has stood up to the cotton consortiums and beaten them. I'm frightened the west Kimberley will be lost. The world's last tropical wilderness a victim to the developers.'

'Joe Ross thinks he can beat them,' Sal said.

'There's no one more passionate about the river. He told me he's got a whitewater expedition planned. When the wet's on and the river's boiling under class V rapids, they're going to run the river from Mount Elizabeth to Fitzroy.' The thought of Joe's plans spurred me on.

'Sounds like Cataract Canyon,' Sal laughed. In Utah eighteen months before a boatman had suggested we do this wild river run on the Colorado. We had declined.

'I reckon they'll line the boats around the waterfalls.'

'Is there waterfalls?'

'I thought Joe said there was. I don't know. I know next to nothing and that's the problem.' I paused, thinking about it. 'What can I do really?'

'Play your old racing tactics,' Sal suggested gently. 'You always said winning was knowing your opposition. You were a tactician.'

She was right. Carrying a busted shoulder that stopped me using the whip and near-sighted I had always won by tactics, never strength. But despite the handicaps, fate was generous and I had ridden more than one hundred and forty winners.

'I know nothing about cotton. When we had the cattle in Queensland and drove up through St George I always thought how prosperous and tidy the landscape looked. In the sixties when I came down with the cattle trains St George was nearly all scrub. Didn't look like the place would ever amount to anything. But now it's one of the most prosperous centres in south-west Queensland. All thanks to cotton.'

'We'll start with health,' said Sal, who was thinking along a different tangent. 'It's rumoured a lot of people get sick in cotton country.'

'I don't think they can prove it.' I was feeling defeatist. 'Every cross-reference check on health disorders discloses people are no sicker in cotton towns than anywhere else.'

'It's out on the farms,' Sal persisted. 'I'll make some inquiries.'

It seemed as good a way to start as any. I telephoned an old contact in Gunnedah and he gave me the name of a cotton farmer's wife. Sal made the next call and we were invited over for dinner and offered a bed for the night. In my lifetime farmers had always been the same, irrespective of what they produced from the soil. I knew people who grew cotton and liked them. I wanted to be fair, dispassionate and unbiased. I felt like a detective posted to a case with no heart for the job.

The Gunnedah district was deeply divided over revolutionary

agriculture practices. Disputes were settled in court, neigh-
bours didn't speak and there was evidence of a 'new farmer',
an entrepreneur, never before known since first settlement.
The politics of agriculture along western-flowing rivers in New
South Wales had shifted to a new course since I had retired
as an amateur jockey and no longer rode at the bush
meetings.

Sal and I had been sheltered from dramatic shifts in agriculture. We lived on the open tablelands, which form the
southern uplift of the Warrumbungle Mountains. It was too
cold for cotton and the risk of cool, wet harvest conditions
discouraged farmers from growing summer grain crops such
as sorghum. The district had become predominantly beef
cattle, with some wheat, fat lambs and wool. Small towns were
in serious decline and only larger towns held steady, propped
up only by isolation.

It was not an uplifting experience to go to any of these towns
but when we topped the basalt escarpment that overlooked the
Liverpool Plains it was like entering another country – an exciting one. In loose terms the whole region was geographically
defined as the Liverpool Plains, with the town of Gunnedah
the principal service centre, but immediately south of the town
a vast stretch of level black soil was known as the Breeza Plains.
It was on these plains Peter and Josie Brown lived.

During my lifetime – given any excuse, and it used to be
horses – I would drive east into this magnificent land of mountain backdrops and breathtaking wide valleys. It had been the
land of the Red Chief, a Kamilaroi man who had reigned here
for much of the eighteenth century. The legend told the story
of a tribe weakened by factional disputes and the attrition of
encroaching hostile tribes. Unable to stand by any longer, this
young man, bearing the totem of a red kangaroo, seized two
young women from another clan and challenged the old chief
to a death dual for the right to keep the girls and become

chief. Following the outcome of the dual the Red Chief went on to build the most powerful clan in the Kamilaroi Nation and the tribe was never threatened again until Europeans arrived.

The Kamilaroi Nation suffered some of the worst documented atrocities in colonial history. It was the clans to the north, in the Gwydir River basin, who were slaughtered. Major James Nunn provided a figure of forty warriors killed at the battle of Waterloo Creek in 1838, but an eyewitness reported three hundred men, women and children slaughtered. Four months later twenty-eight unarmed Kamilaroi people were murdered at Myall Creek. Compared to mass slaughter in Rwanda in the 1990s these figures may seem small, but in Africa the killings were part of a civil war. In northern New South Wales it was a purge to rid the land of black people.

The Myall Creek murders resulted in one of the most controversial events in nineteenth-century colonial history – seven ex-convicts were hanged for the murders. The *Sydney Morning Herald* of 5 October 1838 reported the hangings as an outrage and declared that Aborigines were less than human. It appears that Governor George Gipps almost stood alone in demanding the arrests. In 1834 the British parliament had passed the anti-slave bill, known as the 'emancipation of British slaves'. An awakening of evangelistic piety penetrated to the roots of government and colonial governors – often very religious themselves – were inspired by the new wave of puritanism in Victorian society.

By 1840 the clans of the Kamilaroi Nation had been culturally destroyed and survivors clung to miserable camps on black-tolerant stations. The rich flood plains supported the establishment of some of the most magnificent holdings anywhere in the world.

White settlement of the Liverpool Plains was almost bloodless, a reversal of the circumstances in the adjoining Gwydir region to the north. But it would be mischievous and a distortion of history to imply that the people who settled the country north of the Nandewar Ranges had a different set of values, because they would not have.

I knew many of the old families on the Liverpool Plains. At picnic race time they were too hospitable for amateur jockeys who liked a grog. Following victory in the Ladies Bracelet one afternoon a local grazier encouraged me to celebrate the win with him. Next day I was still drunk when legged aboard a grey gelding to compete in the first race of the program. I covered the distance holding the horse's mane and when confronted by two stipendiary stewards and the race starter as well, I was informed that I was the only jockey in British racing history to go from barrier to post without once holding the reins. I told them they should include Irish racing history and they might find plenty of occasions. All three went bright red – with rage I thought – and I waited for a six months' suspension. Instead, they all burst out laughing, told me to get out and pick up the reins in the next race. They were good sports. I hated to think what would happen to a drunken jockey in the 1990s.

The pioneers a step behind the first to claim these beautiful valleys and flood plains enthusiastically moved on with a vision that land to the north and west would be as good. Sixty years later the dreamers were still searching, far away in the Kimberley. But no land on any horizon measured up to Australia's Liverpool Plains.

In the early days of the wool barons the occasional drought had little or no effect on the management of these vast stations. The Peel, Mooki and Namoi rivers would recede to the permanent waterholes while the buttes of old plains grass provided sufficient nutrition for hardy merino sheep. Bushfires too were almost unknown, for the Queensland wet invariably spilled over and sent a tongue of monsoonal cloud south to the ramparts of the Warrumbungle Range, which for millions of years had fed the Liverpool Plains with rich volcanic soil from every fissure, gully and creek that flowed north from the twisted line of cliffs and lofty spurs. But nature could always provide a leveller and the leveller on the Liverpool Plains was flood. It could come in any season. In the space of ten days it could dash the hopes of every flood-plain farmer from Tamworth to Wee Waa, devastation covering two hundred and fifty kilometres.

In the late winter and early spring of 1998 the three rivers had burst their banks on three occasions, spewing a tide of muddy water over thousands of hectares of winter wheat crops and fallow cotton fields. Looking down from chartered aircraft, television reporters caught camera glimpses of an inland sea. Three times the city of Tamworth braced for massive flooding, averted only by a pause in the torrential rain long enough for flood peaks to roar on downstream. The city escaped serious damage and so did the two big river towns, Gunnedah and Narrabri.

It was the farmers who copped nature's wrath and as we topped a low rise in the road, an hour having slipped by since descending the escarpment on the western perimeter, the scene before us disclosed the heartbreak in a single glimpse. It was the Breeza Plains on the Mooki. With the sun low and almost behind, we could see the land clearly to the monotonous blue line of the great divide. The low angle of the sun reflected on newly formed lakes, sparking a sort of brightness in a brown land with a weak, sickly tinge of green, where patches of the dead wheat crops were taking a little longer to die. The cotton farms stood out. The first heavy rain had arrived in June, before a lot of the cotton modules had been moved to the gin. The wet black soil closed the farms to heavy transport and there the modules lay, exposed to the weather and finally the flood. Still white, they stood out, like hundreds of bogged buses. Where they lay in an unbroken line, near the lakes that pulled in the last of the sun's rays in a final sheen of light before the night, they looked like chunks of glacial ice waiting for the summer sun to make them disappear. It was an alien and unlikely landscape, as though the planet had warmed rapidly and the great glaciers were receding.

At the Brown's it was a nostalgic step back in time, perhaps thirty-odd years. It was a time when men seemed to laugh more than they do now and women rose above the mundane, daily chores of housekeeping and domestic duties and somehow retained a femininity almost lost at the end of the century.

Inside the home, nightfall mercifully blacking out the land-scape, we drank wine and laughed. I had that feeling of being on a ship, chatting and laughing but knowing all the while that outside we were surrounded by a sea, this time of mud. All of us – the women too – steered away from the reality outside.

One of the favourite topics of conversation in the bush was the old characters. I think it was because they were gone. But there was too much disquiet on the land for the old stories and the atmosphere to last beyond the pre-dinner drinks. Taking seats at a dinner table was always an opportunity to refocus, as though everyone was trapped and no one would escape the roving eyes of the intuitive. People exposed some-thing of themselves at that critical moment of taking their seats. Those at peace with the world rarely introduced the next line of conversation. The other male guest slipped into this category and to break the ice I asked him where his property was. It was on the plains north of Gunnedah. With a little prod-ding he explained why he had switched to cotton – water and profitability. He discovered he was living on top of a huge aquifer and the bore he had put down yielded more than 200,000 litres an hour, providing ample water for irrigation.

'The department told me I had to take the water now or miss out.' he said. 'That was only four years ago. I was a cattle-man in those days and grew a bit of wheat.'

'What do mean – miss out?' I asked.

'They'd reallocate the licence somewhere else, I suppose, or maybe just put a cap on it. I never asked.'

'Opportunist cotton grower,' Josie jested, placing roast beef on the tablemat in front of the man. His name was Grant.

'We all are,' Peter added, pouring the wine. 'It's grow it or get out. All my cattle are e-listed.'

Cattle run in conjunction with cotton or grazed nearby on an adjoining property had only days before been placed on what was called the e-list. This was done to protect the beef export industry from the chemical endosulfan, which left a traceable residue in meat. Cattle that consumed grass exposed to spray drift would reveal a slight residue for some weeks, but they had to consume copious amounts of affected matter to exceed international residue standards. Endosulfan, known as the 'soft chemical', killed the notorious heliothis grub. 'Soft' because it did not harm insects, which in some cases acted as predators and helped control other harmful bugs.

Big Jock Newman, a stock and station agent, took a taste of the wine and cast his eye, which never lost that glint, around the table. Being one hundred and fifty kilometres away it was always questionable economics on my part to sell cattle at Gunnedah, but he was such a good-humoured man I had crossed the range on two or three occasions every year with a load of cattle. 'Got a client with a million dollars to spend,' he said. 'He wants to live in this area and run cattle and grow grain, but it's all too close to cotton.'

Grant was close to sixty. He was a practical farmer with no pretensions. 'Reckon I'll go out of cattle. It's not worth the worry.'

'What if they ban endosulfan?' Sal suggested. She knew more than she let on. 'You could run your cattle then.'

Grant chuckled. He was a deep-chested man, and although the hair above his collar was white he'd still play with a 200-litre drum of diesel. 'We'd have a chemical war like they've got on the Darling Downs. Some of them dropped endo and used profenofas. The spray drift half killed the sorghum crops. The sorghum blokes had to kill their bugs and used 2-4-D, which drifted onto the cotton fields and dropped their yields.'

'You don't have to go to Yugoslavia to get bombed.' Josie drained her glass and looked at Peter. 'The glasses are low.' Then in the next breath: 'The chemical bombardment on the cotton got up to eight flights this season. Further north at Moree it was seventeen.'

Peter topped up the glasses with an Amberton shiraz. He'd been quiet since the cotton talk started. The floods had ripped all his wheat from the soil and to survive he was about to plant his first cotton crop. It was do it or leave. The days of the frogs croaking through the night down by the creek and the gentle north-westerly drifting through the plains grass had gone forever. A very private person, Peter hated the new lifestyle – his thoughts at times transparent. His wife, Josie, was disturbed by the changes, as most women out on the farms were. I noted the other two women never spoke when the subject was cotton, a topic so consuming we rarely left it. These people were worried and they were powerless. In the Namoi Valley cotton had become like a giant Kimberley tide – there was no stopping it, you had to respect it, but you knew when the tide had raced out there would be nothing left but stinking mudflats.

'I hope it never gets so bad the guns come out,' Josie said unhappily. She was a vivacious brunette and wanted no part of anything that retarded life and vitality.

We all went for our wine glasses. Jock Newman smiled, but looked at no one. Grant set his empty glass on the table and plastered his fork with potato and his wife, Jenny, froze into a statue. Peter would have to respond with more than another bottle of shiraz.

'Two or three years back,' Peter said gravely, 'someone tried to bring down one of the spray aircraft. There were two bullet holes in one wing. It was when helix contamination in export beef closed off some of our overseas markets.' He paused and took a mouthful of wine. 'I am sure that won't happen again. The ones really feeling the pinch from poor cattle prices know they're prime suspects when it comes to guns. Josie's simply stated the frustration out there.'

'It's a lot more than beef contamination, darling, and you know it.' Josie wasn't a woman easily moved to anger, but her eyes were smouldering, not at what her husband had said but at the thought of what might be left on the Australian land-scape for her children, and afterwards, their children.

It was difficult to define the sadness that hung over the Liver-pool Plains. In my racetrack days I remembered making low flights across them, when red-hide cattle and red kangaroos broke cover from woodland belts bordering the billabongs, and flocks of ducks a thousand strong took to the air. Thirty years later the same flight path cast a shadow of the plane on a treeless land under a maze of water diversion banks. Like a symbol of inherent greed and loss of soul, a confined flood plain provided security for those within and peril for those left out, and those clutching for the threads of justice would find they might as well ask a python to pull them from rising water. Maybe, in human terms, the pioneer families and those who arrived soon after World War II were enduring a similar plight to that experienced by the Kamilaroi people a century and a half before. The carefree plains of their childhood no longer existed. The disappearance of wildlife, tree removal and the early morning drone of advancing aircraft in the spray season, created something alien, something horrible, for once set on target the throttles would open and where sweet smells of the bush were once taken for granted the land gave up a new odour, sweet too in a way but also sinister.

Sal and I decided we should speak to someone from the Kamilaroi community, to find out first-hand how they felt about the devastation of their homeland. Mick Horne quickly impressed me as a man capable of leading hundreds of young people out of a world they felt had turned its back on them. A powerful Kamilaroi man, I looked upon him as a reincarnation of the Red Chief. He had been sent back to rescue his land a second time. God had toughened this man for the task. Six years in maximum security was a taste of hell and when Mick emerged into the sunlight he had a burning passion to lead his people from the darkness.

It was local Gunnedah historian John McDonagh who arranged my first meeting with Mick. Retired from business, John devoted his time to the recording of local history, acted as environmental 'watchdog' for the community and was an active supporter of Aboriginal culture. His uncle, Russell McDonagh, had encouraged Ion Idriess to write *The Red Chief* first published in 1953 by Angus and Robertson. The notes that Russell passed on to Ion had decades before been recorded from the lips of a Kamilaroi full blood known as old Bungaree, who appeared to be the last chief of the Gunnedah clan.

John suggested we meet Mick at his home and see the artefacts he carved from wood and painted. The little porch at the front door was an introduction in itself. There were statues of black people, wood-carved goannas and snakes. When John knocked Mick greeted us so fast I thought he must have sprung from somewhere.

'Come in and have a cup of coffee,' he said cheerfully and thrust forward a hand so big mine disappeared as we shook.

Sal walked quickly across the porch, confirming Mick's ability to carve life-like reptiles. The passage to the kitchen was painted on both sides with bright traditional art. Boomerangs, didgeridoos and shields were scattered on the floor and on a table in the living room. The didgeridoo Mick was painting lay across the kitchen table. 'Sal had a very perceptive eye and was instantly enthralled by all the native animals painted on the wall. Mick told us one of his daughters did all the mural paintings around town. We had already seen them on the walls of the Coles supermarket.

Mick's special love was boomerangs and didgeridoos. The boomerangs he made from gidgee, which was thought to be the hardest and most durable wood in existence. At Longreach in western Queensland, original fence lines erected with gidgee still stood, now more than one hundred years old. It was a stunted woodland tree from the semi-arid lands. To cut his boomerang raw material, Mick had to travel to Brewarrina in far north-western New South Wales. While he explained the various shapes and the special purpose for each category of boomerang, we ran our hands along the blade of one. It had an edge like finely moulded steel. I picked up another from a wooden box full of them and Mick told me it was a battle weapon and could cut a man nearly in half. I knew that to be no exaggeration. Blagden Chambers, a pastoralist and amateur writer in the late nineteenth century, had ridden onto a battle-ground not long after the warring tribes had left. There were several bodies and he had been staggered at the damage a boomerang could inflict. It was 1865 in the upper Warrego.

From the box Mick plucked out a long-handled, hunting boomerang. He said it was a replica of the type he used. He was the only Aborigine I had ever heard of who still used a traditional weapon in south-eastern Australia. If he got tired of supermarket food he took three boomerangs and went to some favourite hunting spots where he could always find feral pigs. It was silent hunting, he explained. He could knock a couple of sucker pigs down before the old sow knew there was any danger. But hunting was a rare diversion, a breath of fresh air from the studio. Mick was an artist and a musician. Entre-preneurs dealing in Aboriginal artefacts had placed orders amounting to seven hundred boomerangs before the start of the Olympics in Sydney. They wanted as many didgeridoos as he could find time to make – or, more to the point, that white ants could tunnel out for him. Mick cut the selected pieces from yellowbox eucalyptus and left them scattered about in the bush on white ant nests. The ants homed in on the fresh inner sap and hollowed out the pieces for him. It was the traditional method, but he did say, with a wide grin that was characteristic of the man, that ants had no sense of deadlines to meet. I gathered the process was very slow.

In between painting the boomerangs and didgeridoos with traditional colours and symbols, Mick trained young people from the local Aboriginal community in Aboriginal dancing. His dancing troupe had taken first prize when New South Wales hosted the world indigenous dance festival. Every year at Katherine, in the Northern Territory, up to 10,000 people gathered for Australia's festival of indigenous dancing in July.

'To get that corroboree feeling,' Mick said enthusiastically, when we all sat down in the kitchen for coffee, 'I take the teenagers down to the big river gums. The new arrivals are often a bit spooked. But I take the ochre paints down there and tell em to paint up. Then I play the music from the car, recordings of Aboriginal singing groups. It warms them up. After that we turn off the music and I teach them to dance to the sticks.' He paused, not sure whether Sal and I understood what he meant. 'The clapping sticks are made from hardwood. Each dance is a story and the sticks beat the tempo.'

The kids would have loved it. All painted up, beating time to the music of the Dreamtime. Time and time again indigenous cultures had provided evidence of how important dancing was to human contentment. People who didn't dance aged prematurely.

In the country it had all but disappeared from our culture and towns and villages threw up a haunting profile of people who had no 'fun', didn't know what it was and seemed scared of its very suggestion.

Sal and I were a generation too late to see the real bush

corroborees. I knew I had missed something and regretted it. When Mick taught these teenagers to dance he was rekindling the flame of an ancient culture and helping haul the Kamilaroi back from the brink of extinction.

Despite an age gap of more than twenty-five years, it soon became apparent that Mick and John were great friends. John had grown up in the town in the early 1930s and due to his love of the river he had made many dark-skinned friends. Back then the parents of the children still fished, occasionally knocked a goanna on the head and cooked it in the coals on the river bank, and gathered bush vegetables. For a white kid whose dad was always away for the day and his mother too scared of snakes, the life of an Aboriginal child seemed more interesting, and I am sure it was.

'I'd like to have a look at the river,' I said, feeling it was time we moved on and let Mick get back to work. 'I've never taken much notice of the Namoi. Rode at amateur meetings on the riverside racecourse for more than twenty years, but never once walked to the bank and took a peep.'

'It's not a pretty sight,' Mick said soberly. 'You want to go home and forget it.'

'I thought it would be like the Castlereagh at home,' I replied. 'I live twenty kilometres from it, but when we go to Binnaway for groceries and meat I always glance down from the bridge. The water's okay.' Further downstream at Mendooran the water had a clear sparkle about it and on a hot day a swim was always tempting. There were lovely white sandbars, and always in the back of my mind was a canoe trip from Mendooran to Gilgandra to see all the bird life. Banjo Paterson too had been inspired by the Castlereagh and had written about it in 'The Travelling Post Office':

The roving breezes come and go, the reed-beds sweep and sway,

The sleepy river murmurs low, and loiters on its way,
It is the land of lots o' time along the Castlereagh.

'You're in for a shock,' Mick said standing up. 'I've got time. Rebecca loves a break away from the house with the tiny ones, anyway. I'll take you to the Namoi–Mooki junction. Only a couple of kilometres out of town.'

I mentioned I had the billies, some pannikins and tea in a little box and somewhere among the river gums we'd boil up.

'You can't boil up on the riverbank Mick. The sight of the water makes yer guts crawl.'

We waited while Mick went to a nearby house and collected his daughter. Sal said she'd do the shopping while we were away. She always took the opportunity to do a big grocery shop when we went to Gunnedah or Dubbo and I think she had a fairly accurate image of what I was about to see.

'It's been a great sadness for me,' John said while we waited. 'Growing up here as a kid the river was our whole life. Beyond the classroom, that is. We swam, fished, canoed and we had those big Tarzan ropes hooked to tree branches for swinging away out across the water before dropping in. The worst thing is the loss of the fishing. My mum would light the old fuel stove late in the afternoon and send me off to catch a couple of jewies. Mind you, I didn't need any prodding. If she wanted fish for dinner she'd have to catch me between school and the river.'

When Mick arrived back with his daughter Rebecca, we all piled into my four-wheel-drive Jeep Cherokee. Rebecca was dark with long slender legs. She reminded me of some of the young Bunuba women. Mick was very proud of his Aboriginal heritage and said he could trace back through generations to the original Gunnedah clan.

'Just pop down to the lagoon first,' John said. 'I know it's a scene repeated right across Australia, but this may be the only example where we can compare an environment one hundred years before the arrival of white man to the present.'

In the days of the Red Chief the lagoon had been the tribe supermarket. Taken from the lips of old Bungaree and passed on to him from successive generations, the story of the lagoon threw up a picture of a water habitat set among reeds and native water lilies, where waterfowl, wild geese, black swans, pelicans, brolgas, spoonbills, herons and several species of duck made their home. In Idriess's recording the lagoon was full of fish as well, along with shrimps, yabbies, shellfish and tortoise. The women and children collected numerous varieties of vegetable foods.

The lagoon was on the lower flood plain, about a kilometre long in an overflow flood channel. From the car where we got out you could look across the water and see a low-lying street, with houses raised on stilts. The water was a dirty brown, with a light shade of green. To the right was an old wooden fence, the wire lying in ugly rust-coloured clumps. The leaning posts were now part of the debris of fallen-down trunks of once beautiful river gums. When I turned the engine off there was silence, save the shuffling sounds of our feet as we stepped through castor oil burr and notorious noogoora burr.

Mick suggested Rebecca remain in the car with the babies. 'I don't know what it is,' he said. 'But if you stay here long you get diarrhoea.'

The place was lifeless. Not even a willie wagtail. With nothing to say we soon got back into the car. Mick's next remark was chilling. 'You haven't seen anything yet.'

We followed a network of gravel roads for about four kilometres. Once covered in native plain grass the river plains now lay under a mantle of noogoora burr and bishop weed. The giant river gums closed ranks behind us, creating a lovely soft riverine atmosphere and if no one had previously uttered a word I would have expected to see big wide sandbars of beach-coloured sand set among streams of crystal clear water.

We stopped and got out.

'Don't go any further,' Mick said quickly, as I approached the bank of the Mooki. Mick had already explained we were two hundred metres from the junction with the big river, the Namoi. 'The banks are falling in.'

This time the scene was frightening. Because this was more than mere pollution in one of the region's principal water-courses. The Mooki had become a poisonous canal. The fluid between the crumbling bare banks was the colour of pea-green soup. I'd seen salt river flats on the Murray, equally as ugly, but they were isolated and had no effect on human habitation. This river of green fetid soup fed directly into the Namoi, and another kilometre downstream were the bore-pumping stations for Gunnedah's water supply. The bore water didn't come from the river. The underground aquifer was separated from the river by metres of solid earth and perhaps even a rock strata, but I had a squeamish feeling about this green fluid passing over the top of the underground streams. I later found out the town's bore had been re-drilled to more than 80 metres, to a deeper aquifer that provided excellent water.

Slowly we all walked down towards the junction, following the river bank. The big gums clung precariously, the soil all eroded away from the roots. Many had already fallen in, creating a tangle of great dead logs in the green soup, flecked with white bacterial froth, like big gollies of spit from a drunkard.

'The whole river's caving in,' I said to Mick.

'The chemicals from upstream have killed the couch and nutgrass,' Mick replied bitterly. 'It's all the shit they're pourin in upstream. Everything but the trees is dead. There's nothing here now.' He began to wave his arms and his passion was moving. 'No fish, crays, frogs – not even a bloody shrimp. It's bad when the shrimps are gone.'

'My uncle died here,' John said, pointing downstream. 'Knew he was dying and wanted nothing to do with hospitals, so drove his car straight in. A few days passed before anyone saw the roof of the car in the water. The shrimps had bared him to a skeleton.'

'Yeah, it's bad when the shrimps are gone,' Mick repeated.

'I turned away. It was a sombre moment, but throughout the course of my life I've found humour can surface at any time.

At the junction the Namoi was a ribbon of water no wider than half a cricket pitch. This former great river, the longest northern tributary of the Darling–Barwon and with a watershed equal to the Lachlan in southern New South Wales, had been reduced to a trickle. A metre above the waterline the banks were dark and wet and I commented on it.

'They've sucked out that since Sunday,' Mick said in disgust. 'Look at that. Three foot of water in a couple of days.'

Downstream from the junction I saw several head of cattle come in for a drink. The flowing stream in the Namoi could at least be called water. Still, the thought of the brown-greenie water filtering through the gut and the kidneys of these animals and forming the juice in the steak killed any desire for a barbecue.

We didn't stay long at the junction. Some yellow-crested cockatoos landed in branches overhead and when they squawked their voices carried through the sad old trees, a plangent reminder that no other native animal or bird had appeared or been heard. Rebecca too, with her tiny baby held firmly in her arms, looked vulnerable. Full of deadly bacteria and poisonous plants this was no place for woman, child and baby.

I wondered briefly what sort of poem Banjo Paterson would have written. I imagined him walking along with us, pencil and pad in hand, for he had been on the Mooki in happier days. From 'The Old Timer's Steeplechase' I quote Banjo:

The flag went down, and we seemed to fly,
And we made the timbers shiver,
Of the first big fence, as the stand flashed by,
And I caught the ring of the trainer's cry:
Go on, for the Mooki River.

. . .

Alas to think that those times so gay
Have vanished and passed for ever!
You don't believe in the yarn, you say?
Why, man, 'twas a matter of every day
When we raced on the Mooki River!

In sight of the Mooki I had ridden more than forty winners. 'You're lucky,' I said to the imaginary Banjo. 'Your eyes will never be scorched.'

On Tuesday, 10 November, the *West Australian*, Perth's daily newspaper, announced that the controversial plan to dam the Fitzroy River to irrigate cotton fields in the west Kimberley had been dropped. The article went on to state that Cotton Australia's chief executive, Garry Punch, had been quoted as saying the cotton industry never supported a dam on the Fitzroy and it was not needed. Clearly the plan had been 'adventuresome' from the start, by one man, but the newspaper didn't add that.

Tim Fisher, who was the natural resources coordinator for the Australian Conservation Foundation, was quoted as saying rivers in New South Wales and Queensland had been devastated by the extra active demands of the cotton industry. He went on to say that some private holding ponds held enough water to fill 20,000 Olympic-sized pools. He knew of one Queensland cotton farmer developing a pond large enough to fill 200,000 Olympic swimming pools – 200,000 megalitres.

Kimberley Land Council executive director Peter Yu was quoted as being sceptical about the abandonment of the plan. He would not be convinced until all references to it were removed from the memorandum of understanding between the state government and the corporation that had initially put forward the proposal. Perhaps even less convinced was a Broome-based environmental protection organisation – Environs Kimberley. The state premier had apparently confirmed that the dam remained on the agenda. Under the memorandum of understanding, the proponent was still obliged to carry out the feasibility study for a dam.

I telephoned Joe Ross and congratulated him, as his personal effort to draw attention to the plight of the river and his people would have had an enormous impact. 'Your hard-hitting talk on ABC radio in Broome pushed the pendulum a bit more too.' Joe responded warmly. It was generous of him to say so, but I think the die had been cast before I went to air.

'I can't help being disappointed about the expedition,' I said. 'I was particularly keen to get into some of those rock shelters and look for art.'

'You can't pull out now.' The eager tone in his voice echoed across 5000 kilometres of arid lands and desert. 'The old blokes are pullin out packsaddles that haven't sat on a mule's back for forty years. The women are talking too. Everyone's excited. Besides, the dam builders aren't going away. It's only a postponement.'

It was at this point a new dimension of the expedition emerged. If the dam was off the agenda, even if only temporarily, there was an opportunity to refocus on the contemporary Aboriginal people in the west Kimberley communities. Did they have the capacity to get tourism up and running? There was already one successful operation in Geikie Gorge, at Fitzroy Crossing. If a horse-based venture could be established it would act as an inspiration to groups throughout the Kimberley. But there was little time. The same economic pressures destined to destroy the great river lands of south-west New South Wales and the Great Barrier Reef in north Queensland were about to pounce on the west Kimberley. Much of the east Kimberley had already fallen to the ravages of European settlement.

It was now or never.

4 A Handful of Wild Horses

Summer passed slowly, sucking in the dust devils, which danced ominously on the fallow for weeks on end. But nature gave clues to the future. It was the ants this time. In February they built numerous nests and all were on little crests of hard red dirt. When the rain came it lasted for days and overflowed every dam. On the low plains to the west of the Warrumbungles paddocks lay under water. I kept a wary eye on the weather charts and noted there was no let up in the big wet in the top end. Three weeks before my planned departure for Broome I telephoned my Aboriginal friends and they told me creeks and rivers were still in flood and the prolonged wet had pushed up barriers of spear grass two and a half metres high. We would have to defer the expedition departure a month.

It was far more than a waiting period for me. Whenever possible I talked to people about dams, irrigation, salinity and, particularly, cotton. With cotton I expected controversy, but on the Kimberley issue I experienced my first confrontation with racism and it bitterly disappointed me. I couldn't believe that people failed to understand the significance of reconciliation. That they didn't perceive reconciliation was not confined to a gesture of good will, but ultimately the future of Australia's long-term stability. Like my people – the Irish – Indigenous

Australians were never going to forget the treatment dished out over the previous two hundred years.

It was disheartening, but it also fired me up and made me more determined. I was raring to go. Finally on 17 April, I arrived at Sydney airport at 7.30 a.m. with one hundred kilograms of gear. It seemed so out of place in the modern world I packed it onto a trolley and pushed it towards the nearest check-in counter with my eyes locked ahead. The polite Qantas staff took no notice, as though they saw it every hour. A riding saddle was strapped to one of the big packsaddle packs and two men had to lift it together. I waited anxiously with my American Express Card to pay the overweight. The check-in man said I could put it away: the old military packs, the packsaddles stamped 1942 and the riding saddles were given a free passage by Qantas.

Watching the gear travel along the conveyor belt made me think of the white explorer Ernest Giles. Here I was with the same equipment, about to follow a section of his 1872 route north-west from Alice Springs and cover in two and a half hours' flying time what had taken him three years to accomplish. That is, traversing the continent from the lower central regions to the Indian Ocean.

My principal contact in the west Kimberley was now Peter Brooking, who lived in Derby. Peter was the man to talk about horses with, Joe Ross had told me. Someone had told me there were not many horses at Millie Windie and I had asked Joe directly over the phone. That was when he put me onto Peter. When I last spoke to him, a week or more before, he had ten horses in hand.

Unable to reach Joe Ross by telephone, I finally sent a fax to tell him I was coming up. Joe telephoned to say there were so many volunteers he would have to put a cap on the numbers. He intended to call a meeting at Fitzroy Crossing, three days after my arrival in Broome.

The size of the party began to worry me. Unfit riders, constant catching and hobbling, rigging of packhorses and lost time with green horses amounted to a rabble. It wouldn't work. From my experience in packhorse tourism twenty or more riders requiring eight back-up packhorses was unwieldy. Joe thought he could arrange a food airdrop from Fitzroy Crossing to cut back on packhorses. Food, however, isn't the problem on overland horse treks. Tents, swags, personal belongings and cooking gear take up eighty per cent of the pack room. Not everybody pulls their weight when it comes to personal belongings.

At Alice Springs, Broome passengers changed planes. Tracking slightly north of the MacDonnell Ranges, the jet passed over Mount Liebig (1500 metres), which marks the end of Giles's 1872 bid. He got a little further to Mount Udor, on the southern edge of the Tanami Desert. The jet would cover that extra bit in five minutes.

Minutes afterwards, ancient watercourses shimmered in the sun, under a crust of raw salt. Further to the south, pursuing other routes, Giles frequently had tried to force his way across these innocuous-looking pans, only to end up digging out a packhorse in a heat blast out of hell. To gaze down upon the Tanami, sipping coffee, I couldn't help but feel bewildered by the spirit and zeal of a man like Giles. But in the coming weeks I was to discover it had nothing to with zeal and character. It was a fever of the mind and all else faded to inconsequence.

An hour passed and the salt watercourses began to weave to the south-west. It was time to watch for the desert mesas, well south of Halls Creek. Those in sight, it's merely a matter of minutes of careful scanning and there it is – the mighty Fitzroy. At 35,000 feet it was visible from eighty nautical miles. Skirting south of Fitzroy Crossing, the pilot tracked close enough to the river to see expansive ribbons of muddy water. The wet was late, ending only a week before, and I recalled Peter Brooking's warning about late rains and the spear grass. But nothing at the moment could have dampened the excitement I felt. More coffee from the hostess, giving all the passengers the treatment in a less than half-full plane, I watched the river swing away to the north-west. Below the country was no longer a dull red in a high sun. The soft green of the Pindan had appeared, suddenly consuming the landscape. Described months before by an astonishingly ignorant journalist as a heap of nothing, the Pindan was home to hundreds of species of birds. It was the sort of vast wilderness that could one day be used to prevent endangered African fauna from becoming extinct – the Kimberley evoked an African savanna without the wildlife.

But the dreaming was over, for the pilot cut the engines and the seatbelt sign was back on. We swooped across Cable Beach and banked over the Indian Ocean. The final glide to the runway offered glimpses of red ridges, pindan wattle, iron-roofed bungalow homes amid green tropical gardens and everywhere tall palms. Close to touchdown the tropical trees and the desert scrubs obscured the human colony, and in every direction but the ocean the Pindan wilderness engulfed and swallowed the most romantic desert oasis in Australia – Broome.

Don Gill from the Manse bed and breakfast collected me at the airport and took me to the old bungalow home built in 1910. On the way Don mentioned that a concert was about to start on the main oval of the town.

With all its greenery of tropical gardens, Broome encouraged walking in the evening before sundown, so after settling in I thought I'd wander over to the oval. I arrived just in time to hear an Aboriginal speaker tell a large crowd about the plight of the local turtles. The four-wheel-drives on the beach were crushing all the eggs and the turtles were disappearing. I could never understand anyone driving a vehicle on a beach, unless it was on Fraser Island in Queensland, where the beach was the only access.

Broome had a typical desert climate and that was one of its charms. No risk of going to a high priced hotel, only to sit in a room while the rain pelted down day after day. It happened every year in eastern Australia, somewhere up or down the coast. Holiday makers returned home exhausted from frustration. But the desert climate can catch you, too, unexpectedly. Very cool air rolled into that hollow where the oval was. Dressed in nothing but a thin shirt I had to leave before the music started. Before leaving I introduced myself to Peter Yu, Kimberley Land Council executive director. He confirmed the government hadn't officially dropped the dam proposal.

Next morning I met with Environs Kimberley secretary Maria Mann. She told me the Fitzroy, King Sound and the Buccaneer Archipelago were under another threat – uranium. A multinational exploration company had acquired an exploration lease about ten kilometres from the river and within its flood plain. Originally discovered while drilling for Kimberlite pipes in search of diamonds, the mineralisation of forty-eight tonnes of uranium oxide was discovered before ground conditions stopped drilling. If the deposit were mined in the conventional manner there would be tailing dams on one of the world's most volatile flood plains.

Before heading into the bush there were a few tedious matters to attend to. Only tedious because I wanted to be at several places at once, except a large supermarket where I had to think carefully about supplies for the next ten days. Choosing a vehicle to hire was not so bad. The sign Topless Rentals struck a chord with me and I found them wonderful people to deal with. While shopping I read that Steve Pigrim was appearing at the Roebuck Bay Hotel that evening, so with my jobs done for the day after a quick dinner, I headed for the Roebuck.

Steve took me back to the old pearling days when he sang 'Saltwater Cowboy'. All his songs contained a story or legend.

To be in Broome and miss Steve singing would have been a sad thing. In between songs I met people and one young Aboriginal man recognised me from Fitzroy Crossing. He wanted to take me reef fishing. As the twelve-metre tides surged out you rock hopped out to the reefs among the deep channels. It sounded exciting. The problem was meeting him at the Roebuck the night before to arrange a time. I didn't fancy having a hangover and scrambling on an outer reef when the second highest tide in the world turned and swirled towards home. When I was a little more than ten years old a drunken drover had made me run from a camp one night to escape all the snakes that he said were falling from the trees. A big night at the Roebuck, I thought, might prompt me to see flying sharks if I went out there fishing. His name was Andrew and maybe we would get to fish together on those reefs one day.

Later that night I asked Steve about the song 'Bullfrog Hole', because I had seen the sign on the Gibb River road the previous June. I only recalled it because it was such an odd location name. In the song, Harry the bull roams alone, his donkey mate shot from a chopper. Steve explained it was an environmental decision to shoot the feral donkeys. It turned out that the donkey shooting was another odious fallout from the 1967 equal wages decision. When the Aborigines were thrown off the stations, these was no one left with the patience or time to handle the station donkeys. Those that were raised for the breeding of mules went wild and bred into tens of thousands. It was said that more than a million had been shot and every dry season more shooting was necessary. Poor old Harry the bull was left all on his own.

Monday morning and a cattle warning sign on a gun barrel road knifing endlessly into the Pindan was all I saw for two hours. I was at last going to meet Peter Brooking, who lived on a small bush farm a few kilometres out of Derby. I stopped for a cup of coffee at the Willare Bridge Roadhouse. At Willare Crossing the Fitzroy did little to evoke the reverence you felt for the river two hundred kilometres upstream. The crossing was at the centre of the delta flood plain, where three or four channels distributed the flood waves into King Sound.

Seven kilometres south of Derby I turned right onto the Gibb River road and found Peter's place not far away. The house was set in woodland, shaded by a large native plum in the front and eucalypts on every other side. The deciduous boabs were there too, now denuded. Peter was waiting at the gate.

Peter Brooking was a road builder. Contracted by the local shire he got the traffic moving on the dirt roads following the wet. Upon completion of that work he did station road maintenance and general earth-moving work. A horse breaker and stockman in the sixties, his eyes lit up every time you talked horses. Slightly balding, he was in strong physical shape and there was a hint of boundless energy. I had doubts about a lot of things, but this man was a lucky break.

Still on the small chat a traveller carries and I was slapping my arms and legs for mosquitoes. I returned to the car for some repellent and we sat down under the plum tree. Peter wore shorts and a short-sleeved shirt and he too sprayed himself liberally. The sweat on my face had already begun to run and for a few moments I thought about Cable Beach and the south-east breeze. The Derby peninsula was long and narrow, lying between mudflats that at low tide stretched for twenty kilometres either side. Every nearby creek was the territory of a salty.

I had the 1:100,000 topographic maps and we spread four of them out on green grass cropped close to the soil by horses. For the moment we made Mount Ord the centre of our calculations. Claiming the highest elevation in the entire Kimberley, it was also the site of the old bullock route through the Lady Forrest Range, when the drovers walked them to

Derby for shipment. For a brief period after the war a vehicle track was pushed through the pass at Mount Ord and it became part of the only road link between Derby and Wyndham to the north-east, until the Gibb River road was formed, which is more direct.

Peter showed me on the map the areas he had mustered some thirty years ago, when he was a horse breaker on Mount House.

'Unfenced country,' he said. 'A couple of times we packed out in the northern valleys looking for cattle. Most of it I don't know.'

'You know where the pass is?'

'Only because of the map,' he replied with a grin. From the start I sensed he had a wonderful disposition. 'It's well hidden. The first white men through those mountains in the 1890s missed it. That explorer bloke, Frank Hann, he crossed to the west of Mount Ord through a very rough gorge.'

'We might see some sign from the old days,' I suggested.

'We may too.' Peter spoke slowly, always thinking. 'Right up until the fifties there was not much access. Not many people around now that remember. Some say the old road to Wyndham went through that pass. It's hard to believe the bush could reclaim it all so completely.'

Fifty kilometres east of the pass the Lady Forrest and the Precipice ranges merged at a point called Jacob's Ladder. The tight grades of the contours on the map left little optimism of a passage out.

'I don't know that country,' Peter said quietly. 'You want to go that far?'

The question left me stuck for a credible answer. The late wet had altered all the original plans. No one had been able to get into the Bunuba station, Millie Windie, to work the horses. Now we were packing out from the Gibb River road at Inglis Gap. From there the ride to Mornington Station was about one hundred and eighty kilometres, in a south-easterly direction. In Peter's mind there was no need to go so far when the purpose was an exploration trek to examine the possibility of packhorse tourism. I hadn't mentioned anything to Peter about the art. Most of those reared in the old days were deeply superstitious about rock shelters and rock art. They were invariably sacred sites.

'I'd like to ride through the country that may one day go under water,' I said gently.

'It's a hard ride they tell me.' When he was serious Peter's eyes faded away and you knew he was back in a world I never knew. 'No one has been down the ladder for a long time.'

'We get to Mornington we can have a spell,' I said quickly, trying to brighten the prospect. 'Hobble the horses out and explore the gorges.'

'We're banned from Mornington.' He looked uncomfortable and I could see he didn't want to ride into any trouble. 'Cur and Joe Ross had a falling out.'

'What happened?'

'No one told Cur about the rafts comin down. But no matter,' Peter added quietly. 'We can stay in the mountains and search for other gorges.'

At the peak of the wet season in February, an eco-tourism company based in Melbourne had financed the first raft expedition to fully navigate the Fitzroy and upper tributaries. Led by Joe Ross, the team of twenty-five men, in five rafts, two kayaks and one inflatable canoe began the adventure at the headwaters of the Barnett River and negotiated the river system for three hundred and fifty kilometres to Fitzroy Crossing. Some of the rapids were rated the maximum advanced 'V' and the mini waterfalls were impassable, forcing the team to rope the rafts down the falls.

Our agendas were slightly apart. Peter wanted to ride for his people. I wanted to ride to save the river. In the end we both wanted the same thing, we simply saw different tracks leading to the same goal. It was a moment of indecision for me. One thing was clear: I didn't want to get offside with Michael Cur. In many respects we were men from the same pod and I didn't want to be up against him.

'There's been a misunderstanding,' I said to Peter, bewildered. 'Do you mind if I ring him now?'

Michael Cur couldn't have been more welcoming. 'As long as I know,' he said. 'That's all I ask. Just the courtesy of being told what the plans are. The first I knew about the rafts was the news on the television.'

'I'll ring you when I have an itinerary.' I was so relieved I was nearly speechless.

'We'll look after you,' Michael said at the conclusion of the conversation.

The February rafting expedition proceeded without incident and that was probably why Michael Cur's first knowledge of it was from the television, when the local news broadcast that the expedition had been a success. In the wet of 1998 it had been a very different scenario, when Joe Ross and hardy white water adventurer Bob Brown mounted a private expedition to run the river from the Hann junction to Fitzroy Crossing. The expedition had all the ingredients of an action-packed novel. Attempting to run the rapids in canoes where the Fitzroy cuts through Mornington Station, they were thrown like bits of debris against the rocks, losing most of their supplies. There's a story that Joe and his colleagues ate a goanna and I suspect Michael Cur may have come to the rescue with emergency rations. One of the participants, Victor Marr, was seriously injured and had to be rescued by helicopter. Victor was a guitarist in the popular band 'Fitzroy Express'. I don't think Joe will be able to cajole Victor from his beloved band to go whitewater rafting ever again!

The year 1999 was a milestone in Joe Ross's life, for he'd

had a passion to run the Fitzroy River since he was a teenager, attempting it first in the mid-1980s. In 1999 when the rafts burst into view at Fitzroy Crossing and the welcoming crowd vented their praise, Joe would have enjoyed the same over-whelming feeling mountain climbers experience on the top of a previously unassailable peak.

With the expedition still intact we got around to the horses. There were a few horses walking around the house yard. They looked a bit like scrubbers who had been on green watery feed. Two or three walked past us several times, looking at Peter and expecting something. He was hand feeding them.

'I've got about ten here,' Peter said. 'Got the boys workin on em. There's another four out at Millie Windie we'd like to get hold of.'

I hadn't put the maps away and I doubled checked the distance from Derby to Millie Windie. 'Its two hundred and eighty kilometres from here. You going to catch them and load them at a set of yards somewhere?'

'Oh no,' Peter replied casually. 'We'll just grab em when we're goin along. There are a couple of little mobs in the mountains out there. I nosebag feed em.' He grinned. 'They never forget the nosebag.'

'What about the horses at Fitzroy? You been talking to Joe lately?'

'There's supposed to be a big mob out from Leopold Downs. Just can't remember the name of the place.' When Peter was sceptical about something he wore the look of trying to hold back a smile. 'Mind you, I don't know who those boys are. Then there's supposed to be another four out towards Halls Creek.'

Halls Creek was another three hundred kilometres further east from Fitzroy Crossing. Even if the horses were only halfway it was a long way back to Inglis Gap. The cost of it all could easily get out of hand. I pinned my hopes on the big mob near

Leopold Downs which was only about seventy kilometres north-east of Fitzroy Crossing. With a few doubts still lingering in my mind I switched to the packsaddles, telling Peter I had two in Broome.

'They're a bit of a problem,' Peter said reluctantly. 'I got one here. There may be two at Leopold Downs. Jubilee Station's offered the loan of one.'

I had the feeling four packsaddles would be the most I could expect and it might prove to be a blessing. With two packs to a horse, a total of eight packs would service ten riders, on a frugal pack list.

It was about lunch time and I knew Peter had other things to do. I asked him if I could set up camp somewhere near the corral. He seemed surprised that I wasn't driving into Derby to stay in conventional accommodation, but I was of the opinion nearly everyone's the same when they're visiting in a town. You had an urge to explore it and see what was offering, and that could lead to a bar. In the bush you made do. I enjoyed reading by lantern light.

I pitched the tent near the set of yards under a grevillea. The horses took an interest and a couple even followed me into the timber when I went looking for some firewood. In colours they went from creamy to black and were all geldings. They were very inquisitive about the camp preparations and I knew a decent fire would make them back off a bit. After I had the fire throwing out a bit of flame I made a point of letting them smell the back of my hand. Four of them didn't want me near them. The whites of their eyes flashed and they swung away. Yet even they were curious. They didn't walk away and after retreating to the other horses for a few minutes I tried them again and again. Eventually they all accepted me, except the black horse.

The horses had the run of the garden in the front of the house, the machinery yard down the back and several acres of scrub that was well grassed. Every time one raised its tail and dropped a few turds a family of turkeys would appear. It was the undigested grain. There were no flies about, thanks to the turkeys, and their droppings in turn must have been quickly dealt with, too, because I never once stepped on them.

In the deep shade of the front garden a hose leaked generously and a flock of fowls camped on the cool wet ground. The horses, restless, waiting and wanting the nosebag, frequently stepped over them.

With the creeks still full, the mosquitoes were a constant irritation. I thought the smoke would shift them but, typical of noon-day heat, the smoke kept changing course. The only thing that worked was repellent spray to hands and face every thirty minutes. Without my books it might have been an unbearable afternoon. Frank Hann's diaries, *Do Not Yield to Despair*, had arrived by special post from Perth two days before I'd left for Broome but so far I had only looked at the maps. Hann's 1898 expedition appeared to cross the three ranges we planned to, which was not all that surprising given the nature of the terrain. What particularly interested me was his trek along the upper Fitzroy and the Hann rivers (the latter was later named after him). I wanted to know the features and gorges he noted along the way, as I wasn't aware of any written records since. Aerial photographs had led to the drawing of maps you could trust your life with, but the draftsmen had no concept of what lay on the ground in the form of rock shelters.

I didn't notice the passing of the afternoon, so enraptured was I with Hann's diaries. The heat gave way to a pleasant autumn evening, and with the sun down, the lantern going and fire burning brighter as darkness grew, I could see the flames reflected in the horses' eyes. The moon rose early and the bark of the boab, like smooth human skin, caught the light. The bottle-shaped trunks had become twisted skeletons and the patternless spread of branches were like arms frozen at the height of a corroboree.

I boiled up some rice for dinner and was lifting the pot off the flames when a bloke climbed over the fence from the road. He introduced himself as Robert and sat on the ground. With him was a little boy of ten or more.

'Biggest wet for years,' Robert said, drawing on a cigarette. 'I've been wanting to get out to Millie Windie and handle the horses. Creeks all in flood. No hope of getting a vehicle through and costs too much to go out in a chopper.'

I offered some rice to him and to the little boy, whose name was also Robert. They declined.

'There's plenty of horses at Fitzroy I am told,' I said to him. He looked worried and almost apologetic. 'We should be right for horses with ten here ready to go.' I didn't think there were ten. There were two I didn't think would be coming and I thought my comment might draw him. He didn't say anything.

The little boy was a delightful child. He had a quick intelligent eye and a sense of humour. His mother had gone away to Port Hedland to live and she was coming back to collect him. People of Aboriginal descent had a unique sense of family and in the event of broken marriages extended families closed around the children.

Over a billy of tea I talked with Robert for some time about what he knew of the past. I had already read some very disturbing accounts of the three-year campaign to hunt down the Bunuba warrior Jandamarra. One of the fiercest freedom fighters in the long tragic history of Aboriginal uprisings against the white invader, Jandamarra had been feared in the Kimberleys by both white and black. Having read everything I could put my hands on, I believed Jandamarra had fought a private war against the white pastoralists and the police. A constable Richardson had fathered the first child from Jandamarra's loved one and analysis of white behaviour towards Aboriginal women in the early days suggested that the young woman probably submitted reluctantly. Such behaviour would have sparked a hatred from Jandamarra never to be tempered.

Some brutal characters were engaged in the police campaign from October 1894 to April 1897, when Jandamarra was finally shot dead by a black tracker. A story Robert told was the most chilling I had ever heard. Robert was articulate and in the coming weeks I developed a great respect for his knowledge.

'The camps had little warning when the mounted police were coming. A sentry would race into camp and there was panic. The police patrol was over the rise, their horses trotting. The women would snatch dillybags of tucker; the men their weapons. The nightmare was the babies. You can't run fast carrying a baby, so the mothers placed their babies in a coolamin and planted them. The police gone they planned to come back. But the aim of the police and assembled possies from the stations was indiscriminate. Many babies were left to die, slowly.'

The Kimberley tribes were defeated by the invaders in a scorched-earth drive.

Next morning I woke at daylight and was fiddling around with a few twigs to light a fire when Peter walked over and insisted I have coffee in his kitchen. I told him I thought it would take a few days to sort everything out. I wanted to inspect the horses drafted for the trek, talk to riders and check transport arrangements. In the meantime, Peter said he and the boys would look around for a few more bush horses.

After breakfast I packed up, said goodbye and set off for Fitzroy Crossing. Joe had planned a meeting of those keen to take part in the expedition at 10 a.m. With two hundred and sixty kilometres to travel I had to push the old Toyota along and I was feeling a bit regretful I hadn't left for Fitzroy Crossing the previous afternoon.

I arrived in Fitzroy Crossing with a few minutes to spare. Joe was in his office. There was to be no meeting. He would call it next week, he thought, and suggested we drive around the village and meet a few of the riders. Next day he was flying to Darwin.

Since the middle of March Sal had followed a fitness schedule. Three kilometres of brisk walking every day, finishing the last four hundred metres with a hard run, followed by ten minutes of exercises. To stand up to long days in the saddle it was the minimum requirement. My program had been more demanding, as I anticipated some rock climbing. So when I looked at the men Joe introduced as volunteers my heart sank. They were not fit and had no concept of what was involved. I certainly didn't blame Joe. He was enthusiastic and had put the Leopold trek before the community, calling for volunteers.

I was relieved when he collected two of the Elders, George and Bob. George was Peter Brooking's brother. Joe introduced them as good drivers and said they knew every track in the vast district. We decided at once to drive out to the station where all the horses were. Joe couldn't come. He was heavily involved with Aboriginal affairs on a national basis.

We went to the roadhouse to fill up and ordered some lunch. I asked for two rolls of tobacco and was staggered at the cost of them. The older people were reared on roll-your-own tobacco and for decades it had served to soften the harsh reality of life. I felt that it shouldn't have been taxed at such a savage rate.

The impact of this was rammed home an hour after we left Fitzroy Crossing. On a gravel road, threading its way through the Oscar Range, a truck approached. Not another dog could have fitted in the cabin, and ten or more Aboriginal people were riding in the back. George and Bob were keen to talk to them, and I stopped. I couldn't understand a word uttered. It would take weeks to pick up their accents. At first I thought they were speaking their own language, but it turned out to be English spoken rapidly in pidgin form. We stopped for less than five minutes. Time enough to share all the tobacco, both rolls. The Elders kept a mere half-palmful for themselves. I hadn't seen such a thing for decades. Irish nuns had enforced it: what you had you shared, and you took no more than anyone else. It was their way, their belief, and it fascinated me to see adult men share voluntarily and so totally. It was the way of these people.

Beyond the Oscars the black plains threw up a dense stand of spear grass. The soil reminded me of the Barwon country around Walgett, in far north-west New South Wales, which was now the wheat bowl of the inland. Bob said it was Leopold Downs Station and the few cattle we saw on the road were fat.

One yearling darted in front of the car. It was unbranded – a cleanskin. 'You bring gun, Mike?' George asked with a smile. 'Up on the Leopolds we'll eat them.'

There have been times in my life when the absence of a gun left me feeling partly dressed, like my belt was unbuckled. But guns hardened the hearts of men. I was tired of them. 'Peter might have one,' I replied.

George nodded. He was still looking at that calf, now behind us. I could nearly smell the steak myself.

A king brown crawled onto the road, head slightly raised. The windows were down and I slowed. They could whip up and back at lightning speed. I saw it happen once on a tractor, in the days of no cabins.

'Them bite yer, you dead,' Bob growled, grinning like a boy.

'Many about?' I asked.

'Plenty snakes now,' George said. 'They eat up big now before the sleep.' He paused. 'Don't sleep too long, them fellas. Warm days back by August.'

'They cranky now,' Bob quipped.

They were delightful characters. Bob was quite fluid and easier to understand than George. Aboriginal people had a great sense of drama and theatre. They loved stories and loved to tell them. A corroboree performed by the Bunuba people was lucidly recorded by R.H. Pilmer in the late 1890s:

> We just sat and watched the show – and with 500 dancers, and the bush lit the brightness of day when the big corroboree fires were at their best, it was a magnificent one. We could plainly see the lubras and old men beating time with their kylies, hear the shrill singing and the 'yack-ai'. I venture to state no theatre in the world could stage a song-scene or a ballet such as Nature herself, in the Australian wilds, presented for us that night.

Cathie Clement & Peter Bridge (eds), *Northern Patrol*

R. H. Pilmer was a mounted police officer working in the west Kimberley in the 1890s.

The black soil held the water, forcing me to lock into four-wheel drive. The spear grass was well over two metres high. I was preoccupied with the spear grass, the heat and the snakes. Would two weeks towards winter make any difference? What would the boys think if they knew what I was taking their mother into? And, more nagging still, was it fair to put her through it? But I needed her support. I needed her expertise with the camera.

At every change in the country, at a creek, or at a rise that afforded a view, George or Bob had a story.

Bob was the most vocal. 'See those big rocks over there. Policeman shoot blackfella there. My father knew that fella.'

George wasn't so much interested in the theatre – when he spoke it was imparting knowledge. 'That tree there – you see that tree, Mike? Your horse or cattle hungry, you feed them those leaves.' Several times George spoke of trees and when I asked he gave me the traditional name. The fodder tree, I checked out later, was the corkybark wattle.

An hour went by, the tyres on stone crunching underneath. I could see the King Leopold Ranges ahead. Where in the hell were we going? But I said nothing, because I knew it was merely my impatience. With the slow going we were probably only one hundred kilometres from Fitzroy Crossing. Now the black soil plains were behind, and we rolled on over undulating foothills where bloodwood trees were dominant. Bloodwood was an apt name and there were several species. The trunks varied from red blotched white to slightly pink, as though the bark had been soaked in watered-down blood. The trees could be an eerie symbol of the past, depending on your mood and the influence of stories passed down. Maybe all the horror stories were true. Maybe some were not. You had to keep appreciating their love of theatre, from which their Dreamtime had evolved.

'You got boys?' Bob asked.

'Oh yes,' I replied, glad to get away from some of the stories. The last one had been about a cave full of skeletons. Robert too had told me about the cave. He could take me there! 'My eldest is thirty.'

Bob's face lit up. 'Mine too.' Bob was said to be over eighty, but there was no such thing as men too old in their culture. After all, a man at fifty is in his prime, in more ways than one.

'What does he do?'

'He's in Broome. He's in the gaol.'

There was an awkward silence and I asked what the young man had done.

'He got on the grog and try taken car.'

In the Kimberley the fate of Bob's son was a common story, like an old record player stuck on repeat. It was another deadly fallout from the social reforms forced upon these people in the sixties. Bob's generation were taught to be skilled horse-men and stockmen. But when the Aboriginal people were deprived of their dignity and their life with the land, those skills and knowledge had sometimes been lost. The people simply languished in ghettos and children half-reared them-selves in a new culture of no pain, no endurance, no respect and no knowledge.

It was about mid-afternoon when we arrived. There were no horses anywhere in sight. On the fence surrounding the house was a sturdy top rail with all kinds of saddle gear draped over it. It looked encouraging, despite there being no horses.

As I drew up outside a young bloke came through the gate to meet us. There was no sign of welcome about him. 'Who are you?' he demanded.

I told him and explained I had come out to look at the horses.

'They're not here,' he said defensively. 'Supposed to be a helicopter comin.'

'Where are they?' I took him gently.

'The helicopter find em. I don't know what day, though. No one's told me.'

There was a fire going in the house yard and a big black camp oven had been pulled to the side, the lid nearby. There was still a large piece of meat left, a bit on the charred side. Seated in old plastic chairs and spread around a bit were three or four young men. A white bloke had his back to us.

'Got any tea there?' George wasn't through the gate when he asked, with Bob close behind.

'We got a jug for boilin up,' the young man said, implying there was tea if we made it. George and Bob walked ahead and greeted the other boys. On the way George tore a piece from the lump of meat in the camp oven. I was introduced. I turned around to the white man. It was Pat Hurst, the bloke who gave me some advice at the guesthouse in Fitzroy Crossing. 'What are you doing out here?' I asked, surprised to see him.

'I'm up in the Leopolds, actually,' he said, with a sort of shy smile. 'I got onto the gold.'

'Oh, be buggered. I thought that was a hundred years ago.'

'I got it all right.' There was a glint in his eye. Where else in the world could you still be a gold prospector, out on the frontier. There was still that raw edge of life in the Kimberley, where free spirits could roam.

We chatted for a while. Both veteran stockmen, we could have talked for the rest of the day. He wanted me to swing the compass point and ride to his goldmine. I explained I had a different treasure in mind and he laughed. It was great to see him again. I took the jug and a billy into the house to make the tea. It was a new home, well built. Not much had been done since the builder left.

This was a new station. I didn't know the circumstances and didn't inquire. The mustering was obviously done using contract helicopters. It was a start in the right direction. Initially it was going to be hard on the young blokes, because the old people from the stations were too old to pass on practical experience.

We drank the tea, then I announced we were heading back to Fitzroy Crossing. Pat volunteered some more advice, quite openly for all to hear. I listened very carefully.

George and Bob made it clear they were very dry on the way home. Suddenly I was too, but I resolved not to have a single drink. There was still a little daylight when we arrived at the Crossing Inn and I suggested they wait in the car while I picked up a carton of Emu Bitter. I wanted to set up a camp and there was no time for drinking at the hotel. George and Bob needed their swags, which we could collect later.

George knew a good camping ground near the old river crossing. Originally the village had been out there. We passed the guesthouse and continued maybe for a kilometre. The bulldozer-levelled camping ground had no appeal, so I followed a steep track to the river's lower bank. The Elders were out before I'd switched off the engine. They were thinking about the beer.

It was a nice spot up on the sand ridge. It overlooked the river, which still flowed bank to bank, but it was a gentle flow, and not a murmur could be heard. The night was coming in fast and I lit a fire to throw some light out.

I made a billy of tea for myself and got busy with some rice, flavoured with tomato and garlic. The mosquitoes were bad, but the Elders never felt them. I watched the insects settle on their forearms. They must have been biting, but not so much as a swat from those gentlemen of the bush.

I quickly put up the tent. Back at the fire the stubbies were moving rapidly out of the box. I got a meal into the two of them as quickly as I could, but to no avail. Bob was calling me 'Boy', which I quietly felt delighted about, and George was continually saying, 'Mike, when do we leave on the big ride?' I could see it was hopeless. Kindness intended, I'd done the wrong thing. They were compulsive drinkers. Already each of them had drunk enough to put me flat on my back. I bundled them into the car.

First house was George's place. Several young men and women surrounded the car in the dark, and when I got out I was shaking hands all over the place. Where did I come from and was I staying? Amid the smiles the smell of alcohol hung heavy in the air. There was something on in another street, near where Bob lived. George got back in, the vehicle filled with bodies and I moved off, crawling for fear of running over someone.

The next street was also poorly lit. I stopped beside a huge circle of people and the light from a torch was focused in the centre. I couldn't see much from the driver's seat and got out. Bob, George and the rest struggled out and I was introduced to literally tens of people. Aboriginal people touch incessantly with social introduction. They made you feel accepted imme-diately, as I had discovered months before. They still lived within the spirit of their old culture.

Deep in the circle, fifteen or twenty people of all ages were seated in the dust playing show poker. Outside the tight peri-meter of the circle children played and any number of dogs trotted about, tails wagging. It was raw community life. I stayed for a while, taking it in. Hypersensitive to people and scene I felt my own mood swing. The Bunuba people had something most other Australians had lost. No amount of money could buy the family spirit of the Bunuba.

The next morning I woke early at my river camp, packed up quickly then went to the roadhouse for breakfast. Afterwards, I went to see George. He was in the shower. In a way I was relieved, because I didn't know what to say. I felt Bob would struggle on the trek, but I knew George wanted to come. I told George's son to tell his father I would get enough horses. I wanted George to ride with me. The boy was cheer-ful and asked me to come in and sit down. It was a spacious house and I could see that the front room was full of bodies under blankets. I declined. He said he would pass on the message.

I arrived back at Peter Brooking's home late morning. Always loyal, he volunteered nothing. I didn't think he was surprised to see me back. I explained the horse situation, that the broken horses hadn't been ridden for years and no one knew which ones had seen the rope from the rest. Even if they were run in with a helicopter, there was a month's work for an expert breaker.

'I think the boys and I can find a handful more,' he said calmly.

'How many boys coming?'

'They'll all come I think.' When Peter spoke very slowly you knew there was some doubt. 'They got families, mind you. Makes a bit of a problem.'

The boys were nearly all men. It was Peter's way of referring to them. The youngest may have been in his late teens; the oldest over forty. Even as Peter and I talked, they worked on a handful of horses in the corral and adjoining yard. One horse was being coaxed around the ring-shaped yard, to get used to the saddle and the girth. Another had a red-hide lasso around its neck, a boy in a sleeveless black top talking quietly to it, as he inched his way along the red-hide rope. The bay gelding stood straight-legged, head high, and prominent was the white in the eye. For a moment Peter and I fell silent and watched. The boy reached the horse's head and deftly fitted a halter.

The square yard next to the corral was where they did the shoeing. Two horses were being shod. The black horse had his hind leg held with a strap connected to a rope around his neck. While I watched from my seat under the plum tree the horse plunged away a couple of times, only to find the shoe was going on whether he liked it or not. The boys never once raised their voices. They worked in pairs, except with the black horse – one tackled the shoeing and two stood at the horse's head, one boy languidly rubbing the horse down the neck. No one gave any orders. One would start work and another back him up.

Peter laughed when I mentioned it. 'Everyone's his own man,' he said. 'One bloke will put a shoe on, then say other one tomorrow. No one will say no – let's finish him. Time doesn't matter. If it's hot and mosquitoes are bad we'll do more tomorrow.'

The clothes and get-ups supported Peter's appraisal of individuality. Two had black hats with red-string bands. One wore a shirt with a crocodile drawn front and back. Another displayed an eagle, and one shirt had kangaroos, emus, crocodiles and a white cockatoo drawn at random. Nearly all of them wore blue jeans, heavily bleached. Caps of any old colour were popular, too, and when they had something on their feet it was sandshoes.

The horse in the corral with the halter on ran backwards until his rump collided into a steel rail. The handler went in quietly, talking to the confused animal. It was just a matter of time, maybe three or four days, before they were riding this one.

'I hope most of them come,' I said to Peter. 'We'll need a few hands with this lot.'

Peter had a sudden twinkle in his eye. 'It's the good old nosebag that does all the quietening down. Mind you, I'm takin no chances with your wife. I borrowed one for her. He's called Shornie. The boys are givin him a little bit of work too. We don't want em real soft.'

Peter was something of a father figure. I got the impression he had taught some of the boys all they knew. Not just horses. Mechanical skills as well, right down to tyre changing. With the horses there was no money involved. They worked them in the corral and rode them out along the road because they loved working with horses.

'What about the tucker?' Peter asked. 'As we won't have any airdrops from Fitzroy, I'll see if George will bring his truck along.' Now that the expedition headquarters had been moved to Derby we couldn't expect Joe Ross to arrange food drops.

I hadn't known George had a truck. It was good news. It looked like he was a certain starter. 'The water's still running in the mountain creeks,' I said. Pat Hurst had mentioned the rivers and creeks were still running high. 'Maybe the last lot of storms dropped a lot more rain up there.'

'I think they'll drop quickly now,' Peter said tentatively.

I had to agree with him. I wasn't worried about the creeks. The long drive back from Fitzroy Crossing had given me time to think. I needed to get up into the mountains and observe the environmental situation at first hand. Were we heading out too early? Was it still hot and was there too much water? In addition I wanted to make a supply dump. To be independent with food at least. I explained to Peter that what I had in mind was to drive out to Mornington.

'Better wait until the morning,' Peter said, looking a little concerned. 'By the time you buy up be getting on a bit. You won't even make the Napier Range before dark.'

I hadn't been back into Derby since the Cup race day the previous June. Aware now that the rumours started by ignorant travellers from back east were groundless, I saw the town in an entirely different perspective. With all the trees and bushy gardens there was a green softness about it, and everywhere I went people were friendly. When a group of Aboriginal horsemen rode through the central business area I was completely won over. I made inquiries about accommodation, thinking of the nights Sal and I would have in the town before and after the expedition. On a tight budget, I couldn't afford the luxury hotel again. I was told about the Kimberley Guesthouse.

With shopping I usually needed a woman to guide me. I tended to have a mental block after self-raising flour, rice, jam, sugar, tea, coffee and powdered milk. Usually lost and irritated in supermarkets, I was thankful for the long aisles in Woolworths that afternoon. A lot of little items were tossed into the trolley, unimportant at the time, but four hundred kilometres from the nearest shop they could be the difference between a happy camp and a miserable one.

When I drove back to Peter's place he was sitting under the plum tree talking to an older man.

Peter greeted me. 'Sam's come out to have a talk to you.' 'He's the only man alive who knows anything about the country you want to ride into.'

Sam Lovell had a presence about him. When we shook hands

he reminded me of Aboriginal stockmen I'd met in Queens-land. They looked you in the eye and spoke confidently. Clear-featured, with a hint of the Caucasian, Sam had a heightened intelligence apparent from the first conversation. Later I found out he was a 'stolen child', beyond doubt a crushing experi-ence and painful beyond any metaphor.

I've been down through Jacob's Ladder,' Sam said, sitting erect in his chair and weighing me up. 'About forty-five years ago it was. You need to know where you're going.' He paused, letting me think about it. 'There's some dead-end valleys.'

'I'll get my maps from the car,' I said eagerly.

Sam produced a map. 'This is an old map. For your purposes it's better than the new ones because it shows the old tracks.' He smiled briefly, a disarming, friendly smile. 'All this country has returned to the wild. Some of those tracks used in the fifties may have disappeared altogether.'

He spread the map out onto the grass. It was Lennard River, 1:250,000, printed by the Royal Australian Survey Corp in 1963. 'The King Leopolds and the Lady Forrest made a formidable barrier to the north in the early days. Frank Hann may not have been the first white man to venture north of the range, but he was the first to do a decent recording of what he saw.' Sam put his index finger on the map. 'He got through the Lady Forrest here – Mount Bell gap. The year was 1898.' He raised his eyebrows, as though to catch my attention. 'That's where the Gibb River road now goes, far to the west of where you want to go. You and Peter have got to find the Mount Ord gap. You can't see it up in that tangle of mountains. Frank Hann missed it. They all missed it for years.'

'No other way?'

Sam shook his head. 'You have to find that gap. Believe it or not there was a vehicle track for maybe two decades. In eighty-three I picked my way through in a four-wheel-drive. Had a load of kids with me. There wasn't much sign of the track, but I knew where to look I guess. We threw the dead branches off it and in a couple of places I had to work with the axe on fallen trees. We got as far as Nugget Gorge.'

Peter had left us to it and gone down the back to his workshop. Maybe he and Sam had already pored over the map.

'The old track swung sharply to the west after the gap,' Sam went on. 'You're going in the opposite direction and if you miss the passage there's no way out. You have to ride back. Once down the ladder you're in the Adcock River country. Bad country it is. Full of washouts. You got to keep away off the river, in waterless slate country. The heat comes up from the ground worse than from the sun.'

Sam was the messenger. No one wanted to go. It was a ride to hell. Maybe there was no need for it. We could pack out for the head of the Lennard up around Pittard Bluff, which was near Dimond Gorge anyway. The boys would get a taste of the packhorse experience. Perhaps a strong movement back into their country and culture tourism with horses was enough to capture people's imagination and save the river. But it wasn't within the country under threat. The advocates for progress and development driven by dreams of great wealth were always powerful and influential, capable of discarding morals and protocols with the same ease they blew their noses. They would rave against such sentiments as Dreamtime nonsense. If the water didn't flood their operation, there was no argument.

I vacillated quietly, tortuously, knowing just a word from me and the search for the galleries was off the agenda. I had two hundred dollars worth of supplies in the car for a dump at Mornington. I had to make a decision. Motivated by nothing more than the need to buy time I raised the subject of rock art.

It prompted a long searching look from Sam – not reproachful, something deeper. 'Someone got up into a remote canyon years ago. Saw a big cave full of drawings like none he'd ever seen before. He said the artists were Egyptian. He's dead now, but Elders spoke of this place too. They said strange people from another land did the drawings.'

This didn't sound like the Bradshaw paintings. It was something to my knowledge unrecorded. I struggled to contain my excitement. 'You know where this gallery is?' I asked as casually as possible.

Sam explained where he thought it was. The area was a long way off the Lennard River map. Somewhere out there was perhaps the Holy Grail of ancient Australian rock art.

'Have you been anywhere near it?' I wanted to assess the nature of the country.

Sam's eyes lit up. 'I was the first ever to take tourists over the range. They were real old-time safaris. No tracks – just a compass. I carried a boat on the roofrack and took my guests through Dimond Gorge. Mornington was a part of Tableland Station in those days and the only structure on the lower Adcock was a stockyard and supply shed. Once a year the musterers came down to brand the calves and collect the new season bullocks.' He hesitated, his expression sober. 'Sometimes on bigger safaris I went up another gorge. More like a gash in the earth – a canyon, I suppose you'd call it. We had to carry the boat around the rapids, and one day we reached a terrible murderous rock fall. I never attempted to go over that one. I expect the gallery was up there somewhere. Maybe many miles. In terms of human effort perhaps days.'

Peter sauntered back from the workshop. He sat down and asked whether we'd figured out a route.

Sam laughed. 'Oh we worked over the map while you were away. Looks like you'll need a packhorse to carry an inflatable raft.' Then he added, seriously, 'Those places are sacred. You should have the consent of the custodians. None of us go to these places without permission.'

'I'll make inquiries, Sam, and find out if any of the old

people know anything about the art up there,' Peter said. 'We won't go looking for it until we've asked them.'

'What if they know nothing about it?' I asked.

'Its just a courtesy,' Sam said gravely. 'Doesn't matter if they know about it or not.'

In Aboriginal mythology and spiritualism there are strict protocols in regard to sacred sites. It was what a social worker in Broome had been trying to tell me. I had met her there in October through a linguist, who had also been very helpful with my general research. They were good friends and they invited me to join them for dinner one night at an open air café that overlooked Roebuck Bay. I couldn't recall her name, but the darkness of her hair and wild laughing eyes had made me think of a Mexican girl. Whatever prompted me she had become in my mind Magdalena, a lovely Mexican name in keeping with her confessed beliefs in spiritualism.

She believed without reservation. I suspected Sam did too, particularly if he had been reared as a Catholic, because there was a parallel. Punishment was not an earthly contemplation, except for trivial things. If you contravened the great laws God dealt with you. We Catholics knew of purgatory and hell, the latter banishment for eternity. Aboriginal spiritualism seemed far more complex, but similar – the triumph of good over evil.

I had no problem with my intentions. I prayed to God to save the land and allow me to be an instrument. My problem was the blind conviction I was being heard. I didn't have that. Magdalena and Sam did. Sometimes I pondered on the ancient cultures across the globe. The Navajo of Arizona and New Mexico believed their lives would be shortened if they told a sacred story to a stranger. The Hopi of Colorado gravely warned strangers about observing sacred ceremonies, stating the God of Fire, Masauwia, would destroy their souls.

The spiritualism of the hunter–gatherer and the tribal sedentary societies was not confined to sacred sites, sacred stories and ceremonies. I found it thought provoking, in a deep spiritual sense, that these societies could be many thousands of kilometres apart, across the world's greatest oceans, and have often very similar beliefs. The Zuni of New Mexico regarded the land as a spiritual relative and all upon it interconnected. We knew this to be the belief of Australia's indigenous people. The Hopi from the high arid lands of Colorado held animals to be intrinsically human, in terms of mythology. They carried messages and warned of impending danger. Aboriginal people may have gone one step further with their belief in the totem. The spirit of each individual was connected to an animal in the wild. The bearer was to always look out for the animal and look upon it as a kindred spirit. The pragmatic could laugh deliriously at such ideas but who were we, wrapped snug in our brand new culture, to wipe aside teachings of thousands of years as mere superstition?

5 The Saltwater Lady

I didn't wait. Sam had fired my zest for the mountains and I took off for Mornington when the shadows were already lengthening. With Michael Cur's blessing I would store the supplies I'd bought on his station. We'd use them to replenish our supplies before setting out on the second leg of the trek.

For a while the bitumen cut through the Pindan, and moving at one hundred kilometres on the speedo I looked like eating time and crossing the Leopolds before dark. Then the sealed road ended. Ahead lay the great black soil plains of Kimberley Downs Station and before me water as far as I could see. Back came the four-wheel-drive shift and I proceeded slowly. There was an old saying in the bush, 'Water never fear, mud beware.' I kept to the middle and avoided wheel spin. It proved to be the longest stretch under water I had ever driven. As the sun lowered the slanting rays caught the termite nests, shaped like teepees.

At the Lennard River crossing the ground looked wet and treacherous. The sun was hovering on the horizon and at the next watercourse, a creek, I pulled off the road onto a hard piece of ground. There was a long waterhole hidden beneath the paperbarks and when I got out I could hear the gentle murmur of shallow water rippling over stones. At the edge I gazed into water so clear I could see my face as sharp as a mirror. I dropped a few twigs onto the surface. The little ripples made my face and hat wobble and within seconds small fish darted in to investigate and a small cherubim, a freshwater lobster, wasn't far behind.

All the trees along the bank were river paperbarks. Frayed bits of bark, the colour of tanned Caucasian skin, clung to off-white trunks and when a breeze whispered through, the little pieces fluttered amid branches heavy with leaves.

The camp was a simple, beautiful place. One of the first to camp beyond the Napier Range since the last big monsoon storms, I found flood driftwood stacked in heaps against the larger trees, and had a fire going in no time. I cooked some steak skewered on a green stick, lay down early to sleep and waited to hear the bush noises, the nocturnal sounds of all the bush creatures. But there was nothing, not a sound all night. It disturbed me and I packed up at daylight.

The country running up towards the King Leopolds was comprised of hard-looking hills lined with granite outcrops. To break a landscape that offered no welcome were boulder tors, and over a low pass I sighted a whaleback of bare rock. It was high enough to offer me a view of the country to the west, which according to the map was rugged and interesting. I was restless to walk. You never feel the country sitting in a car, and my haversack was packed and ready with all I needed for a three-hour excursion, including two litres of water.

The walking at once was tough. Seeds from the spear grass stuck to my shirt and trousers like quills and the height of the grass impeded any movement of air. With sweat trickling down my neck and onto my chest, the ducking, the weaving and the rock hopping forced me to stop and rethink my motivation. The spear grass was so thick I couldn't see if anything lay on the ground, except the big rocks. Peter had told me that nearly all of this station – Napier Downs – was rotten with king browns. I was thirsty, too, not twenty minutes from the car.

The two litres would pass through me like water spilt on sand. It was madness. I returned to the car humbled by my first taste of the Kimberley wild alone.

Soon the terrain changed and the colour invaded the land, like a black and white movie progressing to technicolour. Hog-backs and sheer valley walls marked the southern ramparts of the King Leopolds. Through the Inglis Gap evidence of the fault line appeared in the form of spectacular conglomerates, said to be the result of silt-loaded rivers transporting boulders until impervious formations blocked the passage. Raised and insidious, shaped like black moles on the ancient terrain, these conglomerates appeared like mounting crusts of pillow lava and, mysteriously almost, the morning sun reflected the fire-red of thousands of holes and crevices. To add to this scene of Archaean geological chaos, the starkness of the Leopold pink and white sandstone and dolomite rose above the tattered green of the valleys.

The rugged divide of the Leopolds behind, the road flat-tened out again and the red escarpments tapered away. I arrived at the community of Imintji, where John and Nola Robb owned and operated the only store. It was government policy to assist Aboriginal people to move back to traditional homelands by establishing satellite communities. The village of Imintji cost about 2.5 million dollars to set up, and was com-prised of homes that I thought looked very attractive. John and his wife had recently sold their Beverley Springs Station, about eighty kilometres north-west of the village. A glance at the map showed a station way out on a limb, surrounded by wilderness more or less abandoned since the last of the packhorse police patrols. When I asked John what it was like out there he nearly convinced me I was riding in the wrong direction. With ani-mated enthusiasm he spoke of rainforest pockets and ranges untrodden by Europeans. When asked about the viability of

Kimberley cattle stations he said the region had never been given a chance. The stations were always too big and impossible to properly manage. In the higher rainfall of the western table-land country he claimed improved grass species substantially raised carrying capacity. I had always been of the opinion that conservative range-land grazing looked after the country better than any form of public management and encouraged the horse culture. When men and women rode horses, they lived close to the earth and were more likely to hear the land's cry for help.

Reaching Mornington didn't present the same challenges as the previous June. The creeks demanded a sturdy four-wheel-drive, but the big water had moved on to the Fitzroy. The old camp seemed deserted when I arrived. Standing at the edge of the shed complex I didn't see him in the shadow.

'Good-aye,' Michael growled. He was seated behind the bar. He introduced me to Jake Zahl, sitting on the patron's side. On the bar were a handful of brochures. Jake was a tour oper-ator, and going by the heavy look in his eye he should have telephoned Michael and asked about station road conditions.

'We've had a pretty good go,' Michael added. 'Started about eight o'clock last night'.

I quietly thanked the Almighty I hadn't arrived yesterday. 'Some occasion?' I posed, half ribbing them.

'You bet,' Michael rasped.

'The departure of the tourists from hell,' laughed Jake.

I looked at Michael. I already knew about his capacity to relate a story.

'I was forewarned,' Michael began. 'That's if anyone could warn you about a mobile pantomime let loose in the Kimber-ley. To make it worse they couldn't have arrived at a worse time. I'd just walked out of the generator room with grease all over me, having completed a difficult little job, and I see three four-wheel-drives stop outside the fence. A tall stick of a thing gets out and asks for the proprietor. I tell him he's looking at him. Taken aback, he tells me he only deals with people correctly dressed. I told him that in the Australian wilderness correct dress had varied from stark naked to colonial military attire – which might he prefer? In the meantime, I told him, he and all his entourage were placed in the same unenviable position as the priest who told the sinner he would go to hell. The sinner replied it was not certain he would go to hell, but it was certain the priest would get to hell off the premises.' Michael paused. Shaking his head with the same flabbergasted disbelief he'd felt two evenings before, he said, 'But they didn't go! They couldn't light a fire and took over my kitchen. They carried their own grog over and used all my bar facilities. Then to cap it off they wanted a corroboree. "Money no problem to us" – it became like a chant – "Money no problem." Our wines are very expensive, the best in the world and when we give you a plate of spaghetti you never again taste food like it. Well I got even on that score – told em it was shit they were eating. On the money no problem bit I rang Wallace, told him to come with the community and jump up and down for a few minutes and charge a thousand bucks. But he didn't come.'

'To soften the blow did you make any money out of them?' I asked.

'You lose money with a group like that,' Michael said soberly. 'They disrupt everything. Make it uncomfortable for other guests and you know they aren't the slightest bit interested in the gorges. This is eco-tourism at its best, among Australia's most colourful gorges and canyons.'

It was a one off. Michael would probably never see the like of it again. In the packhorse days I copped a similar group. They complained about everything and burnt cigarette holes in the inflatable mattresses.

Jake owned and operated Hot Land Safaris. I picked up a brochure and saw it was a six-day package. Guests did everything from swimming in the Lennard Gorge to exploring Dimond Gorge by canoe, and Jake knew some barramundi spots on Mornington. No worries about tyres, bogs, wrong tracks – it had great appeal. After a mug of coffee with me, he left for Derby, his home and tourist base.

'The barramundi fishermen have been here ten days,' Michael said, when I asked how the fishing was. 'Last week the camp was full. Water and mud won't stop those blokes. Some nice fish were taken too.'

'I hope we get some, too, because the supplies I've got aren't very exciting. I want to drop some food out here. In one of the sheds.'

'Have a look around. Please yourself where you put them. How are your plans going, anyway?'

I told him there was considerable reluctance to trek over the range and down the Adcock.

'I feel I should offer a bit of caution,' Michael said thoughtfully, 'The country here is terrible on horses. When I first came here I brought eighteen thoroughbreds across from Queensland and not one saw the mustering out.'

'We'll go quietly,' I assured him. 'Trekking's vastly different to mustering.'

'What about Sal? Hell, she was half scared here in the camp last June.'

'I told her you'd fly her to Broome if it got to her.'

'God struth, I've got a business to run!'

'You could back load with a cook. Get one about thirty-five. Experienced enough to run the kitchen and young enough to knock you up.'

Michael pretended to be horrified. 'You're a bad influence. Actually, I am waiting on a cook. Due here next mail plane.' Then he added, shaking his head, 'I don't know her age. God blow you – if she's thirty-five I'll feel guilty now every time I look at her.'

The thought put a bit of colour back in his face. He got up and went over to the store.

'Seven for dinner tonight, including you. I'm cooking a turkey. What do you think of that?'

I got up and walked over. The fat bubbled in the baking tray and the gamy smell reminded me I hadn't had any lunch. It looked big enough to cater for twenty people.

'I wasn't a bad mustering camp cook,' Michael said. 'Cooked a lot of turkeys in the Gulf. The wild ones – plain turkeys. Now I protect them. In fact everything's protected – not a firearm allowed on this million acres. I've even got a bunch of wild donkeys hanging around here for people to see.'

'How do you view galleries? The rock art.' It seemed as good a time as any to bring it up.

Michael sat down again wearily. It would take a brave front to get through the evening. If it were me after a night on the grog, the safari tents beckoning would have been too much. The tourists would have fended for themselves. 'To tell you the truth, I have nothing whatever to do with them. I respect the wishes of the Elders and keep away. Maybe there are galleries here. I don't know. If there were and I knew about them, I would never let tourists near them.' His face cracked into a grin. 'I really believe they're sacred, you know. With no disrespect to the ancient cultures I'll tell you a story about a tour operator. Someone dared him to take tourists to a sacred site and announce admittance was strictly naked only. European attire would displease the spirits. So in the company of three strong German women he popped the gauntlet and they sure as hell picked it up. When his gear was off, and they'd got theirs off, they gave him a lesson or two. The spirits were angry, he said, and today he believes in the Dreamtime mythology with a passion.'

'He was all bluff to start with,' I ventured.

'I don't know really,' Michael said persuasively. 'A lot of

women have been raped over the ages. Not many men. Serve him right, anyway.'

'You were a bit ambivalent towards Fitzroy irrigation when I was last up here. Mind you, I understand it. When I first saw irrigation in south-west Queensland I thought it was a wonderful thing. I didn't realise what was about to happen to the western water system.'

'By gee, that industry's cost me some money this year,' Michael replied vehemently. 'I took some agistment at Goondiwindi and sent the road trains off full of young cattle. It was all done in stages. The final drop off before Goondiwindi was Tambo in central Queensland. There I got word the agistment station was e-listed. I had to sell the lot on the spot, and the cattle market's been going up ever since.'

I asked him about the dam. I had a lot of respect for his view on every subject.

He frowned, staring into the bordering savanna with an expression of very private nostalgia. 'If I am standing here in twenty years' time I'll need an aqualung. You watch and see. They'll get going in a small way, then like everything else the money will shut the eyes of the politicians and the job will explode. They'll demand every ounce of water these mountains can supply.'

That's the way it was with Michael. This ex-Queensland Gulf cattleman had seen more in his life than most saw if they lived ten times over. He was a hardened realist. A man who could talk a lot without throwing the bullshit. There was also a decency and humbleness about him that was rare, for I don't think it ever occurred to him that he ran the most stringently controlled eco-tourist operation in the west Kimberley. He offered comfort and protection in the heart of one of the world's last remaining great wildernesses. The rough road in, the minimum three-night stay, the compulsory central camping arrangements were all part of the plan to protect the wild.

Under Michael's regime the million acres would be as wild in the year 2009 as it was at that moment.

I sat with him and drank coffee. He had created an outstanding role model for Australian tourism and I knew he was unaware of his contribution. 'Maybe I'm clutching at straws, Michael,' I said, 'but if the Aboriginal people can get eco-tourism up and running it would present an alternative. I've seen it work in Arizona.'

'Different cultural background though,' Michael countered. 'I read a lot. You have to in the wet. There's nothing else to do. I read once where the Apaches raided the Mexicans for three hundred years on horseback.' He hesitated, knowing what I wanted to hear. 'Look, I'd love to think that it could happen, but I don't believe it will. This game's no picnic. You've got to be everything from a cook to a wildlife expert. You've got to enforce your own law. Take this place, up around the million acres. If I were to go slack for just one week people would be camping in the gorges, leaving litter about and shooting. If someone gets lost I could be in the air for three hours, which would cost me seven hundred and fifty dollars. Then there's the breakdowns. Never a week passes that I don't lift a spanner to some vehicle. Like the time you came in last year and we put the tyre on the rim. And that's not all. I'm the first-aid expert, my plane's the ambulance and I'm the pilot. It happens. I've done some mercy dashes with Aboriginal patients and seen what the top of a silverleaf bloodwood looks like after a propeller has chopped through it.'

We talked for a while before dinner. I realised I was out of my depth and I couldn't volunteer an opinion. I asked myself – could I run the Mornington operation? The answer was no. I hated doing the same thing week after week. I couldn't fly a plane and I couldn't help with breakdowns if the problem was anything more than a fuel blockage. Yet deep down I wasn't convinced. The Navajos did it and did it well.

I wished I had paid more attention during our two-hour stop at Monument Valley, eighteen months before.

Next morning I dumped supplies, wrapped in plastic food bags, in the generator room. I left Mornington Camp about mid-morning. Michael suggested I go and see old Teddy. Known as the 'Mayor of Imintji', Teddy was thought to be in his mid-eighties. He had a war story about a Japanese fighter plane.

About noon I found his house, guarded by several dogs, none of which seemed to be of any recognisable breed. With the man eaters of Halls Creek still fresh in my mind I had adopted a safety procedure for these occasions – stand by the car with the door open and if none of the dogs growled, go to the gate and let them smell you through the fence. Teddy's dogs accepted me and I proceeded towards the cement verandah just as Teddy's sallow face rose above a windowsill. He'd been asleep on the floor. I glanced beyond him into the room, wondering whether he had any furniture. Household possessions appeared to have a low priority.

I felt rude disturbing him and suddenly my prepared lines for self-introduction seemed a little arrogant, as though he were a wind-up toy available on demand. Instead, I asked his permission to camp on the creek, which he gave instantly. His eyes lit up when I suggested he join me for a cup of tea later in the afternoon.

Just off the road, about a kilometre from Imintji, was the little creek and camp. I could hear water falling onto stone, like a bore pumping into a tank. Flowing water usually promised a pleasant camp. This one was in a disgraceful mess. It took me half an hour to pick up the litter and burn it. Satisfied, I erected the tent and prepared a damper. I went for a slow cook, putting the glug of flour in tin foil and warm ash. I wanted to share it with Teddy.

The official community leader drove him out, a young man in his thirties, and he gave me a very sincere welcome. They were both about my size. Still warm in the ash, the damper had been cooked for some time. The billy I kept simmering, just off the boil. I made the tea immediately. Arriving so late in the afternoon I was hoping they might stay for dinner. I had been reading Frank Hann's diaries, which gave me a penetrating insight into that period in the west Kimberley. The gap for me was the mid twentieth century.

They both sat down in traditional style on the soil and waited for me to speak. In old language Teddy was still the chief. I explained to them both what I was doing here and how they could help me.

Teddy looked at me knowingly. He'd seen a few like me in his time.

'I've heard Tableland's not worrying about the cattle any more and they're chasing goannas for tucker.' Tableland Station on the Hann River had been handed back to the Gija people in the early 1990s. It was a hard straight left and he didn't deserve it. But it would get him going.

Teddy's eyes were like burning coals. 'Well that's a savage appraisal of the people,' he said. Michael had told me he was articulate. There was some mystery about his origin. Some said he was full Afghan, others thought half Aboriginal. In soul and spirit he was Aboriginal.

'No offence meant,' I said. 'For all I know it might be a viable cattle business out there. If not, I guess it gets down to what you'd sooner eat.'

'Whatever's going on out there it isn't that,' Teddy corrected. 'Even for the big white station owner there's no money in it anymore. I reckon my people will survive in the long run, because they don't mind eating goanna. But it is a shame Aboriginal stations weren't made possible twenty years ago when today's old people could have taught the next

generation. Now they're too old and there's a middle-aged generation out there who don't know much about anything. It's a
tragedy. You can hear what you like and a lot you hear is not
the truth. But I know the truth. I was moving cattle through
these ranges as a drover long before those who knew what was
best for us were born. A terrible tragedy happened out here
and the world took no interest in it.'

'Moved off the stations you mean?'

'You gotta go back to the tribal days. Life here in the inland
was hard. Before white man there were seasons that drove the
tribes to the brink of starvation. White man brought a new life.
It was on his terms, but there was food – no hunger any more.
They didn't need money. That would have all come in time.
What made their lives rich was the horses. My people loved
horses. You hear what you like, but I was droving cattle when
the Japs bombed Broome. You give my people horses and they
love them as an equal. When they left the stations and the
horses were shot, the people cried. I saw old men cry. No white
man ever loved a horse like my people. A great evil befell this
land and it may be a long time before the spirits are appeased.
This is a sad land.'

Teddy was the last drover to drive a mob of bullocks up
Jacob's Ladder and on to Derby. The year was 1948. 'They'd
follow the mules,' he said. 'The mules always took the climb in
their stride. One mule's worth ten horses.'

'The country wasn't fenced,' I said. 'It's got me beat how the
herds were kept separate.'

'Cattle stay where they're born.' Teddy looked happier now,
talking about the cattle and the mules. He was a little man,
withered and gaunt like a dry thistle. Nature toughened old
stockmen with powerful immunity and I expected to see the
mayor of Imintji about for some time.

I opened some damper and the prunes. They both shied off
the prunes. The younger man in his thirties hadn't said

anything, except occasional grunts of approval when Teddy was speaking.

'You try and shift an eight-year-old bullock and he'll lie down and die,' Teddy continued. 'Heat, thirst – no matter. He waits to die rather than be moved from his territory. Nothing on earth will make him stand.' He paused, his deep eyes fixed on me. 'There are forces at work we don't understand.'

The younger man drained his mug and declined a refill. I had a feeling he was ready to leave.

'You mentioned Broome was bombed,' I said to Teddy. 'Were you in the area then?'

'I was working for Vestes in 1942. They paid a pilot with a tigermoth to collect me at Derby. They had a mob of cattle on one of their territory holdings ready to move. To fuel up we had to go via Wyndham. We were passing over the Precipice Range when a Japanese zero pilot spotted us. Even before it dipped and came after us we didn't expect it to be one of ours.' Teddy began to illustrate the story with his hands. 'The pilot dropped the nose – the ground rushin up at us. Our only chance was the mountains, he yelled, close to the ground. He levelled out and hit the power. Very manoeuvrable little bi-planes they were. Then he yells above the roar of the engine – the gorges. We went around a bluff like a young fella fired up with grog takes a turn and oh, my mules might kiss, I thought, it was a tight corridor of rock he flew up. Is he still there? He's closer, I yell back. He hadn't shot at us. We must have been still out of range. I'll drop him at the Estaughs, the pilot yells over his shoulder. The Estaughs were still several miles down the range and the zero's getting closer. The pilot yells, the zero pilot won't fire while the cliffs demand every ounce of flying skill. Also, he might have got close enough to see we weren't military and not worth the risk. Anyway, at the Estaughs we shot between the spires and banked hard towards the cliffs of Mount Hamilton. The zero aborted and changed course.'

'What happened then?' I was riveted. I wanted the whole story.

'We were too scared to go on to Wyndham. The zero was headed that way when we last saw it. So we flew south-west to Noonkanbah on the Fitzroy. Not many strips about those days but the pilot knew the land. All he did was fly managers and stockmen from station to station.' Teddy grinned for the first time. 'Those that were prepared to get in. Flying was a very new form of transport.'

'What are the Estaughs?' If someone talked about a spire I always needed to know more.

'Sharp-pointed peaks,' Teddy said, not very interested. 'The big one at the point's an ugly thing, like a canine tooth. You'll see them when you come down the Adcock. Bad country in there. Like a mini desert.'

'How do you think horses will handle it?'

'I never went through with a packhorse. We rode horses, but the mules carried everything.'

I wanted them to stay, but rice and tin stew probably had little appeal. Maybe they had wives who were cooking a meal.

It was a long night and at daylight I left for Derby. The low coastal plains baked under a pitiless blue sky. Ten days in the heat had still had no effect on me. I wasn't acclimatising, but I had overcome the negative impulses that heat to which you're unaccustomed caused. What chance poor Sal? Arrive on Saturday evening and out on the horses Tuesday. It began to worry me a great deal.

I stopped off at Peter's place. At the corral there were signs of activity everywhere. Shoeing gear lay on the ground, bridles and headstalls were draped over rails and the red-hide rope lay on the ground in several scattered coils.

Standing among the trees and listless from the heat, I noticed horses that were not in the mob three days ago.

I walked on past the house and found Peter in his workshop. I don't think Peter ever stopped. Trained in the days when Aborigines did all the work on the cattle stations he knew nothing about recreation. 'Black people were not included,' he said to me one day, and if there was a trace of bitterness he didn't show it.

'You weren't up there long,' he commented, no doubt remembering I had planned to do some exploring on foot.

'High grass and heat,' I said, feeling a bit despondent. 'Not even half-day foot excursions are on. I am worried about my wife.'

'Perhaps your wife could remain in Broome,' Peter said sympathetically. 'There's a young woman in town into photography,' he added thoughtfully. 'She's got her own horse, too.'

'Oh no, Sal will come,' I said. 'She'll stick. She'd go with me into hell if I asked her to.'

'Well hell's where we're headed,' Peter said blandly. I searched his face for a trace of humour.

'I'll go and see this young woman,' I said finally. 'Sal won't feel so isolated if there's another woman in the expedition.' But another woman exposed to the rigours of heat and long days didn't ease my anxiety. I changed the subject. 'How did you go with the horses?'

'The boys got some more,' Peter said quietly, looking past me at a group of them. They heard him talking and a few hopefuls had assembled at the open side of the shed. 'Reckon we're about right now. What day do you want to go?'

'We'll have to train four of them for the packs,' I replied, thinking about something Michael had said. Half wild horses, he'd told me, went berserk sometimes when first packed and smashed everything, including the packsaddle. Old racehorses were the packhorses in my tourist outfit in the seventies. Most would be asleep by the time they were packed up.

'I've been thinking about that too,' he said, smiling at what probably seemed to him an over-anxious call. 'They don't like the croppers much do they – the first day. If I can get George's four-wheel-drive truck over the Lennard we don't have to pack the horses for three days. Just put the packsaddle harness on em and if one wants to pigroot and buck it won't damage anything. They won't get rid of the harness.'

I had a vision of the truck rock-bound in the middle of the river, all our gear on board and the current too strong to shift it. But there was that item that goes almost everywhere with me, like my wallet – the climbing rope. Rigged up, we could unload the truck if the need arose. I was all for it.

In Derby I tracked down the woman Peter had spoken of. Her name was Heather Harrison and she worked at the newsagency in Derby. With long hair and unblemished skin she looked to be in her twenties. She was tall and strong and there was more than a hint of determination about her. She told me photography was fast becoming more than a hobby in her life and she would come with us if she could get the time off. We got talking about horses and she said there was an aged gelding available. She thought maybe Sal could ride him. A live weight is much easier on a horse than the dead weight of packs and Sal only weighed sixty kilograms. As an ex-jockey I was very conscious of weight.

I camped back at Peter's corral that night and left for Broome next morning. The horse handling was on schedule. In Broome I would need to buy, or possibly order from Perth, small inflatable rafts. I was still on the learning curve with the satellite phone and I needed to bury my head into the instruction book. I still had a lot of research on trees to do: trees could tell you much about the country. But the most time-consuming research of all would be Frank Hann's diaries. It was a thorough diary, with a record of every day's principal events. The problem was trying to plot his 1898 expedition on the map. His attitude towards the wild tribes was most disturbing and when two of his packhorses fell down the side of Mount Broome I began to wonder whether he was a good pathfinder after all. The diaries were well named – *Do Not Yield to Despair*. He certainly didn't.

At the Manse in Broome I could stay for a long time with my books, pads and pens. For dreamers, poets and writers the old pearling town was something of a paradise. It throbbed with life, as though the tide itself was the surge of blood. Take a haircut in Chinatown a couple of hours after breakfast and behind the quaint corrugated-iron buildings, erected when high tides still surged into the street, the mangroves and mudflats were drained of the sea for five kilometres. Return six hours later and the sea would have invaded all but the streets of Chinatown. Levees now held the tides at bay. A hint of the evening in the air, you could sit out on the pavement under an umbrella, drink coffee and read the paper. Two hundred metres away the water teemed with aquatic wild creatures. Below the surface and into the sea, Broome was a jungle on par with Africa. The underwater mystery became, in the minds of guests, another dimension of the charm. Yet like the embrace of an imaginary saltwater lady, nature had made Cable Beach the safest for swimmers in Australia. The tide run was fast, but there were no deep channels for perilous rips. No one ever spoke of bluebottles or stingers, and the sharks appeared to respect the human domain, as they were never sighted near the surf. The gentle tropical nature of Broome was thought to have lulled Dutch refugees from Java into a fake sense of security on 3 March 1942. The day before the Japanese had undertaken low-flying aerial reconnaissance. Australian military personnel were alarmed and echoed their fears to the Dutch captains of the flying boats that were anchored in Roebuck Bay. The tranquillity of life in Broome, exhaustion from long, slow flights and the perception of safety on Australian sovereign territory led to the total loss of the fleet and fifty Dutch lives. In addition, thirty-one American servicemen died when a troop carrier was shot down after take-off and crashed a few kilometres off Cable Beach. Japanese zero fighters based on Timor launched the attack.

My days in Broome waiting for Sal to fly in were full enough and I would have missed a lot if the Bundaberg rum had forced me to wallow in the soothing surf of Cable Beach all day long. To stroll through old Chinatown before the shops open was the time to look into the bawdy history. The sun would be warm and the air still. The coconut trees in the street centre encapsulated the tropical atmosphere. Behind the buildings was the sea channel where the pearl luggers once berthed. The divers never really escaped from the sea. If the tide wasn't in, it was leaving at a rush or returning like a flood. Their lives at sea hung by a thread. A twisted air hose, a fouled rope or a surface rise too fast due to tidal change or a monster shark was all it took. Men with no future lived hard and dangerously. Their only passage to a better life was to gamble to take all. Mostly it was lose all. Fear and uncertainty stimulated the sex hormone. They took the prostitutes like there was no tomorrow, fell instantly in love with them and killed out of jealousy like I might blast a crow sitting on the fowl house. The merchants, too, were hard, with a tenuous future. Most carried guns and if they weren't slung from hips, they were under the counter or in the drawer of the desk. North, south and east of Broome the pastoralists were still fighting a guerilla war. There were spearings and massacres, and any number of white men who purchased supplies at Broome were never seen again. Early white historians tried to quash the truth of Australia's frontier in the west between 1885 and 1930. Old police records were not considered reliable. It was a colourful and violent time. Only now were men and women challenging the records and rewriting history.

By nine o'clock a few business premises would have opened their doors, but the streets would still be empty. On one such morning, I decided to pay a visit to Maria Mann, secretary of Environs Kimberley. I knew she'd already be on the go. I walked to the high end of the street and found her office.

'There's a protest meeting today,' she informed me briskly. 'We're trying to save the old bungalows, which housed the divers in the off season. There's been an application to demolish them.'

It was a full-time fight to save old Broome and the Pindan wilderness beyond. There were volunteers who worked tirelessly, giving up weeks in the year, and their only reward was a decision reversal, often only temporary.

'You been to the paper yet?' she demanded. Maria had suggested I go and see one of the journalists with the *Broome Advertiser* and see if they would like a story on the packhorse expedition. She knew I would raise some environmental concerns that impacted on Broome. With Maria the fight was every day. She was passionate about Broome. She was passionate about her people.

'You don't have to save the bars,' she added, when I admitted I hadn't. I thought she struggled not to smile, but I wasn't sure. 'No one's going to demolish the bars. I know someone. I'll ring up.'

Maria had helped me research every aspect of life in the west Kimberley, from giving me the names of environmental experts to explaining complex social issues. She was single-minded and very intelligent. If the lure of the brewery and the saltwater lady at Cable Beach distracted me, I only had to go and see Maria to be snapped back on track. Broome was about to plunge into one of the nation's great environmental battles and no one would be waving the flag more brazenly than Maria.

At the paper – the *Broome Advertiser* – a pretty young woman took the notes and I struggled to concentrate. She took my photo out the back, near where the luggers once berthed. If the divers of one hundred years ago could have seen her they would have thought she was an apparition. I told her I'd be back with a report.

Out on the front verandah I felt the morning sun passing from pleasant to a little warm. It was coffee time at the bakery. Time to pull out a chair with Kali Balint and Mark Zehntner, who I'd arranged to meet. Both whitewater enthusiasts, they had only eight weeks before been in the successful expedition down the Fitzroy. They were avid environmentalists. I asked them about their worst moments.

'Whirlpool holes,' Kali said, his eyes glowing. 'In a kayak you're sucked under and it seems forever before you resurface. That's scary.'

'High-standing waves give you a bit of a beating too,' Mark reflected. He was a wiry man with tattoos. 'They flip the rafts. You fly over boulders in boiling white, trying to hang onto the stern rope and hold the paddle in your free hand. You can't afford to lose that paddle.'

Over the coffee and the scones I related our plans to them.

'The river was wild and all consuming,' Kali said soberly. 'We didn't have much time to look at galleries. But we did see one very interesting drawing. It was a boat with high bows. A boat one would not expect to be used by people living in the Stone Age.'

'Can you give me a map reference?' I asked hopefully.

He hesitated. 'Can you remember Mark?' he asked finally.

Mark shook his head. 'It was rough in there in places. I never took my eye off the water. If I marked the spot on the map and was kilometres out I'd only make it harder for you.'

'That's the way I feel too.' Kali said soberly. 'Its all such a blur now.'

It was disappointing. But the canyon was well off my

intended course with the horses. Time would beat me. I had to forget it.

The boys' love was adventure. I didn't dwell on the art for long. Mark was a rock climber and we traded some stories. The hard stuff was over for me. Nothing to do with age – the age clock is stored in the mind. But an accident had left me with a weak knee.

The Chinatown bakery was one of the most cosmopolitan cafes I'd been in. At any time of the day there were people seated at the tables from at least four or five countries. Unlike people in so many big towns today – hanging around, filling in precious time – the people who moved through Broome were vibrant. The atmosphere was abuzz with activity and it was infectious. When Kali and Mark left me to go back to work I could have sat there for a long time, dreaming about white water, unclimbed mesas and ancient galleries.

Staring blankly out through the double doors onto the pavement I saw her coming. She stepped through the doors and I waved. A look of surprise flooded her face, almost disbelief. It was the social worker I had met in Broome the previous October, who had explained so much to me about Aboriginal beliefs.

'You were serious after all,' she said with a fresh, little-girl smile. 'I thought you were full of bullshit.'

I still couldn't recall her name. I liked the name I had given her in my mind – Magdalena – mysterious, strong willed and with a passion that burned beneath her skin. She was petite, with brown hair falling to her shoulders and unwavering brown eyes.

'The expedition moves out Tuesday from Derby,' I said with some degree of pride, especially as it refuted the bullshit. 'My wife arrives from Sydney tomorrow. We'll have a day on the beach and then it's off into the wild.'

She sat down opposite and put her handbag on the table. 'Did you bring your horse?'

'No,' I replied lamely. 'That was a rush of blood. A transcontinental haulage of 5000 kilometres was not on. Anyway, he's got a suspect tendon.'

In October I had been invited to join a group at a beach cafe. One of the men was a racing enthusiast, and charged with a few drinks I had announced I would bring a racehorse from New South Wales for the Broome racing season next winter. At the time I was contemplating bringing my own saddle horses across for the expedition.

'And after all that time we gave up to you,' she taunted. 'Running you out to the racetrack and discussing trainers.'

'It was madness,' I said, forcing a smile. 'Transport the horse 5000 kilometres. I must have been still half drunk.'

'Is it still the gallery with the ancient drawings?' she asked, suddenly serious. 'The expedition, I mean.'

'The possibility of getting Bunuba packhorse tourism up and running is a big part of this job. But I do want to find the gallery – yes.' I paused. She looked to be in a hurry. 'Like some coffee?'

'Thanks, but no. I'm flat out. I just popped out of the office to buy a take-away sandwich.' She picked up her bag. 'I've seen so much Aboriginal superstition in my job that it's influenced my thinking. They believe in the Dreamtime with a conviction we never knew.' She hesitated and looked away. 'These sacred places are more than timeless rock. You may confront great danger.' She looked me in the eye.

'Like what?' I demanded.

She shrugged. 'I don't know, really. I knew an Elder from the old Beagle Bay Catholic mission. He said the benevolent Dreamtime spirit and the God of the priests were one.' She paused, her eyes lowering to my belt. 'Your cross. The one you keep in the pouch. Perhaps that's enough.'

I felt uncomfortable. The cross she spoke of was a very private spiritual object. I remembered clearly why she knew.

Back in October she had asked me why it was necessary for me to carry two pocketknives. I had showed her the cross. It was a brass one, with a cross dominant above an Indian Pueblo. On the bottom was inscribed 'New Mexico', a land claimed by Archbishop Robert Sanchez of Santa Fe as the 'land of faith – the holy land'. Those who followed protocol may have argued it was not a cross of the sacraments, but to me it was powerful. If I had it with me, I could venture into most places.

'I believe it is,' I said and was tempted to kiss her. But I didn't know her well enough. I didn't even know her name. 'I'll remember when I get there.'

She smiled. 'Be careful.' Then she got up and walked over to the counter.

I was wary of the occult. If you had faith you acknowledged the power of the devil as well. With faith I believed you went on to the next life, but you had to earn it. Perfunctory attendances at church services were merely a willingness to listen. It was what we forgave and sacrificed that counted. I didn't know the nature of the ancient beliefs, but forty thousand years of survival demonstrated their love for the earth. Based on our current treatment of the earth, I gave the human race three hundred years at best.

Instantly, I decided I would go out into the bush for the rest of the day. I still didn't know much about the Pindan. From the bitumen road it didn't look much. It had been author Pat Lowe who first told me about the native wildlife in the Pindan wilderness. A very busy, enthusiastic little woman who still spoke with a clear, arresting English accent, her husband was Jimmy Pike, an Aboriginal man from the desert and a traditional artist who in 1998 sold almost every painting at a London exhibition. On the same trip to England Pat and Jimmy were invited to a Buckingham Palace garden party. It was uncertain whether the Queen had read Pat's little book, *Jimmy and Pat Meet the Queen*. The book was beautifully illustrated by Jimmy and was an enchanting short story about the moral of native title.

When I had met Pat she told me the Pindan was often denigrated by white people who had no idea of its real natural qualities. She described it as 'old-growth, semi-arid forest', and no one with writing skills knew it better than Pat. She gave me a copy of her most recent publication – *The Boab Tree* – suggesting I take special note of the trees in the Derby district, which I already had. But I knew nothing about the tree until I began reading her book, searching for a clue that might relate to a human crossing of the Indian Ocean in prehistory. The baobab had its origins on the large island of Madagascar and palaeontologists were in general agreement that the seed drifted across the wide expanse of the Indian Ocean. When brittle dry, the baobab fruit would float for long periods. In Madagascar water was the natural source of distribution. The plant also travelled west to Africa. The mystery surrounding the Australian boab was not where it came from, but when it arrived. Scientific evidence suggested the crossing was long before the evolution of modern man, but Pat's book had one short paragraph that fascinated me. It was the established fact that Coco de Mer palm pods from the Seychelles Islands had been found washed up on the Western Australian coast, an ocean current float of approximately 6400 kilometres. The Seychelles lay only 1200 kilometres from Tanzania in east Africa, the origin of Homo habilis (who lived 1.9 to 1.6 million years ago). I believed the discovery of these huge buoyant pods sealed the lid on a human prehistoric crossing from Africa to Australia. Early humans in Africa were exposed for nearly two million years to the possibility of some freakish and extraordinary event that could have led to a crossing of the Indian Ocean on east-flowing currents. Over such an expanse in time, the possibility to me seemed more likely than the negative.

The Egyptians in Sam's mind, Magdalena's visions of the

spirits, Peter's dreams of the homeland, Joe's wild passion for the river, Mick Horne's ghosts of the Kamilaroi and the mystery of the boabs: it was all welling up in my mind and I knew if I headed for the Roebuck I'd be throwing down the rums. I left instead for the Pindan – Pat and Jimmy's country.

The bird sanctuary road was about ten minutes' drive north of Broome. It was a dirt road that led back to the coast, south-east of the town. I parked the little hired Jeep in sight of the water and followed a walking trail back into the Pindan. The forest was explosive with wildlife. The lovely red-necked brush-tail wallabies and grey forest kangaroos were continually hopping out of my way, obviously not too perturbed by my presence. The wallabies invariably stopped within sight and watched me pass through. The birds I didn't know, except the Brahminy kites. Two pairs glided gracefully over, so low I could see their eyes. They were strikingly marked, with white chest and head and rufous brown plumage on the tail and wings. In my haversack I carried a copy of *Plants of the Kimberley*, and was amazed at the diversity of vegetation, including the billygoat plum tree.

Back at the Jeep a couple of hours later I met an ornithologist returning from a rocky point with a group of tourists. He told me 700,000 birds migrated from Siberia, Alaska and North America to feast on the edges of the mud flats. Known in broad terms as high arctic or tundra breeding birds, they returned to the northern hemisphere at the height of the northern summer. The mud crustaceans doubled the body weight of the birds for the long flight home, which took four days to the first nesting spot in the wetlands of China. In China humans plundered the big bird populations and a percentage was lost every year. It had been assessed that half the world's population of migratory tundra birds fed between Broome and Port Hedland in the southern autumn and early winter.

I began to think about what would happen to these migratory birds if the ecosystem of the Pindan was drastically altered.

All the surface water deposited either by rain or technology – such as irrigation – ultimately drains through the Broome sandstone to Roebuck Bay (Broome) and Eighty Mile Beach to the south of Broome, which is the feeding ground for the tundra birds on their way back to the Arctic. If the Pindan were to become polluted with chemicals, the wide variety of worm fauna would absorb the poison and either poison the birds or, more likely, deprive them of their essential food supplies for their migration back north. The worms – or in biological terminology, benthic fauna – are available in their millions on the intertidal mudflats and any man-made disruption would spell grave consequences for the tens of thousands of birds that circumnavigate the globe according to season. Maintaining the free flow of the Fitzroy River was only part of the ecological battle to preserve one of the world's most fragile ecosystems.

With these troubling thoughts in mind, not helped by a hangover, I headed for Cable Beach for a swim. The salt shrinks the lines in your skin and for a little while you look younger, but more importantly feel younger, for a long time.

Later, back at the church guesthouse in Broome the night had gathered in the streets and the forest. At dusk, much of the residential area reminded me of a forest. The houses melted out of sight, as if the Pindan had rolled in like the tide. I dropped the hatch on the fowl house and told the chooks it had been a deeply spiritual day.

Everything was in order now for our flight to Derby on Monday. The rafts I had found in Broome. I had been talking to Sal and the family on the satellite telephone. It proved to be quite easy. For satellite communication the globe was split into zones. According to the instruction map Broome could choose between Indian Region or Pacific Region. Through trial and error I found the correct antenna angle for Pacific

Region and after that it was simply a matter of pressing the correct digits.

Tomorrow Sal would arrive and the day after we'd be heading inland. It seemed that at last everything was coming together. The expedition was almost up and running.

CHAPTER

6 Bunuba Land

On Wednesday, 10 May 1898, explorer Frank Hann left Derby with an undisclosed number of horses and several Aboriginal assistants, the boys principally for horse-tailing and packing, the girls for cooking and washing. Four days later, he was exactly one hundred and one years ahead of the Bunuba Expedition. The Bunuba people were the heart and soul of the expedition. They led the way, provided the horses, all the humour and the stories. I recorded it all. So I called it the Bunuba Expedition.

In his diaries Frank Hann reflected a lot upon himself. He shared his fears, doubts, ambitions and depression. Without that component in his recordings no one would read them, as diaries were otherwise no more than a series of entries. Hann, in his crude writing style, produced the saga of an adventure. His whole life was an adventure and the similarities between us were quite extraordinary. Like me, he was a lousy business-man. We both went broke at one period of our lives. Hann simply rode away from his station in the Queensland Gulf – Lawn Hill. He blamed drought and I blamed the wool crash. Later, when the pain had gone and you could look at the deci-sions dispassionately it was an error of judgment. Going broke was a mistake somewhere. Always would be. By middle age we were both plagued with old horse injuries and both had a reluctant penchant for the melancholy. I think Hann's moments of depression were far more severe, as he had no escape from the rigours of frontier life. He was an explorer at heart, but I suspect he searched for gold nuggets to elevate his spirits. He was a man with a passion for corners unexplored by white men and I guess he was lucky those corners still existed. Today those corners don't exist. The nearest would be the unclimbed side of a mountain. Where we would have differed profoundly – had we ridden together – was his attitude to Aboriginal people. Hann was a good man but his attitude to Aborigines was typical in 1898.

Sal had arrived the day before, and together we flew to Derby with enough gear and supplies to half fill the twin-engine plane. Wherever we went, airport staff were wonderful. At Derby Peter gave me the disappointing news. The boys weren't coming. In the final draft, only seven horses were suitable for the 320-kilometre trek. Thanks to Heather, we had one extra aged gelding. It had become an expedition solely to find the ancient art. Where was George? Peter shrugged when I asked. Maybe too close to Saturday night, he suggested with that wide boyish smile. Two men; two women. Well, if we were never heard of again, it was at least a good balance. But it was very sobering news. It was to be a Bunuba expedition. It was Joe Ross's idea and I had wanted to keep the concept alive. As an adventurer I was more than happy to ride along with Peter and lap up some of Australia's most spectacular scenery, but that was far off-track from the plan. Now I wondered what I was going to achieve.

On Tuesday 6 May, Heather's Dusty and Trigger were loaded at Derby showground. At Peter's block the big single-deck truck reversed up to a mound of red dirt. We were ready to load the other horses. I perceived a problem from the start. The mound was higher than the floor of the float and horses loathe stepping downwards into a stock float. With all the boys turning up to farewell us we had plenty of manpower. In fact, we needed the boys to catch the horses that morning – they had sensed something was on and were galloping through the scrub like wild animals. One by one we cornered them but it was only Peter who could gently walk up and secure a headstall.

All finally assembled at the mound, the game began. Not one horse would have a bar of it. Had they ever seen a truck? I didn't ask, because I think I knew. We tried force walking: lift a front leg, a rear one – sometimes two front legs stood on the truck. We were nearly there with one horse! Then he would dart backwards and we'd start all over again. We tried waving a stockwhip but that made them more piggy. I suggested locked hands behind the rump like race-day barrier attendants. 'No,' Peter said. 'Get yer head kicked off.' Eventually, Peter brought over a nosebag and he managed to feed one of the little bays called Johnny. The old donkey and carrot trick. Surely the rest would see him and think it safe. We went through all the procedures again, while sweat poured off us and mosquitoes homed in on the smell. It was hopeless.

'Are there any yards with a loading race?' I asked Peter.

'The old bullock yards near the boab tree gaol. We better take em there. It's only three kilometres away.' Walked in by the police, Aboriginal prisoners had been housed in the boab tree on their first night into Derby. The tree, thought to be 2000 years old, had a hollow trunk big enough for about ten people to sit inside. The only entrance was through a hole a metre or more above the ground.

Six horses were released onto the road and two boys – Shannon and Shane – jumped on a couple bareback. Sal, Heather and the other boys went to the yards in the truck. I followed on foot with the horses. The black one – which I'd dubbed Blackjack – seemed very wild and I wanted to make up the third man.

It was every bit as bad as I had anticipated. Blackjack had his heart set on freedom. Marked by a defiant white blaze from ears to bottom lip, I watched his rump slide into the scrub with the other four in hot pursuit. If the road hadn't been fenced we would have lost them then and there. When he reached the fence he had the brains to try and break back through us. That's where I came into it. I would be waiting for him, waving a big stick. Not deterred, Blackjack would spear towards the open road where one of the riders waited. It was a close go on several occasions. My shirt was soaked with sweat and running headlong through the snaky long grass filled every stride with dread. But tough as it was, I didn't miss the riding skills of those boys. Never once was there a trace of daylight under their backsides and their knees and legs remained relaxed. No tight gripping. They rode with superb balance and their hands allowed their mounts to move in long fluid strides, as though no one sat upon them at all.

Out on the black soil plain they galloped, with Blackjack still showing the way. With no scrub to impede them it was easy for the boys. Beaten, Blackjack shot through the open double gates into the yards. The truck was already in place, backed firm against the loading race.

There was a smile on every face. No animal – horse, mule, bull or buffalo – could defy the long narrow race with a handful of eager men intent on loading. Still blowing a bit, I walked around to join Sal and Heather. Peter and the boys would load them in a minute flat.

Twenty minutes later and still only three horses were on the truck, including Heather's. They were penned in a small partition up the front. It looked like it was going to be very hard going with these horses, for apart from a bit of hand feeding, they were more or less wild. A wild animal won't go out of the sunlight into what it perceives is a trap. The float was roofed, which for these horses must have seemed like a cave with alien smells. One of the boys stood away a little and I asked him quietly where the horses had come from. He waved his arm out towards the Pindan. 'These bush horses. Some quiet fella. Some buckjumper too.'

'Which one buckjumper?'

A huge grin broke over his face. 'Them the packhorses.'

'Boys not coming because food all bucked off?' I inquired, grinning through my teeth.

He threw his head back and laughed, then quickly turned in case the frustrated group up around the loading race saw him. 'We got wives and girlfriends,' he said over his shoulder.

In my time I've seen a lot of horses loaded one way or another. Never had I seen such a stubborn bunch. Once again we tried the fear tactics – the whip. You didn't hit them. Apart from the cruelty of it they could go into shock and that was definitely the end of the road. The boy cracked it in the next yard and let the red hide buzz above their heads. All they did was circle the forcing yard in a tighter bunch. Peter then did what he had wanted to avoid. He caught the two most handled – Shorny and Creamy. With a lot of gentle coaxing Shorny went on and Creamy quickly followed. That left the wildest looking ones to load. Blackjack was so wild there was a possibility he'd bolt up the race to get away, provided there was only one other horse in the yard with him. Peter caught him and the three-year-old One Sock. It worked. That left the chestnut with an old bullet wound in his nose and a grey horse of thoroughbred stock. We worked on them for ages and were close to admitting defeat when a white man drove up. A good friend to the Derby Aboriginal community, his name was Michael Wand. He was a strong man, and at once he took control and set up a plan with a long green-hide rope. It was a combination of two men pulling on a headstall from the front and roping the horse in from the rear. On the first go it worked with the chestnut. Then it was the grey's turn. He went berserk and broke the headstall and the rope in three places.

'They pull him on with a landcruiser last time,' one of the

boys said, exasperated and looking at Michael's vehicle.

'Oh no, we're not going to come to that,' Peter said. He was always quietly spoken.

'Where was that?' I asked suspiciously. The grey wasn't a wild horse from the bush. He had too much class about him. This horse had been turned into an outlaw. 'After Fitzroy rodeo,' a boy chuckled, knowing how pleased I'd be to hear it. 'Him Flying Fox. Throw em good too.'

'Best packhorse you got,' Michael threw in quickly. 'Only bucks when someone gets on. Very strong horse. With the packs on he'll climb Mount Ord. You need him.'

We tried twice again and went so close. Ironically, if we had all walked away and left Peter on his own I think Flying Fox might have been coaxed on. Top horse handlers were the same all over the world. They had something from birth, and no amount of will and determination would ever compensate.

Working up on the back of the supply truck Sal made a pile of corned beef and tomato sandwiches. With the horse float finally ready to go, we fell upon the sandwiches and ate them standing. There was no time to boil a billy. Allowing for steep climbs and equally slow descents in low gear, it would take the horse float four hours to the Lennard River turn-off. Two of the young blokes, Buddha and Harold, were going with the driver. Peter said they would help us with the horses until we swung north towards the Mount Ord Pass. Peter was exhausted. Right from the start he had been in the thick of the loading battle. I took over the wheel of the supply truck and with me in the cabin rode Sal and Heather. Peter slumped into the back and fell asleep on top of all the gear. The only bonus for the day was the temperature. A gentle south-easterly had arrived. I took Sal's hand and gave it a squeeze when we felt it. 'The south-easter couldn't have timed it better,' I said.

Sal was being very brave. She had watched, sometimes in horror at the horse-loading antics. On more than one occasion she had muttered to me that the horses would go bush the moment they smelt freedom. She clutched the satellite phone, convinced we would be calling up the Derby-based operators to be rescued.

The horse float had a good start on us. We dropped the boys off at Peter's place. I had eight kilograms of corned beef to collect from the fridge. It was about four-thirty when we hauled up over the King Leopold Ranges at Inglis Gap and I down-shifted gear for the descent into the fault-line country. On the floor of the ancient valley we caught up to the horse float, parked on the side of the road. The old yards had been taken down. All that remained was an unloading race and several scattered posts. The horses would be bewildered when they came off and unpredictable.

I don't know how many times my fifty-metre rope had come to the rescue. Working off the standing posts as stays, I had enough rope to go around twice. The rope stretched three times its length and was designed to save a climber's life in a fall. Reefing back hard, I was able to make the yard horse-proof.

The horses refused to walk off. Dusty and Trigger had endured a long stand and Peter threaded them through his own horses to get them off and give Heather a chance to take them to water and let them feed. We were all hoping the other horses would follow them. They didn't. Peter, his two men and Robert, who drove his own vehicle out separately, had to steel themselves for another battle.

With only an hour's daylight left I took Sal with me to set up a campsite. The first thing we always did was collect the firewood. All other camp preparations can be done by lantern and torchlight if necessary. At first it struck me as strange there was so little dead wood with so many bloodwoods, until I noticed the charred stumps. Man-made fires every season burnt almost every stick of dead wood. Picking the campsite too was a problem. The spear grass had turned to hay in a matter of days and would explode at the strike of a match. The only bare spot was a pile of rocks by a creek. It was going to be a rugged night. To get a tent placed we had to stamp the spear grass with our boots and use heavy rocks to jam the pegs. The ground was like cement and the first peg I tried buckled like rusted wire.

While Sal and I struggled with the campsite, we could hear constant rattling from the truck one hundred metres away. No one got cranky. Aborigines of the Kimberley rarely yelled and never ever swore. Whenever there was a 'look out' or 'grab him' I saw one of the horses come out backwards or sideways. There was a wide gap between the door and the top of the loading race and in retrospect it was a blessing as all of them jumped or fell out the side. It would have taken a powerful forward scrum to push each one of them backward down the race. When the last one was shouldered out the door it was starting to get dark. Before each horse was half carried off, Peter put a halter on and kept hold of the lead rope so they couldn't gallop away. Creamy tumbled out on his back and for a few seconds Peter lost the rope.

The hobbles were put on immediately, and after the last horse stumbled out Peter waved the truck driver off and they all walked down to the supply truck to collect the nosebags. Anticipating a late finish Peter had measured each ration of horse nuts in Derby, before the loading debacle. There had been no time to educate these horses and Peter's nosebag method of quietening down was a clever bit of horsemanship. After their first ride in a truck and bewildered by high mountains never seen before, the horses would have been very disturbed. But at that time of day they knew it was nosebag hour and when all the munching began inside those little home-made hessian bags they wouldn't have cared if the Leopolds were the surface of the moon. The only horses to go into my rope yard were Heather's. She was nervous they would wander and I agreed with her. Pampered horses were always the most unpredictable.

The pass over the King Leopolds lay behind us. Hann would have said we cheated and to this point we did indeed. No one alive today knew Hann's original route and upon reference to the diary that was understandable. The only other pass through the Leopolds was Millie Windie Gap, occasionally used by horsemen riding north from Leopold Downs. But there was nothing to learn, observe or enjoy from following the Gibb River road on horseback. It would have been a waste of time. Hann crossed the Leopolds near Mount Broome, approximately thirty kilometres south-east of our camp.

Monday, 30 May 1898
Shod Jimmy and Tom Tit. Packed up and started. Went up the range, had a great job. Joe and Sultan rolled down the range, smashing everything, but we got them up again. While at them the blacks were singing out on the range above us. I had a shot over their way so heard nothing more of them. Going down the range we had to make a track, very rough but got down all right.

I expected to ride past Mount Broome on the second day.

I had run packhorses for years and looking at my campsite that evening I had to admit it was the worst ever. We did at least have fresh water at hand's reach. Both Sal and Heather got to work on the dampers and I boiled up a kilogram of corned beef. The women placed the dough into tinfoil and covered them over with hot ash. With hot tea and coffee served, everyone was gathering in around the fire when a vehicle with powerful headlights rounded the bend on the Derby side. It stopped on the road, near the camp. The Toyota Landcruiser was towing a horse float.

'It's George!' Peter exclaimed, obviously thrilled.

'Told you I'd come, Mike,' George said, beaming as he got out of the passenger side. 'Brought my girl too and her friend. You said you wanted to write about our country and our girls. What the girls did when we all out here with the cattle. I brought em.'

The driver was white. I invited him for dinner but when he declined I didn't blame him. The girls Priscilla and Rachelle, on the other hand, were very excited and I quickly popped another half kilo of corned beef into the big billy. Meanwhile Peter and Buddha unloaded the two horses from the trailer. Both were eye-catching. The larger animal was a whitish-grey stallion; the other a stylish grey mare with a black mane. Their names were Stallion Tom and Possum. They were led over to Peter's group, which hadn't wandered more that fifty metres after the empty nosebags were removed, and hobbled out.

I felt a bit concerned when the driver left without even a mug of coffee. They had come from Fitzroy Crossing via Tunnel Creek and Windjana Gorge, a distance of three hundred kilometres, half of which was a four-wheel-drive track. But I was delighted to see George. If Robert found his horses up around the headwaters of the Lennard, he and the girls might ride with us all the way.

The dampers emerged from the ash with a rich brown crust, and the aroma lifting from the corned beef billy had us all standing and casting long shadows from the two lanterns. I tested the beef with a fork. It went through the meat almost on touch. Our first campfire meal was ready. In a camp atmosphere everyone ate quickly, as though the dark released the inhibitions of table manners. Another mug of tea and we dwindled towards swags and tents. If I hadn't read a full account of the police patrols to the foothills of the Leopolds in the mid 1890s I would have suggested to Sal a tent was unnecessary. About fifty kilometres south-west of our camp a police officer woke in the middle of the night to the sensation of something moving over his stomach. It was a three-metre-long king brown. The snake didn't bite him and, killed by one of the men, it became breakfast.

The punitive police patrols rarely entered the Leopold country during this period as the ranges were the fortress of the mountain tribes.

The history was significant to me at that moment, as we slept in old Jandamarra country. Jandamarra was the only Aboriginal guerilla fighter to effectively use guns in defence of his people. I saw him as Australia's Geronimo, and like that great Apache chief, his fierce resistance was the last gasp of freedom for his people. The nature of the frontier war in the Kimberley, however, was vastly different to the one fought by the Americans in Arizona and northern Mexico. There were never any peace offers, and Aborigines wouldn't have trusted them anyway. Instead, the white pastoralists were bent on extermination. In October 1893 Alexander Forrest put a rhetorical question to the Western Australian parliament: 'I ask whether the life of one European is not worth a thousand natives as far as the settlement of this country is concerned.'

During his three-year campaign, Jandamarra took refuge in the Leopolds when the police patrols closed in. Not once did the police attempt to track him and his band of warriors into the deep gorges of these rocky, twisted mountains. Instead, the police and the possies plundered the women, the children and the old men on the river camps.

It was a full moon. I woke several times to horses squealing. George's Stallion Tom was asserting his authority right from the start. Every time one squealed I felt relieved – they're still there!

At five-thirty there was just a trace of light and I heard someone breaking sticks. I got up and found Peter by a little fire with the billies on. 'The horses didn't move,' he said, and added with a chuckle, 'Course, they didn't know where to go, anyway. Nothing like a long truck trip to confuse them.'

I squatted by the fire for the warmth. 'How far will we get today?'

'We might make a big run today,' Peter replied in his slow way of speaking. 'They'll be fresh and full of go. Let em knock emselves out a bit. Then when we put the nosebags on they'll settle for the night.' He looked around in the slowly gathering light. 'Don't take any notice of last night. They didn't know where they were. But when they get thirty kilometres up the Lennard some will want to come back here. It's a strange thing that.'

'How many days unsettled, you reckon?'

'Maybe three or four. Then again, the nosebags might do the trick.'

We were moving out with a mixed team: at least five were semi-wild, George's two were well broken in and Heather's were like two big overgrown pets.

The catching took ages. Without the nosebags Johnny and George's stallion might have been the only two to feel a saddle between sunrise and lunch. Heather's horses had spent a very contented night in the yard and after a mug of tea I rolled up the rope. Dusty was one of the most outstanding saddle horses I'd ever seen. Buckskin, lovely dark mane and a little white marking on the forehead, he could have been on loan from the producers of *The Man From Snowy River*. There was a heart-rending story about him too. Heather said she had first noticed him in a paddock on the outskirts of Broome. A half-grown foal, he was so malnourished there was doubt about his chances of survival. She nursed him back to strength but just when she thought serious breaking could commence he fell into a septic tank and a council crane had to come to the rescue. Over the days that followed I would often catch this gelding looking to where Heather was. Given the choice, he would have had her sleeping on his back.

Trigger wouldn't have got a role in the Snowy Mountains film. He was one of those aged snow-white geldings who have skin like a fairy maiden. I'd been caught with a few over the years. One still lived on Myall Plains at the age of forty-one. He'd gone through the winter of ninety-eight better than ever, and I was sure he was on target for Australia's record age, which I understood was fifty-six years. Cloudy was my lead horse in the packhorse days of the mid-seventies, even then aged. I never hobbled out thanks to Cloudy. A little oats in a tin bucket and I'd follow the tracks in the grass, wet with dew. In the Warrumbungles dew descended on the high valleys year round. Sometimes I'd see that bold white head on a terrace three hundred metres above me. All I had to do was tap the tin bucket with a stick. He'd face up, look down sometimes for a minute, then he would come, always fast with the others lagging far behind. He was Arab, of course. I didn't know of another breed that had their strength.

I suggested to Heather that Sal ride Trigger. Shorny looked quiet enough, but the old white gelding was strong, in good condition and it seemed pointless to mount Sal on anything else.

With Sal moved onto Trigger, Peter suggested I ride Shorny. A bay gelding with white socks as long as street marching girls, he had one vice – he was hard to catch. I was warned to hobble him at any moment of non-attendance, toilet included.

The first day was more than horse and rider introduction. The packhorses were to be identified and broken in. Johnny was the first. He took no notice at all, not even when the cropper was hooked under his tail. Next was Creamy. He wasn't at all sure about the cropper. Tail coiled underneath, almost to his brisket, I expected him to go off. He didn't – two from three. Blackjack, however, looked a very bleak prospect. I went forward to help Peter.

'Better not come close, Mike,' he said, almost whispering.

'He can kick frontways, sideways and if behind, God help you. I gotta do this alone.'

Blackjack snorted, blew and ran backwards a couple of times. It took great patience. We all watched breathlessly – even the young women went quiet for a few minutes. When Blackjack was released I thought he'd bolt. Instead, he ran away, turned to look at us all and then commenced to eat the curly bluegrass by the road. We had three packhorses. The plan was to let them run along for three days with no packs.

There was one final drama before we broke camp, on a scant breakfast of tea and toast. Peter didn't look like being able to mount his horse, Star. Soon as he put his left boot to the iron, the bay gelding spun away. George, Robert and Harold had to put shoulder to horse. Peter gave the word, the men went down with their shoulders and Peter went for it. He got on, but if he wanted a pee he'd have to stand in the saddle.

The truck went ahead with all the gear. Priscilla and Rachelle were in the front with Buddha, and Harold travelled with Robert in his four-wheel-drive ute. We were to assemble at the Lennard and Peter would make a decision.

It was a perfect morning. Cool, pleasant, like the Warrumbungles in late spring. The horses ran with the freshness of the air in their faces and overhead corellas squawked from the bloodwoods. The sun lit up the Leopold rock and the deep green of the scattered Mount House box on the lower slopes produced an artist's backdrop. The Kimberley Ranges were unique, with no replica on the face of the earth.

After three kilometres we left the Gibb River road for a track no one had been on since last season's dry. Overgrown with grass, the wheel tracks provided a tunnel through the high spear grass. The grass was dominant in this area of the ranges and without the wheel track grass seeds in the horses eyes may have been a problem. The density varied. Sometimes it swallowed all sign of Peter at the lead, who was followed by

Heather. Sal quickly discovered she had no say in the line of order – Trigger followed Dusty and defied any attempt to split them, so Sal came next. Behind Trigger came Blackjack and the four Derby horses behind him jostled for position. George's Possum sedately followed the four geldings and George and I brought up the rear. Where possible George and I rode side by side, but when the spear grass was heavy I fell in behind him. Shorny was the quickest walker in the pack, but provided he was up with the horse in front he steadied himself, which saved me from continual restraining.

George looked very impressive in the saddle. Without effort he sat straight as a ramrod. His left arm hung away a little, with the stockwhip handle between thumb and forefinger and the coils loose over his wrist. It was a stance of readiness, established over decades of bush riding. His knees too denoted years of sudden, hard, balanced riding. From my school he rode short. On the sheep stations we never had to explode from walk to gallop. Instead, trot off, break into a hack canter and stop again. Sheep men rode long. I never broke the habit, except on race day when the knees rose right to a horse's wither. George's inherent readiness for sudden action was demonstrated every time Blackjack baulked at something and veered away with the four geldings and Possum following. George would be there in and instant. Never moving in the saddle and whip lifting skyward, you had to look smartly to see his hand move. He only cracked the whip when Blackjack put on an act and refused to cross a ditch or a soakage. Up and down went the red hide and the report was like a 303. Blackjack would bolt and if he went the wrong way we had to sit and wait. We never quite knew with Blackjack.

George loved to chat along. I had to concentrate hard. To some degree it was my hearing, as he spoke so deeply it was almost from the chest.

'Mike,' he would say. If I wasn't abreast I'd stride up level.

Dig Shorny in the ribs and he'd be off, me standing in the irons. I think the boys in Derby might have had a pony race or two when Peter wasn't about.

'Mike,' he'd say again. 'This beautiful country. You can ride long time in our country. I don't know the country on the other side. I never been there.'

'We gotta cross the range, George,' I said, two or three times. 'We gotta save all that country. Go to Dimond Gorge. You got to tell all your people how beautiful it is.'

He would think about what I said for a while. He had no interest in development and western society's supposed need of it. His world was right now. He was on his horse, which he was so proud of. Round him were the mountains of his childhood and ancestors of 40,000 years. The rivers were flowing and full of fish. What more could you possibly want? In the end he came up with needs that were maybe mine.

'Michael Cur got a bar,' he said, grinning widely. 'You go to the bar, so am I.'

'We'll have a beer all right.' Spear grass smothering us and the mountains growing in height on either side, Mornington seemed like the other side of the world.

I never spoke of the art. I was waiting to see George with his purple shirt off. I expected to see the initiation scars. If initiated the hoodoo would be powerful, like his own presence. Black hat with a wide green band with Fitzroy Crossing written in white, purple shirt with sleeves rolled, white trousers and a big strong white horse. George was some man. A gentle giant.

We could hear the Lennard before we saw it. The bloodwoods gave way to red gums, plum trees, freshwater mangroves and river figs. When we walked out of the grass a stream fifty metres wide looked like the end of the road. The horses were thirsty and walked into the shallows to drink. The flow wasn't strong. It was the depth you couldn't tell. Robert already had a plan of attack and Peter agreed. Eager to try, Robert put his ute to the test. It had a high snorkel exhaust. The ute lurched, dropped into a hole and the water swirled inches below the window line, but it never stopped moving. He got through narrowly. It didn't look so good for the truck, and the wet and boggy ground on the far track didn't offer any anchorage for the ute to tow from. Peter edged Star deeper into the river and called on Buddha to follow. Harold and the girls were in the back of the truck, relishing the excitement. The truck, with all our gear and food, rolled into the water and looked more like a punt. Peter guided Buddha around the hole that nearly claimed the ute, but submerged were some big boulders. The truck began to spin helplessly and everyone cheered – 'Go for it, Buddha' – as though he were a jockey carrying all the money. The tyre lugs somehow gripped onto something and the truck lurched forward again, the water slowly and surely dropping away until we could at last see the spare tyre. Buddha had got through.

Now it was our turn. Had these horses ever crossed a river? Wild horses would roll in the water, paw at it or simply stand in it up to their bellies while they cooled off, but they didn't like their feet to lose contact with the ground. Too often in flood situations stranded wild horses had waited too long, and when the inevitable swim was forced upon them by rising waters it was often too late. The currents were strong and the distance to safety too great. Blackjack smelt the full stream, stretched his head right out, blew a snort and surged through the current in strong strides. His feet never left the river gravel and the rocks. If Blackjack went, they all did.

We rode on for another two hours and about twenty-eight kilometres from our previous camp we dismounted for a very early halt to the day. Soft from urban living we were all stiff. The horses were hobbled immediately and let loose to feed on patches of bull Mitchell grass. Very popular too was the Kimberley couch on the creek banks.

The horses weren't the only ones starving, and I lit a fire right on the water's edge. On Kimberley criteria it was a little creek, but Sal and I couldn't get over the clean running water. We had forgotten what it looked like. In New South Wales only high tableland streams that ran off phosphate-free soils were clean. On our farm the watershed divided and there were no streams at all.

George had brought some meat and it wasn't going to keep. I cut most of it up for a big stew, and the steak cuts I organised Priscilla and Rachelle to barbecue on a green stick. Grillers are heavy and with the packs in mind I hadn't brought any.

The girls were still a little unsure of me. Nearby was a bull-bush. The wood has a thin layer of nectar, which attracts a tropical green ant. They're very active and very tasty, with a distinct lime flavour. I shook a branch of the bullbush and some ants dropped onto my arm, which I proceeded to eat. The girls were pop-eyed. Minutes later I had them shrieking with laughter.

Priscilla and Rachelle were in their late teens. They were alike in figure, manner and expression, and it was easy to mix them up at a distance. They were lithe, quick and had a spontaneous sense of humour. Priscilla was George's daughter. She adored him and when George sat down on the ground he didn't have to move for anything. She would have fed him if he'd let her.

Harold and Buddha went fishing in a hole downstream and we didn't see them again until late afternoon. Buddha was mid-forties, had done station work in the seventies and eighties, and had decided it was time to retire. In other words, it was time to return to a more traditional lifestyle. A fishing line, the stars overhead and a place to sleep. I envied them. If life could be that simple, every day was a pleasure to live. Harold didn't know his birthday, but Peter thought he was about thirty.

George and Peter weren't hard to find after lunch. They'd

rolled their swags out in the shade and were asleep within minutes. Heather moved her horses to another feeding tree. She was still worried Dusty might get restless, especially if he couldn't see her. Sal and I went for a swim in a hole upstream. You never had to walk far. The little streams opened up into swimming holes after every bend. It was very warm at this time of the day, making the water feel surprisingly cool – a little too cool – but when you got out the sun was an instant radiator.

The camp's high noon peace was shattered by a donkey-jack. We'd made camp in his territory, apparently! The agitated braying was like a bugle out of time. I walked through the spear grass to try and see him. Maybe I'd seen wild donkeys in a zoo. I couldn't remember, but I wasn't prepared for this donkey's ears. He shook his head and stamped a front foot. I knew nothing about wild donkeys so I didn't venture closer than thirty metres. Peter told me later the jacks would chase you off their territorial holes. After an hour this bloke decided there were too many of us and vented his annoyance from the nearby range until nightfall. Oddly enough, the horses took no notice of him, which made me think wild donkeys roamed the Pindan near Derby.

Heather had a swim too and she suggested Sal take a walk with her downstream. Peter had told her about an expanse of water like a mountain lake. I wished I'd gone too. Swimming in the middle of this hundred-metre stretch of water was a three-metre crocodile, which was about as large as freshwater crocodiles got. I'd never seen one swimming. Mostly they were seen lying in the sand, at water's edge or drifting like a log, motionless. Sal said the huge tail propelled him, in long graceful sweeps. He disappeared when he became aware of the human presence. Aborigines ate crocodiles as a delicacy. They were shy and difficult to spear, so a warrior took them from underneath.

When night fell I realised there would be separate fires. I

Peter Brooking adjusts the packs on Blackjack.

L–R: Priscilla, Rachelle and George.

L–R: Mike, Peter and Robert with the spooky Blackjack, who humped our supplies over the three ranges.

L–R: Harold, George, Priscilla, Rachelle and Buddha take a break.

A sandbar crossing on the Adcock River.

'You're on my territory!' This wild bull of the Leopolds may never have seen a human before.

Waterfall at Millie Windie.

Spreading grotesquely, more like a prehistoric monster than a tree, a boab
shades our horses.

Mount Hamilton seen from the Jacob's Ladder on the Precipice Range. Beyond it is an unnamed range.

L–R: Sal, Peter and Heather under Mount Banggalarowi. According to Bunuba legend, 'This hill he nearly collapsed and bats pushed it back again.'

Heather cooling off with her horses Trigger and Dusty (right) at Nugget Gorge.

The packhorses thread through the spear grass with the long mesa of Mount Hamilton behind.

Top: Mike and Harold take a spell from paddling in Dimond Gorge.
Centre: A white-necked heron at Dimond Gorge.
Bottom: One of the Fitzroy's remote and beautiful gorges.

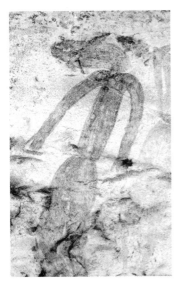

Mystery figures in an ancient gallery. The riddle may taunt archaeologists for decades to come.

Classic Bradshaw Art. Recent work conducted at James Cook University dates the art style from 1500 to more than 4000 years old. Note the 'mounted warrior' on the left.

didn't understand for a while. I began to think divisions between white and black had been so entrenched in the Kimberley for so long that we would eat in separate camps. The prospect appalled me. It was later in the evening when I discovered the reason. Aboriginal people traditionally slept near a fire.

After the Lennard crossing we hadn't seem Robert for the rest of the day. It was dark when he returned. He'd only seen four horses. Fat and shiny, he told me. And full of buck, too, I thought to myself. The good news was the truck would make it as far as a place called the Rocks. Peter had said some of the creeks were boggy for weeks after the wet and the advance up the valley with the truck was a creek-by-creek proposition.

Next morning the nosebags were all on by six-thirty. On the track again, ears were back and mouths threatened as the horses sorted out the order. Like their riders, they were stiff from muscles not tuned to several hours work. Blackjack was in a piggy mood. He baulked at every ditch and creek crossing, the others taking his lead. The routine became monotonous. Peter and the women waited patiently on the eastern side. George and I crowded in behind, urging them over. When words failed George cracked the whip. At one very muddy crossing Blackjack galloped away for one hundred metres. He turned to face us, hoping the little pack would follow him. George held them with the whip and I rode back to bring the black rogue in. Peter rode back and helped us, but Blackjack wouldn't be bullied.

In single file order Possum pranced up behind Blackjack. I had a sneaking suspicion she was very impressed by this powerful black gelding. Creamy dropped in behind her, followed by One Sock, who was still the wild card in the pack. He'd been broken in, I knew that much, but a young horse freshly broken could be a handful if it had never been ridden out. Johnny was the next in order and made to stay there by One Sock, who put his ears back and chased Johnny away if he got anywhere near Possum. The chestnut ambled along behind these two, not happy at any stage of the trek. Bringing up the rear, George and I were able to ride side by side for much of the morning.

We rode into some rich basalt country and the spear grass was replaced with a mixture of barley Mitchell grass and curly bluegrass. If it were not for the high wall of the King Leopolds to our right and the Lady Forrest to our left the open wood-land undulations would have resembled much of western Queensland. But alas, something was missing – the native wild-life. On three occasions little groups of donkeys trotted away. They headed for the remaining clumps of spear grass and all you could see was their ears, floating through the foxtail top of the high grass. Not a kangaroo, wallaby, emu or plain turkey was sighted. On my own twelve-hundred-hectare block in central New South Wales I had more kangaroos than a million acres of the King Leopolds. Kangaroos were essential in the management of native grasses. They did a lot of scratching in the dirt, unlike feral pigs, which uproot floodplains, sometimes so extensively it looked like the work of a tractor and ground ripper. I remarked to George on the lack of native wildlife.

'The emu gone, Mike,' he said sadly. 'Bunuba people burn after wet. Now the new people burn too late. Make big hot fire. Emu lay eggs early in the dry and fires cook em. Same thing plain turkey. Not many turkey now.'

'Not a hawk or eagle ever sighted,' I said.

'Small animals all burnt too. You see plenty rock wallaby up there in them gorges, Mike. They and a few kangaroos only ones to escape fire.'

'And the donkeys.'

'They climb up mountains, too. Get away from fires. I show you, Mike, an old donkey camp, back when they everywhere in the mountains. Nothin grow for years.'

About noon Mount Broome filled the sky to the south-west.

My water bottle was made of muleskin, from Arizona's Grand Canyon. George and I had drunk it dry. I began to scan ahead for the truck, when I saw a pulley chained to the bough of a grey box. I drew George's attention to it.

'Mount Hart Station came all the way down here one time,' He said. 'I work here in the sixties. We used that pulley to brand.'

A little bewildered I glanced around for any sign of an old yard, a white-anted strainer post or the shredded remains of old rails. There was nothing. I asked George how they did it: from my urbanised perspective of the land the concept of running a herd of cattle onto an open stretch of ground and branding the calves was impossible.

'We bring em here from top of the Lennard,' George explained. 'Be fifteen of us blokes on horses in those days – maybe more. No white fella with us. We knew our job.' George paused, gazing across the little plain under scattered clumps of spear grass and patches of sweet curly bluegrass. 'The bullocks come out first. Everyone hold mob and the best cuttin horse wheel em out, one at a time. The mob of two hundred or more lookin for the break and every bloke dancin back and forth on their horse tryin to hold em. It was hard ridin' Mike. Then when we got them bullocks out four blokes move em away and hold em. The rest of us start the brandin. A red-hide rope put through the pulley which was the lasso. Big strong mule on one end and cowboy carryin the lasso loop. He had to be a good man the cowboy. It was tough enough without someone missin. He throw lasso over a calf, it run and when rope grab big mule know to run backwards. Rope run easy through pulley and calf pulled up to a log ramp. Ramp probably made a few seasons before, couple of posts in the ground and some rails. Calf hit ramp two men rush in and throw him, another lassos hind leg and another bloke lassos top front leg. Then the marker bloke comes in with the knife – if it a bull.

One bloke earmarks and another brands. All done very quick and calf let go to run back to the cow. That's how we did it, Mike. We were young men then. No one could do that now.'

'Where were the bullocks taken?' The talking kept our minds off the water and food. We were soft and we had to pick up at least twenty-five kilometres for the day.

'They held in a bullock paddock near Mount Hart homestead and when musterin finished a drover take em to Derby. There they get loaded onto boats.'

In the sixties the bullocks were shipped to Robb's jetty at Fremantle, the shipping port for Perth. They were sold at auction.

Late noon we had to cross the Lennard again. On the eastern side we dismounted and drank a tiny mug I passed around. Here, the river had cut through a basalt layer of rich soil. The plum trees were enormous and mingled among them were the conspicuous Leichhardt pines, tall and heavy with dark green foliage. It should have been an ideal spot to camp, but we weren't welcome. Overhead thousands of flying foxes clung to every limb in the plum trees and made a raucous din. I didn't recall anything near its equal in the wild. The black clusters seemed to extend downstream hundreds of metres and if the flying ones circling above were any thicker they would have shaded the sun. We kept riding, to enter our sixth hour in the saddle. For semi-urban riders the fourth is the hour of pain. My damaged right knee was aching and I could see Sal holding her left side. George had gone quiet, his head sinking down into his neck. I couldn't feel either foot. Finally I called a halt.

Peter was clearly embarrassed when I spoke to him. 'Where did you tell the boys to meet us? We haven't even got a billy to boil.'

'I told them to stop at one of the creeks. We'd have lunch and go on a bit further.'

'Any good camps soon?'

'Next creek's good enough,' he replied, always calm. 'We'll pull up there and I'll ride ahead and bring them back.'

'How far?'

He shrugged and, as always, smiled. 'First big fishin hole, I suppose.'

Peter had asked for some Deep Heat cream at breakfast to rub into his swollen ankles. I didn't have any. It should have been the first item into the medical kit for a packhorse expedition. He wouldn't take any Panadeine. Star was a vigorous five-year-old of fourteen hands, but Peter would have weighed nearly eighty kilograms. Another twenty kilometres on top of the forty kilometres just completed would have exhausted both man and horse.

'I'll walk,' I said firmly. 'I like walking. I'll reach them in three hours.'

'They'll come back in time,' Heather put in quietly. She was used to the vagueness of Aboriginal people.

We rode on to the next creek and hobbled out. It wasn't a bad camp. The creek was still running, that lovely clear water, and within easy walking distance were two deep swimming holes. Our campsite was a horseshoe, which helped to confine horses. Not that they should have wanted to wander, with stands of Mitchell grass half the size of a tennis court. Heather tied Dusty and Trigger up again. Peter rode ahead. No one would hear of me walking and we couldn't simply hope Buddha would return in the truck. Under water for months, the springs and soaks were only just beginning to dry out. Both vehicles could be bogged.

Quiet as a mouse, Sal fell asleep on the rocks by the creek. Nearby George flattened down some grass and was soon heard snoring. Heather went for a swim. She was in better riding condition than all of us. I was too irritable to rest and gathered some wood for the camp.

Time passed slowly and I refocused my thoughts on Frank
Hann. He must have made camp somewhere about here. To
the south the dome shape of Mount Broome dwarfed the
surrounding bluffs and crags. Between the camp and Mount
Broome a narrow reef of quartz ran parallel with the Leopold
Range, one hundred metres high.

Sunday, 22 May 1898:
Gins and I started to go up on top of Mount Broome. Grace's
shoe came off so left Minnie and Dora at water. Mina and I
went up, great job in doing so. My glass make it 1800 feet
above the flat.

On that Sunday, Hann was camped at the foot of Mount
Broome, on the south side of the Leopolds. For a week he and
his Aboriginal contingent panned for gold. He remarked in
this diary that they found only specks of gold. On 30 May he
crossed the range, which in 1898 was the outer boundary for
white men. Beyond was Bunuba territory. The defeat of the
Jandamarra rebellion had claimed the Fitzroy River country
for the pastoralists, but beyond the Leopolds the Bunuba
remained in command.

Enough firewood stacked for two nights I lay down beside
Sal and tried to sleep too. The hoof sounds of a lone horse
made me jerk upright into a sitting position. Peter was back.
Standing in the creek mid-stream, Star sucked up mouthfuls
of water. Peter looked up as Heather and I advanced on him
for news. He looked very weary.

'They were up in a gorge fishin,' he said. 'Coming back now.'

'I hope they have some fish for us.' Sal approached, every
step revealing the stiffness in her legs.

Peter grinned. 'I think they ate them as quick as they caught
them.'

I lit the fire and twenty minutes later both vehicles lurched across the stony creek. Everyone seemed in great spirits. We were so pleased to see the food packs all was forgiven without a murmur. I suggested to Sal we boil up a big meat stew and have it with heaps of rice. Damper would be too slow after nine hours in the saddle. So intent was I on the cooking I didn't hear the deep-chested rumbling from across the river.

'This is his territory,' Peter said warily. 'The country's full of wild bulls.'

I left the fire and followed Peter. The bull pawed the ground in a clump of cane grass. Dust lifted, like smoke from a grass fire and when the bull raised his head high, he displayed a set of horns wider than the length of a golf stick.

'He could wipe us off this flat,' Peter said, worried. 'Hobbled horses can't escape the horns. These feral bulls can be bad news.'

Hearing the threatening sounds – half bellow, half growl, like a domestic bull about to fight the unwelcome neighbour's fence jumper – George strode off quickly with his stockwhip. Robert and the boys dropped what they were doing and spread out, cautiously moving towards the creek.

The first crack from George's whip echoed along the range. Then another and another.

'Everybody, now,' Peter said hoarsely, forever calm. 'Bawl your lungs out at him.'

But the whip cracking and yelling had no effect on this bull. He moved out of the spear grass and onto the creek bank, vigorously shaking his head. The ivory-tipped horns were like giant skewers. He raised more dust and I could hear the saliva gurgling deep in his throat. In full view on the bank, we all stood vulnerable to one thousand kilograms of hard muscle. Under a rich tawny coat, with a shade of charcoal down the shoulder and in the setting sun, it looked like the bull was wearing armour.

'Look for a tree,' I yelled.

Peals of laughter came from the girls and George cracked the whip with every twist of his wrist. He was too close – a matador on the morgue table. Wanting to offset the danger we all advanced a little more. It was very dangerous. If the bull didn't back off someone wouldn't get away. Any second he would leap down into the creek and explode upon us. Suddenly George had stumbled forward, a suicide dash at his age, and whirled the whip in a vicious circle above his head. No cracking, the vibration more felt than heard as the red hide cut the air at high speed. The bull lifted his huge head, the last of the sun catching the white tips of his horns. This was a sound he had never confronted. Helicopters had appeared many times over the seasons and donkeys dropped dead, but no harm came to him. He didn't fear that sound. But this new one threatened him. It was all around him. A terrifying vibration of the air he had never heard before. He turned and in a second the cane grass swallowed his massive rump.

'Wild animals usually bolt at the crack of a whip,' I said to Peter, thankful I could return to the cooking.

'In the wet these mountains are bombarded with lightning, days on end. He's used to it. The wild bulls out here fear nothing.'

The bull gone we were all laughing and joking. A rum would have gone down well, but we had no alcohol. A few of us in the camp, myself included, needed to dry out. But on occasions like this, one nip would have soothed our nerves.

We broke camp early again. This time Star didn't have to be scrum-held for Peter to mount – he was tired and George only had to hold his head. Peter too was suffering with swollen ankles and George was so crippled with stiffness he put his saddle on Creamy and legged up Priscilla, who sat in the saddle as naturally as the boys back in Derby.

About mid-morning Peter left the track and led us into a

deep valley with a rich floor of woodland. When he dismounted I could hear the tumbling water ahead. We didn't
hobble all the horses. Lush feed under big trees and the
morning already warm, it was hard to imagine a horse wandering away. The vehicle crew had already arrived at the waterfall and were baiting their hooks when we stumbled up over
the little rock fall. It was where they had come yesterday and I
instantly saw why they'd wanted to stay. Some people felt a
sense of God in places of worship. To believe in the pure and
the holy was to witness what we were so privileged to see. Red
dolomite cliffs towered above a crystal clear waterhole half full
of emerald green water lilies. The water mirrored the red cliffs
in a profusion of colour. It was the most beautiful scene in
nature I had ever witnessed. Nothing humans had ever made
or painted throughout the ages could hold a candle to some
of the hidden gorges in Australia's Kimberley. If nothing else,
they existed to humble the arrogance of civilisation.

I sat quietly and let myself be mesmerised by it all. Sal stood
at the water's edge, capturing every angle with the camera.
Heather delicately mounted her tripod, Harold hauled in a
half-kilogram cherubim, Priscilla caught a bream seconds afterwards and Buddha rebaited his line. Even crippled-up George
was fiddling around with a line.

Robert observed my pensive mood and invited me to eat
some native fruits. First I had a wild, yellow-skinned passionfruit
about the size of a small mandarin. It had a sharp citrus taste.
Next was the purple-coloured fruit of the rock fig. The pan-
danus palm was too green. Late in the winter, Robert told me,
the fruit shaped like a small pineapple would mature into a
red-orange colour. The plum trees grew in profusion and their
fruits would mature in the spring.

'When I come out here to live in the winter,' Robert said
seriously, 'I don't bring any supermarket tucker. It's all here.'

Nature's supermarket didn't end there. The stems of the

water lilies had been a staple diet for the Aborigines and Robert urged me to look for insects. Could I see the little bush bee? A non-stinging bee, it had nests everywhere in tree hollows. Did I know the boab fruit?

We had ridden into paradise. The most pure water in existence, fish rushing to be hooked, delicious edible fruits, water tumbling from a natural reservoir in the cliffs and below, our horses dozed in the shade of river gums.

'Sure you still want to tackle Jacob's Ladder?' Peter said with a glint in his eye, struggling not to smile.

I had no answer at that moment.

CHAPTER

7

Fragile

'There's smoke. I think the fire's up around Dimond.'

We were preparing to eat lunch when Peter rode back into camp. He'd been out searching for Possum, who had mysteriously bolted, but he now looked like he had more than Possum on his mind.

Sal opened her mouth to say something then caught the slight shake of my head. When Peter rode Star over to the other horses to hobble him, she looked at me a little alarmed. 'If it's Dimond Gorge, we're riding straight into it,' she said sharply.

'Say nothing,' I said firmly. 'Ignore it. They're luke-warm anyway. They don't know the country and don't want to go. I hesitated, staring east into a sky no longer blue, like a distant rain front. 'If there's a fire we'll go around it, sneak through a gap or hold up in a damp gorge. We mustn't turn back.'

Possum's bolting had cast a bit of gloom over the day, and the pleasure we'd taken in the beautiful setting had begun to dissipate. Possum and One Sock were our spares. Without Possum we'd have to rely on luck to cross the next one hundred kilometres of rugged terrain. And now it seemed like Peter and the boys didn't want to continue.

But I felt we had to continue. I had no difficulty in imagining the one hundred metre high dam wall destined for Dimond

Gorge. To put a crack in that imaginary dam wall we had to ride on: cross the Lady Forrest and Precipice ranges so that we could tell everyone what beautiful country it was and that none of it should become the backwaters of a dam. You could fly over mountains, buzz the very gorges if you like, but you would never see it that way. You had to be on the ground to smell the trees and the animal camps and hear the birds. From the air a jagged landform could look next to nothing, but on the ground, with the sun bathing shades of light on the cliffs, that landform might be one of the most striking features you had ever seen. We had to ride on, too, to look for ancient galleries. To Peter and George the galleries were so sacred they never spoke of them, and it was this very strong feeling of reverence that I wished to capture. Here was art that was mysterious, hidden, sacred and very ancient. In my mind its discovery was another wield of that giant sledgehammer against the imaginary dam wall.

Sal knew me too well to talk about retreat. Instead, she silently unrolled the hot tinfoil from the dampers and pulled the fish off the coals. Rachelle and the boys had just caught them and they'd thrown them whole onto the fire.

I'd never eaten unscaled fish with the guts left in and went for the blackberry jam and damper. Heather didn't have one either. Sal put our urbanity to shame and loved her fish. The scales simply peeled off with the skin. Buddha and Harold didn't have anything but big mugs of tea loaded with sugar and a tablespoonful of powdered milk.

We packed up again and prepared to leave. No more was said about the fire. Possum hadn't turned up, but George didn't seem at all worried. An Elder now, he was very philosophical. At the worst, the mare would only be lost for a few weeks. After shortening Shorny's stirrup leathers for Rachelle I left in the truck with Buddha and Harold. Robert set off in his ute for Millie Windie, which was another fifty kilometres further up the track. He looked upon Millie Windie as his real home. Back in Derby any conversation with him always swung back to Millie Windie, whether it was about horses, bush tucker or the spirit of the place itself. I thought he would have lived out there permanently and braved the wet and the wild squalls of wind and rain that went with it if he was not left out there alone. But Millie Windie was just an open shed with no power and no sanitation. Feeling stiff and tired, George decided to go with Robert, and took Priscilla along. I could see Peter was worried about them. If they drove into a quicksand bog their vehicle would have to be abandoned for weeks. We agreed to meet them at the Rocks before nightfall.

For much of the way the going was only marginally quicker than a horse's walk. We collected logs and sticks along the way. Peter had warned that the Rocks had been a popular camp for decades and firewood would be scarce.

About an hour from our lunch fire we sighted five horses. They stood with their heads high, alert and in peak condition. With a toss of the head from the one in front they bounded through the woodlands with the gracious ease of kangaroos.

To our right and to the south another high reef of ancient dolomite rock emerged from the surface. A narrow gorge cut through the reef, sharp and vertical, like a giant girder split in the middle. When clear of foreground trees I could see the green shape of the palms against the amber rock. Obviously another spectacular gorge.

Boab trees sometimes developed into the weirdest tree shapes in existence. The tree Buddha took a mark off reminded me of a giant bunch of bananas. The tree itself covered as much ground as a two-storey building. Buddha pushed through high kangaroo grass to the Lennard. Close to the headwaters the river had become a creek, but the water-hole was magnificent, a rock pool one hundred metres long under big shady plum trees. The lower bank formed a natural terrace, with areas of freshly washed sand and Kimberley couch grass. The Rocks was a perfect campsite.

When the others rode in two hours later I had a billy of rice, laced heavily with garlic and a damper ready to eat. Buddha and Harold disappeared. They did that. There one moment, you turned around to move a log in the fire and they had vanished without a sound.

It was another blissful late afternoon. Time for long swims, slow coffee drinking and yarning. The shadow in our thoughts was the fire, but no one uttered a word about it. Occasionally Peter and George gazed away to the east. They were worried. If we got a strong easterly it would fan the flames over the Leopolds and it would be like a great army storming the land. Millie Windie could be burnt out in a day and if the flames licked over the Lady Forrest Range the narrow peneplain to the north would become blackened – our passage through the ranges. We had to have grass for the horses.

When the boys returned I was grateful for their disappearance. Skewered on a green stick they had nine bream, all weighing more than half a kilogram.

'They your fish,' Harold announced proudly. 'We ate plenty.'

It was a warm feeling. Gradually, we were breaking down the old barriers. Peter announced he was going to cook a big damper, stock-camp style, buried in the hot ash. The fish were tossed in the ash too. I took the plunge this time and ate a big bream cooked blackfella way. I wouldn't bother scaling and gutting ever again.

An hour after sunset the mournful howl of a dingo added growing unease in the camp. The others should have been back. They could have been bogged fifty kilometres away with no tucker and not even a torch to follow the wheel tracks back. Peter was wrestling with indecision. He didn't want to risk the supply truck, but after a time he would have to look for them.

Knowing the bushfire would probably gather intensity on top of a land rapidly drying out, I had developed a dread of any delay. I suggested we wait until nine o'clock.

We sat around the campfire. The flames licked high and reflected off the water. The night was full of shadows cast by a half moon tipped on its side. We listened to Rachelle's Dreamtime stories centred on Geiki Gorge. It was the dwelling place of spirits, she told us, her eyes wide with conviction. There were monsters in the caves and the crevices which could be seen on moonlit nights. People who ventured too close disappeared, according to the legend.

Similar legends persisted across the continent. Palaeontological excavations had revealed a giant goanna once existed that exceeded a mature length of five metres, equal to the longest of saltwater crocodiles. It would have been a formidable creature, perhaps surviving until the onset of the last ice age. There was some speculation that it might have been the 'bunyip' in Aboriginal folklore.

Just before nine Robert, George and Priscilla arrived, tired and very hungry. They had been seriously bogged at one stage. Using logs for sleepers, Robert had had to jack each wheel and place any old timber they could find underneath. That done they had to fill the wheel trench cut in the mud by the tyres with more old logs. Carrying the old material from piles two hundred metres away had been exhausting. It was the last thing George had needed. Everything in place Robert had reversed out of the quagmire, and not to be deterred, had walked the final stage to Millie Windie camp. Everything was in place. No one had been there since he left it in November. He hadn't sighted any more horses.

Fires in the autumn dry were not like bushfires in Australia's south-east, all-consuming and equally voracious at night. The early dry season Kimberley fire picked up at noon when the sun had sapped the last vestige of dew at ground level. By mid-afternoon the flames devoured the land as though laced with petrol and then when evening fell the dew rose from wet subsoil and the fire abated, to smoulder through the night like a jilted woman in love.

At dawn the sun rose like a giant red neon light, the rays deepening across the land with no warmth. There was no smoke smell, but when Peter hadn't lit the pre-dawn fire I knew something was wrong. I got up and looked around. Heather's Dusty and Trigger were by their little allotted trees, standing like statues, but the others had wandered. I pulled on my boots and stumbled down the bank to light the breakfast fire by the big rock pool. We'd had to erect the tents on a little bare patch, back away from the river. There had been too much sand on the lower bank to hold tent pegs. The Aborigines had made a sleeping fire a few metres upstream, right by the water. I stared into the deep gloom cast by the plum trees and saw charcoal-coloured heaps on the white sand and a lazy drift of smoke from the dying remains of a campfire with enough hot ash to bake a boar.

Robert appeared at the moment one of the billies broke into a bubbling dance of water and I dropped in the tea leaves. The fire was cheerful and warm and we talked more about the pack-horse tourism potential for Millie Windie. Robert thought the tourists could be met at the Lennard River crossing and taken on from there on horseback. It would take three days' easy riding to get to the Millie Windie base camp. From the base camp day rides could trek out into the ranges. From experience I preferred to keep people on the move, providing new and interesting campsites. It would be a matter of trial and error for the first few safaris.

We knew Peter had gone looking for the horses and we heard him wading through the grass before we saw him.

'I don't know where they are,' Peter said. Whether problems were big or of no consequence, his demeanour never altered.

'We better take your ute, Robert, and drive down the track. They're headed that way.'

It looked like a late start the very day we'd planned to look for the Mount Ord gap and that prospect was disappointing.

The others all drifted in for a leisurely breakfast. Heather always attended her horses first. She took them for a drink and long-tied them to another tree where there was fresh grass. Rachelle and Priscilla were not morning girls. An hour from sunrise they still looked as though they should have been tucked under a man's arm. When I handed them a hot mug of tea I worked hard to extract a smile but failed. A naked dance in the sand might have done the trick. I glanced at the two white women and discarded the thought.

The delay gave me time to think carefully about the packs. I knew if Frank Hann was beside me drinking a mug of tea he would have gravely shaken his head and told me to drop the plans. Johnny and Creamy were too small. Blackjack was too wild. But he wasn't riding to try to save the Fitzroy River, merely panning for gold and naming every mountain and gorge he came upon.

Compared to the two ponies, Blackjack would hump almost double the weight with ease. He would carry all the food and the mess gear. Creamy would carry the two light tents, three sleeping bags and Heather's personal gear. That left Johnny with the two inflatable rafts and a small plastic bag of spare clothes for Sal and me. The rafts were bulky, but the heaviest only weighed eight kilograms. Peter's swag would ride on the top of Blackjack's packs and George's on Johnny's packs. Used to lifting lead bags in the jockey's room and guessing the weight before going to the clerk of scales I could assess weight within a kilogram. I set Blackjack for forty kilograms, Creamy at thirty and Johnny at twenty-two. Any more risked a breakdown or foot soreness.

Problem was, I still had a heap of sundry gear. Sal insisted on carrying the satellite telephone in one of the haversacks. It weighed about three kilograms and at the end of the day would feel like ten. I had three sets of dual saddlebags. One I set aside to go onto Star, one onto Trigger and the elaborate leather one for Shorny to carry. I had bought it off a saddler in Mancos, Colorado, and placed in it the shoeing gear, insect sprays and fishing gear. We all called it the Colorado bag. Sundry items still left unplaced went into my haversack, including the camera bag. Heather had most of her camera gear secured behind the saddle.

A couple of hours passed before Peter and Robert returned. The horses were on top of a hill about two kilometres away. It was the mountain horses that had confused the search. Peter and Robert had tracked the wrong horses for a while, admitting the months spent in Derby during the wet had put some rust into their tracking skills. Shod horses leave a deeply edged print on the ground.

Sal made Peter eat breakfast. By nature he was entirely selfless, which was a rare condition in the modern world. I sometimes wondered whether the nuns had trained him as a small boy, but I never asked. He was quite prepared to set off for Mount Ord with nothing more than a mug of tea in his belly. After some damper and jam and a big mug of coffee he and the boys set off again with the nosebags. Those magic nosebags! George stayed by the fire. He was cheerful and I admired his mental resilience. He had every excuse in the world not to look forward to the day.

With plenty of female help I had all the packs loaded onto the truck and drove it up to the seven boabs all in one tree out on the little plain. We didn't have to wait long. With a couple of nosebags tucked under his arm Peter led the way and the horses followed like a pony club bunch at any country showground. With the hobbles removed for walking, the boys rushed to put on the nosebags as soon as Johnny – the glutton of the mob – reached the truck. The mountain horses only had to show and the expedition would be finished. Our little mob would bolt and join them – except maybe Johnny. Peter put his nose into the bag and gave him a pat. While they all stood still, the euphoric effect of the nuts showed in their half-closed eyes. We slipped through them and secured the hobbles.

Before saddling we checked the shoes. Stallion Tom was only half ready – no rear shoes. Peter at once set to work on him. Dusty had a loose shoe and Robert got his hands to the spare gear in the Colorado bag. I was sorry he wasn't coming to share all his bush knowledge. Bush tucker men are increasingly rare. But Robert's love was Millie Windie. He didn't like the country over the range and was equally disappointed we were leaving.

With the gentle tap of the farrier hammer in the background, Harold and I began the packing. The horses were broken into the packsaddles. The real test was when the packs were mounted. I didn't expect any trouble with Johnny. He took his load without a flinch. Next was Creamy. He had a rounded back, like an over-fat hog, the worst conformation for a packhorse. I got Harold to reef down on the overall strap and we held our breath as the little horse walked away, unhobbled. We had to know before we left! It was when they walked off that it dawned on them how different everything felt. But there was no reaction – Creamy simply stopped and smelt a clump of coarse grass.

Blackjack we had to leave to Peter, who was copping it from Stallion Tom. The hindquarter muscles flexed on occasions and Peter let the leg drop rather than fight him. Horses rarely shod put one man to more effort than a rugby lock giving ground. The task finished he then had to confront the big black horse with the packs. We all watched.

Each pack had two big O rings, which were slipped over front and back hooks on the packsaddle. With any horse of suspect tolerance it was wise to hook the packs on and lead the horse in a circle before reefing down on the overall strap. If the horse rejected the packs and bucked he might at least throw them clear and avoid damaging the gear. Once the big long strap went over the packs it was a straight-out test of durability: exhausted horse or packs and packsaddle requiring a day's stitching. In some respects it was a catch-22. If an unsecured pack dropped one hook only, the pack dragged under the horse's belly, with the potential to fire a berserk performance. With Blackjack there was no option. He didn't lead one step, for anybody. Peter tightened the big strap and stood back. The black outlaw had all our food. Those hell-bent for Mornington prayed to God. Those who didn't want to go murmured to the devil. God was listening. The big black horse strolled away, lifted his tail and did a shit.

It was time to get the compass from the Colorado bag and with the attached string hang it from my neck. I had the map out after breakfast, when all the packing was completed. The bearing for Mount Ord pass was three hundred and fifty degrees north by north-west. From Cape York to King Sound, across 5000 kilometres of Australia's northern wilderness, a bushman could survive with a fishing line, a box of matches, a handful of maps and a compass. Saltwater crocodiles and snakes were a daily threat. A wild bull, surprised in his favourite camp, could be deadly and in very remote pockets dingo packs demanded respect. But statistics proved the dangers existed more in the mind, for lives lost to wild animals in Australia were less than ten a year. However, the odds could tumble drastically depending on the circumstances.

No one said anything when we were all mounted, about to leave. Star was back to his old trick, but the scrum performance to get Peter aboard failed to arouse any mirth. Joked about as a ride to hell, I felt the girls, Buddha and Harold were sorry not to be coming with us. We had all become good friends and the camp atmosphere wouldn't be the same. Buddha was taking them back into Derby for the weekend and we would meet up again at Mornington.

Peter told me quietly he had instructed them to bring back some fresh supplies, such as vegetables and meat. 'But don't hold yer breath,' he said. 'Twenty Ks out of Derby they'll be half-drunk on the thought of the stuff and they'll be sick for days after.' I was glad I'd made the big effort to take supplies out to Mornington.

We had been spoilt on the track up the valley. The first barrier was the spear grass. Peter in the lead, all I could see was his hat. Heather followed then Sal, who had no say in it – Trigger never left Dusty. I brought up the rear behind Stallion Tom. The plain soon gave way to a steep rocky ravine. For horses it was almost rock climbing. My heart sank a little. They wouldn't last long in this. Peter too was feeling desperate. He zigzagged back and forth, trying to find a passage clear of boulders.

We got through unscathed and the country levelled out again into a tableland. The Lady Forrest Range hugged closely to our right and ugly boulder-peppered hills hemmed us in on the left. For half an hour we walked along in short grass, free of a stone, and at one point Peter reigned in.

'Here's the old track,' he exclaimed. 'See where the boulders were once pushed? I'll try and stay with it because Sam says some of the creek crossings are bad.'

The first one pulled us up where the tableland closed into a deep narrow valley. Blackjack wouldn't jump down the little embankment. Herding the others in tight didn't induce him either. If he didn't go, they didn't. George wheeled the whip and the report echoed along the range. Blackjack turned and bolted at full gallop with his tail between his legs. The food's gone, I thought. Then suddenly he stopped and turned to see if the others would follow. They were bluffed by the whip and remained at the bank, sulky and frightened. I suggested to George he watch them while I ride back behind Blackjack, who walked back quietly.

We tried another tact. Peter kept talking to the horses from the other side and I threaded Shorny through them and urged him across. Blackjack followed, but there was no key to the black outlaw with a white blaze. Every bad crossing was an exercise in extreme patience.

Creamy was the one who scared us most that morning. Distracted with Blackjack I saw the shift in the packsaddle too late. The lower pack slipped under his belly and terrified, he flew into panic, bucking. For the first half-minute a packsaddle in shreds looked certain. He paused just long enough for me to grab him. That not a single strap was broken seemed a miracle. While Peter held him I rearranged the packing and jammed a bit more gear into my backpack.

It was a long hard morning and the only moment we relaxed was when Peter spotted a copse of scarlet gums. A beautiful tree with yellow-red bark and thick pale-green foliage, it was a little out of its territory here. As we slowly gained altitude the silver-leaf bloodwoods became more prolific, marked by their pale erect trunks and slender branches. The steep slopes on either side became precipitous. There was no need to consult the compass – this had to be the passage through.

No wonder the pass had eluded so many early pioneers. At the foot of the final peak, which was Mount Ord, the narrow passage swung at right-angles to the north-east. At no point, either from the south or the north, was the gap visible. It was most spectacular, and my eyes roved ceaselessly for hidden rock shelters.

For most of the way the old track had vanished without a trace. The final scramble over a dividing ridge led into a deep corridor, which in the winter would have seen little sun. Growing here were trees as strange in shape and character as the boab. Neither Peter or George knew what they were. Ancient in appearance, and untidy, the leaves were half as broad as a human face. They conjured up images of Conan Doyle's lost world. Only later, that evening, did we identify them as twin-bloodwoods.

It was a lovely place. The grass was green and showing no signs of turning colour, and the air felt cool, like early morning. It was almost appropriate that the chestnut gelding with the bullet wound should choose this little glen to drop off and bid us farewell. He could recover here in peace and eventually graze his way back to the Lennard and join the mountain horses.

The pass opened out into a high plain, nearly six hundred metres above sea level. When I looked behind there was no sign of the gap, as though the mountain walls had drawn back on a giant hydraulic lift and closed again behind us. Frank Hann had missed it. Under extreme pressure he had clambered through a tight, boulder-strewn gorge about twenty kilometres to the west. The wild tribes didn't want him in their country. It was probably the Unggumi people who were deliberately spooking him. To put events into perspective, the Jandamarra rebellion of the adjoining Bunuba tribe had been crushed only fourteen months before.

12 June 1898
Started, course E SE half a mile. Crossed the Eva Creek, gorge close, then three miles further divide, very high ranges on each side of us. The blacks were on the main range to our left and was very cheeky. They thought they had us. I put a few shots over them which blocked them for a time. We had to go through a gorge. Had the blacks come on us there was no help for us as they could see us and we could not see them. After some trouble we got out all right, no one could believe there was such a pass through the range

with (out) seeing it. Half a mile from the gorge is the
Lennard ...

Hann named the pass Brownrigg Gorge, after a doctor in
Broome. The west Kimberley was full of names of people Hann
did business with or had some minor social contact. The pass
was so rough no one ever used it, but the Bunuba people were
aware of it. I couldn't pay tribute to Hann's choice of names
for geographic features. My admiration was for his horses and
the Aborigines who rode with him. Plotting Hann's track on
the map revealed some extraordinary equine ascents and
descents in the mountains. I didn't think anybody today would
remotely contemplate some of the routes he forced over the
ranges. Hann was eager to return to Derby in order to stake a
pastoral lease claim for more or less the whole of that area.
Had his party been cornered in Brownrigg Gorge by the
Unggumi they would have been subjected to spears from above
and may have all been killed – the men anyway. Yet this did
not deter him from taking up a lease, virtual proof that the
gun was law in the Kimberleys in 1898.

We rode into a light northerly. Smoke filled the sky above the
east-running Lady Forrest Range. North and west the sky
remained blue. At an upland stream we let the horses take a
long drink and Peter felt us out about an early halt for the day.
The haul up the pass had taken a lot out of the horses. It was
unanimous. The horses were always the first consideration. We
unsaddled, took them for a drink, washed their backs and when
there was nothing more to do for their comfort, we put the
hobbles on. Confident now her horses wouldn't stray, Heather
hobbled Dusty and Trigger out with the rest of the mob.

George was the first to wander off and look for a swimming
hole. A lover of fresh meat, we knew he was staring at a delicacy
when we heard him yelling for Peter and I to come quickly
with a stick. It was a nursery of little black pigs, all cuddled up

together in a patch of reeds. We both had a stick of sorts, the first piece of deadwood we'd seen, but when Peter saw the suckers he called wait.

George was too stiff to do anything. Peter's attention was on the thick kangaroo grass beyond the reeds. My hearing a little down, I didn't hear the large pig at the time.

'It's not worth it,' Peter said to his brother. 'They've got filthy mouths and infection moves fast.'

Seconds later it wasn't an issue. When they heard their mother's warning grunts the suckers leapt up as one and darted into the thick stand of grass.

'Should have brought a gun,' George said, annoyed. He was stripped to the waist and his bare chest gnarled from initiation scars caught my attention. Not so many years ago it might have been a spear that was urgently needed. Either one would have been useful, as we slowly backed away.

'I only got a 22,' Peter replied. 'Likely to get us into more trouble than give protection in this country.'

'Would have baked up good,' George said, still disgusted that a hind leg of succulent pork had literally jumped out of the camp oven. I felt it too. It was like arriving at a gourmet restaurant to find it shut. We later settled down to garlic rice and damper. There were no fish up here. The stream was typical of a watercourse close to the source – shallow, no banks and cold.

About sunset Peter contacted his wife, Geraldine, on the satellite phone. Even out here in the wild his road business couldn't be put on hold. From Geraldine he got some unwelcome news – CALM wanted to know where we were. From the air, they wanted to commence the seasonal burn across the range.

'If they ring you again,' I heard Peter say, 'tell them we need another four days.'

Geraldine had asked for the satellite phone number. 'We

can't leave the phone switched on,' I said quickly. 'If we flatten the battery we lose our safety net.'

Peter smiled and passed the message on. If they couldn't contact us, they had to wait until we were safely out of the mountains.

Sal wasn't so sure.

'George says the mountains are already ablaze around Dimond Gorge,' she said anxiously. 'What if they don't wait?'

'Oh, they'll wait,' Peter said grinning. 'Burning people is bad politics.' Then he added seriously, when the last vestige of blood had drained from her face, 'They'll want to know exactly where we are before the incendiary capsules are dropped.'

Our conversations moved from one menace to another. The fires solved for the moment, a muffled rumbling downstream heralded another bull coming.

'We stay put,' Peter said. 'It's nearly dark and he won't come near the fire.'

Next morning Peter and I consulted the map again. We had to ride north-west for an hour, find a gap in the escarpment and proceed north towards the Precipice Range. Sam had told us to get close to the range before swinging east. When we got there we found ourselves on an ancient floodplain between two prominent ranges. Once again the vegetation changed. The Kimberley was a botanist's paradise. Mountain bloodwoods, rusty-leaf bloodwoods, bauhinias, kurrajongs and a new one, the Kimberley Christmas tree, in a splendour of golden leaves.

'Don't think we'll follow Sam here,' Peter said, reigning in. 'Plain's so flat it's hard to spot at times, but there's a watershed. One lot of water running north and another south. We head east we might have to get these horses over some bad washouts.'

I didn't argue. Peter had an uncanny eye for country. He also had great faith in mule pads. Where water was plentiful, he said, cattle grazed out and back from their camps, but mules would walk in single file to the best feed.

Two hours out from the night camp I observed another range and but for Peter I may have lost a day. There appeared to be two wide valleys ahead and the map didn't tally with the visual scene.

'It's a big box canyon that northerly one,' Peter said confidently. 'If we rode north for half an hour I think we'd see the cliffs at the far end.'

Behind us Mount Ord dominated the landscape. Fortified by a lower cliff band, it formed a conical peak on the eastern side and a slightly higher peak to the west. From sunrise the colour of the mountain had kept changing and Sal and Heather had taken a snap every half hour until the massive uplift of red rock was too far away. Mount Ord was the highest point in north-western Australia.

Following a mule pad, we rode through savanna country of principally blackbox. There were mobs of up to fifty feral cattle. Unbranded cows with calves, mickeys as big as their mothers still hanging around for a suck made up the herd scene as they trotted away from our path. Danger from bulls became constant.

'Ride on,' George said, when we formed into a tight little pack. 'And don't stare at them.'

The bulls never yielded ground. Territorial and spooked by the weirdest combination of animals ever to set foot in their valleys, they stared with a combination of fear and bewilderment. None had the weight of the one defeated by matador George, but all had lethal horns. They instilled in us a feeling of helplessness.

The soil on this upland plain had an alluvial component in it. It grew a profusion of grasses and proof of the sweetness of the country were the cattle numbers. But it should have been home to more than feral cattle, donkeys and pigs. Two hours from campsite and in such ideal ecological conditions we should have by now spotted several mobs of red kangaroos. By mid-morning we still hadn't seen a native animal. While no doubt a combination of many factors, fire was surely the principal cause. Cattle could consume a wide range of grasses. They had what was known in lay terms as a 'first stomach', where digestive juices broke down coarse material. Burnt stubs of grass, islands of spear grass spared from the flames and old kangaroo grass hugging creek banks too damp for fire would keep cattle alive until the new growth sprung from the charred land. Kangaroos, wallabies and wallaroos or mountain kangaroos were forced to move on to survive.

I wasn't qualified to say what should be done in the Kimberley and I wasn't criticising existing authorities, because they were so undermanned, burning procedures other than those adopted would have been difficult to carry out. Corridor burning on a 'cold' fire policy following the wet would require enough field staff to form a platoon and a fleet of support vehicles. No one was more aware of the difficulty than I was, but the Kimberley was Australian sovereign territory, not some backyard annexation that no one visited or cared about. What was the region's potential value for international tourism? What was its preserved form worth to human kind? These were urgent questions that should not have been left to future generations to answer: it would be too late.

The fire in the ranges ahead of us began to throw up palls of smoke, like the belching puffs from a volcano. We could smell it, yet the traces of smoke carrying the odour were invisible. Like dark storm clouds, the distance of a fire was always hard to assess. Many firefighters had lost their lives by trying to rely on smell and visual location. When Peter spotted Nugget Gorge appearing suddenly as a deep gash in the Precipice Range, he pulled the left reign and we rode straight for it, seeking the water and dampness.

Inside the final kilometre to the gorge we rode over a scalded piece of ground the size of a football oval. 'Remember, Mike?' George asked, leaning back to make sure I heard him. 'Said I would show you a big old donkey camp. Nothing grow here now.'

Ironically, two dead donkeys lay bloated on the far side, their legs stretched hard and stiff as though frozen in a stance of full alert. A single bullet wound through the forehead showed traces of dried blood. A CALM marksman had taken them out from a helicopter.

Nearing the gorge we entered a damp, green area with a hint of jungle. It was in pockets like this we could escape the fire if faced with a wide front. Shorny and all the other horses had their heads down in green Mitchell grass. All of them were gaining weight fast enough to put feedlot statistics to shame. Every time we stopped someone would whisper 'paradise', better than the one before.

'Let the fire come,' George growled, as he swung to dismount. His left leg faltered and he fell to the ground, foot sliding out of the stirrup. Sal rushed over.

'The bed where I landed will do,' he groaned, always finding a smile. The thick green grass was like a mattress. Peter led Stallion Tom away, unsaddled him and secured the hobbles. I was quietly concerned and thought about holding up for a day. We were safe here from the fire. Depending on the availability of bush tucker, the problem of falling behind schedule could be food. At the last minute, conscious of how unsuitable Creamy and Johnny were as packhorses, I had unloaded some of the food from Blackjack's packs to make the other packs a shade lighter. I had been influenced by the number of fish caught the evening before, and almost every day Frank Hann had recorded big catches of fish: 'Boys and gins caught more fish than I ever saw caught before. Will salt a lot of them.' They had also feasted on possums, but normally vocal at night, we never once heard them.

It was surprisingly hot. The Precipice Range rose vertically a stone's throw from our camp and behind us the high ramparts of the Lady Forrest Range pressed in, trapping the air. Evaporation from a magnificent jungle-clad waterhole into the heavy overhead green foliage created a greenhouse. Heather hopped on Dusty bareback and rode him into the waterhole, followed by Trigger. Dusty drank, pawed and finally dropped onto his knees and rolled, giving Heather a swim as well.

Peter was first up over the rock fall and into the gorge. He announced it had been a lifetime ambition to swim in this gorge. Elders now dead had mesmerised him as a boy with stories about a lost gorge that cut through a range as sharp as a knife could split a lump of butter, where a strong swimmer could swim from the southern entrance to the north in a corridor of cliff so deep the sun entered for no more than minutes each day.

Sal was close behind him and from the rock fall she called me. 'Bring one of the rafts, darling. It's unbelievable.' The water flowing out of the gorge tumbled over much of the rock fall, like a mini cascade. Beyond the rock fall the cliffs closed in like great walls. Excited, we took it in turns to pump up the raft I'd carried in. It was the first raft ever into the gorge. Of course, Aborigines had been coming here for thousands of years, and it was probably sacred to them.

Sal and I paddled through to an amphitheatre, deep in the roots of the range. Here the sun's rays penetrated long enough to create a tropical garden. Fan palms with long slender trunks lifted the fans high in search of extra minutes of sunlight. Beyond the amphitheatre the corridor of water stretched to a flare of sunlight at the northern edge of the range, but we didn't venture there. Peter and Heather did, though, going all the way through after we returned from our paddle to the hidden garden. As we got out of the little raft I could see something was amusing them.

'A croc followed you all the way down and back,' Peter laughed. 'Imagine the shock he's had.'

'Oh God!' Sal exclaimed. 'I am so pleased you didn't say anything. I know they only eat fish, but . . .'

When we returned to the camp the horses with full tummies were asleep in a copse of Leichhardt pines. George was snoring. Anywhere else we may have all fallen asleep in the noon heat, but time seemed somehow precious. When Peter and I began to collect firewood we disturbed a brown tree snake. It slithered about a metre up a small jungle tree and hooked its head in the strike stance.

'Venomous,' Peter warned. 'Don't know its real name. I suppose it's a documented snake. Out here you just wouldn't know. When Sam came here nearly twenty years ago he said the place was full of death adders. He had to keep reminding the kids.'

'You think it's too late in the season?' I asked.

'No I don't,' Peter said. 'Right now it's hot. But whatever those snakes ate is no longer here. That's why they're gone. No one feels sorry for a death adder, but even he can spell big change in the country.'

Enough wood for the night, I drank as much water as I could force down and shouldered the rope. It was perfect rock for climbing. The extremes of temperature, causing any weakness in the rock to crack, followed by the tropical downpours, had rid the rock face of all debris and half-fractured projections. I sailed through the movements with confidence, careful to avoid taking centre weight on my weak knee. On the old scale I estimated the climb at three hundred feet and did it in under thirty minutes. A series of walking ledges speeded up the climb.

From the top of the cliff the enjoyment of free movement ceased. The broken rock was covered in limestone spinifex. The spiky perennial tussock half smothered the boulder-strewn surface and the tiny spikelets tore into my trousers at every stride. Forty minutes later I reached the summit of a range formed by shattered and eroded boulders. I was soaked in sweat and wondered vaguely whether it had been worth the effort. The Precipice and Lady Forrest ranges seemed to almost merge some thirty kilometres east of where I stood. The fire appeared to be on top of a range. The flames were obscured from view and the smoke pall filled the sky to the south. I felt confident the fire was beyond Jacob's Ladder. To the west of where I stood, only metres away, the gorge dropped away in a vertical plunge to the dark ribbon of water. I could hear the water flowing over the rock fall. Looking north, I was confronted with another range. There was no sign of the Adcock River country, or the safe haven of Mornington Station.

CHAPTER 8

Wild Horses Don't Swim

We went to sleep that night listening to the water on the rocks above. For the first time in the Kimberley Ranges I heard the hooting of an owl. At last everything was peaceful and normal. For some reason the cattle hadn't been in here. There were no droppings. Maybe something spooked them, but I couldn't think what. I'd forgotten about the dead donkeys and if there was any movement of the air it was from the north, carrying the stench away.

About midnight Sal and I woke to an ancient chorus – a pack of dingos were wailing together, somewhere near the rock fall. One would start, then several let forth, creating a noise as arresting as a car horn. In between the long wailing bursts there were silences. When they howled again they were closer and we could hear the snappy snarls.

Sal pressed hard against me. 'I don't like them,' she whispered nervously.

'It's not a peaceful orchestra for me either,' I whispered back, thinking about something Robert had said. With the smell of cooking in the air and no reason to fear man, they will come into a camp and scavenge like African hyenas.

'They wouldn't attack us would they?' Sal gripped my arm.

'Oh no,' I said firmly, but I was dreading the thought that the big yellow dogs might come into the camp.

They delivered a couple more encores and we heard no more.

Next morning Sal and I slept in. When we woke Peter had brought the horses in and George was saddling up. It was cold. A combination of the cool water along the creek and the heavy cold air from the mountains had created a transparent mist above the jungle waterhole. I breathed in deeply to test for smoke odour but smelt nothing but the fragrance from the trees. I would have gladly gone back to sleep, but there was no chance of that. The billies had boiled and Peter had made a damper. There was an urgency to leave. I didn't feel the fire threatened us at this stage. Maybe they both simply wanted to get on with it and complete the task.

We got away about normal time. It appeared George had broken through all the pain barriers. He looked a different man and when Blackjack turned in one of his usual antics he was after him on Stallion Tom like a keen jackeroo.

We rode south-east along the foot of the range, which loomed higher and higher as we gradually lost altitude. The softness of the upland valley dissipated with every kilometre. By mid-morning the heat was rising noticeably and I began to think more about the fire. Yesterday the smoke pall was dead ahead. Today we couldn't see more than a paleness in the sky. It indicated a strong wind shift – a north-westerly. Maybe it would be the break we needed, but that was tomorrow or the day after. Today we had to steel ourselves for a possible impasse. Sam hadn't said much about the descent at all. With its tightly graded height indicators the map said much more. But before we faced the test of the ladder we had thirty kilometres to ride. Sam had spoken of the washouts and afterwards stone, endless stone and desert heat. We had entered the first stage.

Blackjack behaved badly at the deep washouts. Refusing point blank to go down the steep banks and cross, he forced us to cross and recross the east-flowing creek. It became increasingly obvious the creek would twist its way into some very rough country. Not even the footsure cattle wanted to run ahead of us any more. Wild-eyed, they broke away from the narrow creek flats. Some blundered into gully deadends at the foot of the 300-metre wall of the Precipice Range, bolted back and exploded across our path, the cows mock-charging with a low swipe of their horns and throwing cheeky half-bucks, with tails cocked vertical with a little curl at the end.

Past noon there was no end in sight and we were all sagging into our saddles. The summit skyline of the Lady Forrest had disappeared. A new, ugly, broken series of ridges pushed us almost into the creek and we rode into a harsh land where the heat rose. Long past lunchtime the creek meandered sharply, south, east and north, and at every bend George and I urged the horses into another jagged crossing. Star and Trigger were noticeably weary. Peter also looked exhausted when he turned and asked us to hold up.

'I hope my ears are playin tricks,' he said gloomily. 'But I think I can hear a waterfall.'

He was only gone about ten minutes. The creek dropped over a waterfall and flowed on through a gorge. 'Short of wings our horses won't get down there,' Peter confirmed.

Sam hadn't said anything about a waterfall. Somewhere we had missed a valley.

Heather jumped off Dusty and encouraged Sal to go with her. She was always enthusiastic. It was her strong point and under expedition conditions such spirited people were invaluable. Without her optimism at that moment we may not have photographed the waterfall and the breathtaking gorge below, which I later discovered had never been documented or named. I never saw it. I only knew it was breathtaking later, from Sal's photographs. I regretted forever not hobbling out the horses and joining the women.

The problem was my deeply troubled frame of mind. The fire was close now. No longer did we scan the horizon. The smoke was overhead. We couldn't camp here. The passage through to the low country had to be found quickly, or else we'd have to retreat back to Nugget Gorge, riding well into the night. Peter and George rode off to search for the ladder and I waited with the horses.

Time seemed to drag. Sal and Heather had obviously climbed down into the gorge. The men not back was a bad sign. A retreat spelt failure. I was just about to hobble the horses and check the women out when I saw the white form of Stallion Tom threading through the woodland of grey box. A little behind a tired Star followed.

George's smile was enough. When Peter reigned in he focused my attention on the northern skyline.

'If you look carefully,' he said, 'there's two ranges. Take note of the size of the trees.'

At a glance the skyline looked unbroken. The spur beginning on the other side of the creek rose steeply for four hundred metres. Then I saw the difference in the Mount House box trees. From one point upwards they were like matchsticks. From the same point down their branches were distinguishable. There was a rift valley in between. It wasn't the first time I'd seen such an illusion. I thought of it as a characteristic of the Kimberley Ranges.

We waited another ten minutes until Sal and Heather returned. The men were happy to have a drink of water and rest for a few minutes.

'You've got to go and see it, Mike,' Sal called excitedly as she approached. Sal was very persuasive and usually I responded.

'They've found the ladder and it's late.'

'It won't take long.'

But I didn't go and I regretted it ever after.

We mounted up. Peter led the way across the junction, where the creek we had been following and another from the north merged. To the east a steep slope ran to the summit of a minor peak and beyond was the rift valley. To enter the little rift valley we had to track away from the southerly flowing creek. The entire geological formation was the result of massive conglomeration millions of years ago during the process of erosion in a mountain range that may at one time have been as high as the Himalayas. The start of Jacob's Ladder was a saddle between the Precipice Range and an unnamed, unimpressive bluff rising steeply from the waterfall.

My old packhorse trail up Mount Blackheath in the Warrumbungles was steeper and far more memorable. The Jacob's Ladder was loose and huge boulders dogged the horses at every turn, forcing Peter to zigzag all over the place, which I presumed gave rise to the name. Looking eastwards the Lady Forrest Range still foiled our attempts to pinpoint the fire. To our relief the fire didn't appear to be in the low country: my observation from the summit of the Precipice Range was more or less confirmed – the fire was in the mountains and driven by a gentle northerly it was moving south. The smoke had made it all seem worse than it was.

The descent was slow. The horses stumbled occasionally and sometimes groaned, their legs feeling the pinch when awkward steps had to be made around boulders and, worse still, stepping down from a rocky ledge onto loose gravel.

At the bottom we crossed a gully and rode out onto an open plain, overgrazed and burnt dry from the sun. The horses' shoes left imprints on the grey, sallow soil and in patches here and there coarse grasses were gradually claiming the plain. We rode into shadow. The Precipice Range now rose nearly six hundred metres above us. Peter switched course, directly towards the daunting cliffs. There was a line of box trees below the darkening rock. It had to be a creek. We didn't know where it came from and we didn't care, as long as it had water. Fish would be a bonus.

Close to the tree line a lone donkey-jack trotted out from the trees. When Peter got near he swung away, trotted another twenty metres and faced us again. He did it again and again. He just couldn't believe his eyes. Presently Johnny broke away and trotted after him. George kicked forward and cracked the whip. The charade continued for the length of a street, until finally the donkey ran to the side and watched us pass. Soon after we rode onto water, an excellent waterhole with pure sand along the banks.

'When I saw the jack I knew we were close,' grinned Peter.

We hobbled out and Peter took both fishing lines from the saddlebag and went looking for a hole. George selected the fire site – I simply watched to see where he dropped his swag and that was the place.

Peter soon strolled back with six bream, two weighing more than a kilogram.

'Fish out of the creeks baked in the coals, strong mountain ponies and scenery second to none in the world,' Sal stated brightly. 'Tourists will go on waiting lists for this.'

'I know,' Peter said, his eyes catching the flame as he squatted by the fire. 'We gotta get up and running. I want to get those boys fired up. Get em out of the town and into something they love doing.'

'Mike's comin back,' George said from his swag.

'What do yer reckon, Mike?' Peter asked. 'Get the vehicles into a central place and take em out from there. Have a big camp like Mornington.'

Over the days I'd been thinking about it. Mornington was a rare concept, made possible by two huge water-filled canyons. It took strong leadership and will to run it, or tourists would get lost by the day, start fires, shoot and overfish.

'I don't believe Mornington's for you people,' I began. 'You have the opportunity to do something unique. To be the first Aboriginal community in the Kimberley to undertake genuine packhorse tourism. You can provide something no white can, which is an insight into your culture. Without them even aware of it, you'll be educating people to the earth and those people will go away and talk about it.'

'You mean run the operation ex-Derby?' Peter queried.

'If you want to keep the country wild and clean you keep the vehicles out, I reckon. Let the vehicles in and you lose control. There aren't many Michael Curs in this world. He's straight, definite, fearless and has a plane for surveillance. When he goes Mornington may not be the same.'

'If we start the horse treks from the Gibb River road we could take the first group early in April,' Peter said. 'Some reckon the best time to be out here is when all the creeks are flowin and the grass is still a bit green.'

'You could make somewhere near the Rocks your base camp,' I suggested. 'You need a better grazing flat for the horses. I used to have a base camp in the Warrumbungles and from there I did various trails.'

'Sounded a good set-up,' George commented, flat on his back. 'Why'd you stop, Mike?'

'I didn't own the land. One day a property changed hands, the bulldozers arrived and the land was civilised. It's been happening for two hundred years now.'

A wild bull broke our thoughts and conversation. Grumbling beyond the firelight he patrolled up and down. There were so many of them, every section of a creek was territory to a bull. When we later lay down to sleep the deep-chested rumbles were still coming out of the dark. I didn't pitch the tent. We all slept around the fire.

Today we would cross the desert. I didn't know whether it was a freak rain shadow or a deposit of unproductive soil cover. In my country we called them sandhills, blown up in severe climatic periods never seen by Europeans. There was one near Gilgandra, in the midst of some of Australia's prime farming land, a sandhill bearing countless species of hardy wattles. Lock a herbivore on it and the animal would perish within a month, water provided.

Sam's instructions had been clear. We were not to try and run the Adcock down from the south side, or the washouts would block us. Cross the river somewhere upstream from a high mesa, continue north to the west of the mesa and look for an arid plain between two ranges. Ride east for about thirty kilometres until we struck the Adcock again.

I expected the first confrontation for the day to be Blackjack at a washout, but it was a bull. This one was lean and mean, and although I had never been to Spain this bloke faced us, moved, turned and refaced us as though the gates of an arena had sprung open. Peter and George were riding together at the lead. They reined in when the bull shot out from a copse of box trees to eye us over. Remaining calm, George turned his mount and rode back to Sal and Heather, ten or so metres behind. I was behind them.

'We swing away,' he said. No smile this time. 'We move all at once. This one bad. He make no sound – no bluff about him. See way he hold his head, Mike? High up and stretched. It's the sign before the charge.'

'What about the whip?' I suggested.

'That bloke's a loaded gun,' George mumbled grimly. 'He's just waitin for one of us to do somethin wrong.'

We urged our mounts simultaneously back out onto the open plain. The bull followed, not behind, but out on the flank, as though he was selecting a target. Not Trigger, please – that aged gelding had no chance. Shorny would escape. Dusty and Stallion Tom would be too sluggish off the mark. Star had the pace, but he was tired. The seconds ran into a minute. The bull was clearly undecided and the gap between him and the nearest horse widened – twenty metres, thirty – at forty the danger had passed.

Peter switched course back towards the Adcock. The bull followed for five minutes, then gradually drifted away and finally he stopped. We began to laugh with relief.

The Adcock still had a big flow. From the south bank we looked across forty metres of deep water.

'We better head downstream and look for some sandbars,' Peter mused, then chuckled to me. 'Wild horses don't swim.'

We rode on downstream for about half a kilometre. Peter reined in where the river split into three shallow channels. It was an ideal crossing. Peter was just about to urge Star into the first channel when another bull strode out of a thick patch of cane grass on the other side and faced up. George kicked forward on Stallion Tom and cracked the whip. The standoff lasted about five minutes. The wild cattle had taken the country over. Now they thought *they* owned it!

Safely across the river we dismounted for a long drink and topped up the water bottles. Sam had told us to do that. He had said the next water may not be until we reached the Adcock again, thirty or forty kilometres downstream. Leading away from the river on the north side a cattle pad took us through a thick belt of timber, which was home to the first significant number of birds since the Lennard. The galahs made me think of home. Corellas squawked from the river gums and dense flocks of budgerigars darted across the water. The forest was riverine and narrow but when we burst out into the savanna the grass cover was instantly sparse. The mesa towering above us instantly caught our breath. Back in the trees it was merely a shadow through the foliage. Now we looked at a daunting tower of rock. It was the only time in Australia I had ever seen anything remotely reminiscent of the stark mesa formations of Arizona's Monument Valley.

Peter thought the mesa may have been known as Minnah Point, after one of Hann's Aboriginal assistants. If he was correct it was a misleading name, as a 'point' in geographic reference is the termination of a range. I dismounted and spread the Mount House map on the ground. The feature bore no name.

I believed geographic names should have a spark of imagination and I was always disappointed that so many dull Anglo names had been plastered across the Kimberleys, as they had in the Blue Mountains west of Sydney. In the Warrumbungles of New South Wales we were more fortunate, with such names as the Tonduron, Barrumbuckle, Mopra, Wedding Cake, Breadknife – to mention only a few. The traditional Aboriginal place names are beautiful too.

It was a perfect spot to photograph everybody, including the packhorses. With the mesa in the background, the camera lens promised to produce some striking photographs. In good spirits we rode away from the flood plain, heading towards an unnamed range. Sam was spot on with his directions. Before us was some hard, undulating country.

The nature of the terrain altered quickly and drastically. It didn't appear to be lack of rain: the change was too quick. We rode into desert and the heat bounced back from the surface. Only hardy scrubs grew, turpentine wattle and prickly acacia. It was the unnamed range that provided the clue, guttered from its jagged skyline by fearsome erosion. We had ridden into the slate country, with flattened, sheared rock in stark contrast to the hard quartz-sandstone. Dolomite country. It bothered me that a range of such distinctive geological formations might enter the twenty-first century without a name. In honour of the mules who served the Kimberley so well in the pioneering days, I named it the Mule Range for the moment, but I felt sure the traditional people would volunteer a name from the Dreamtime.

The horses walked as though on stilts and Creamy threw a shoe. On our left the Mule Range on our right the scaleless cliffs of Mt Hamilton, a narrow plateau extending as far as I could see. Yet the desert-like land between the two great escarpments was beautiful and alive. Bare grey land, covered in the slatish gravel, the stark aridness broken only by the prickly acacia, would be dissected by a watercourse meandering down from the Mule Range. Sweet short grasses grew from the silt and wild cattle bolted away in little mobs, lifting dust whispers like the devil-devil whirlies in the hot spring. Against the backdrop of the red cliffs of Mount Hamilton they conjured up images of old American westerns. I had a sudden urge to take off and go hell for leather for the lead, although that lead was far away and only an old stockman in his dreams would wheel them. Some of my best days of living had been in the Warrumbungles when cattle strayed into the foothills and defied my efforts to send them home. A man had never lived until he had galloped a horse where some struggled to walk. Load of rubbish, of course, but the thought reflected my mood.

We rode under the high point of the sun and the sight of the Estaugh spires gave us no joy, for they were not even the halfway mark. A cool morning and some water left in my Arizona skin bag, I might have studied the most easterly spire for climbing routes. Instead I gazed across the horses in front, to Sal, hoping she wouldn't start holding her side and to George, who rode in the lead, the pathfinder. Star was footsore and was struggling on behind.

Nothing changed for twenty kilometres. Hann had called it fair cattle country. Returning to Derby he had taken up 793,000 acres on 25 June and paid the under secretary for lands one hundred and ninety pounds and ten shillings for it. It was doomed from the start, as he was never able to acquire sufficient capital to stock the station. It appeared he intended to disperse the traditional owners with the gun.

16 July 1898
At the end of Mount Clifton [the bluff at the most westerly point of the Mule Range] we saw a lot of blacks. They all went up the mountain but after a time a lot of them came down to us. We went down the creek to a very strange mountain which I have named Mount Hamilton. We then came back. Blacks still on the mountain. Country all good but only about four miles wide. Blacks had not been at at the camp . . .

17th July 1898
Blacks were still on Mount Clifton. We got one black-fellow. Came onto Mount Hamilton, had dinner. I went to go through the ranges to the Fitzroy. We came on, leaving Mt Hamilton on our right. Country rather stony but fair cattle country.'

'Got one black-fellow.' It appeared to indicate he shot one man dead. There was no record of the tribes ever actually attacking him or looting his camp. Right across Australia, whites had shot Aborigines more or less on sight until the law arrived, sometimes decades later.

I believe we should not judge Hann by these extracts. We should judge that time in history, for the same thing happened in the Americas and in Africa. Men of the old imperialistic days were taught that it was right to take land that belonged to no other white man. Today there remains a hard-core that still think it's right to confiscate land from Aboriginal people.

Frank Hann was an explorer who mapped the last of the blank spaces in Western Australia. He was one of the greatest survivors in Australian history. Thrown from a horse, he died from the injuries in 1921.

About 2.30 p.m. a wide belt of trees marked a watercourse. The situation would be very uncomfortable if it turned out to be dry. We knew the distance to water from the map, but the heat was getting to us. We hadn't anticipated temperatures in the high thirties. Sal was sagging forward again. For four days now she had carried the Telstra telephone kit, which would become heavy after the first hour. We had swapped haversacks briefly, but mine had equal weight and didn't sit well. Sal never once complained – without the telephone every member of the group was exposed to the dire consequences of a bad horse accident, attack from a wild animal or snake bite.

The watercourse was marked on the map as the Thossell River. It was drying up fast. Had we ridden onto it a month later we may have been disappointed. There was nothing appealing about this miserable stream or the surrounding country. We only stopped because we were hungry and exhausted from the heat. I found a little rice left in one packet and boiled it up with a soup packet to flavour it.

The same monotony plagued us again after the lunch break. Trigger had a swelling on his back so Sal rode Shorny, Peter saddled up One Sock and I went onto Star. Dismounting for a casual pee, I forgot about the problem of getting back on. The last horse had disappeared over a stony ridge when I zipped up and Star didn't like being alone. I had to suddenly tell myself I was round at the barrier, about to be mounted on a ratbag and no matter how bad it was I had to cope. With one foot in the irons I angled sharply for the rails and took up a forward position. In big bounding strides Star overtook the horses and went to the lead. He wasn't tired at all, the fox!

'Gee, Star's got a new zest for life,' Peter said, grinning. 'You better stay on him.'

'Next time I'll pee down the side of the saddle and wash my trousers,' I bawled breathlessly to an audience nearly doubled up.

With an hour of sunlight left we struck a channel of the Adcock. It appeared the gravel from the upstream washouts had forced the river to spread wide in a series of channels. We crossed, back tracked and recrossed. Not anywhere could we find a suitable campsite. With daylight fading we unsaddled by a waterhole beginning to turn. Traces of algae marked half-submerged logs and a large freshie sank below the surface as we watched. It was our first bad camp. We spread our beds out onto the coarse river gravel. The horses were given a drink and led away to a rough flat of reasonable grass.

The only food left was a packet of rice, which Sal flavoured once again with a couple of soup packets. In my Colorado bag I found a big packet of nuts. Oh for a drink – George and I were gasping. I took a compass fix on Michael Cur's bar. 'Bar course 95 degrees,' I said, hoping it might cheer him up.

I contacted Michael on the satellite. Not to ask if his fridge was stocked up – Peter wanted to know how to get through. The horses were footsore and the shale in the channels could break them down. Away from the river the undulating ridges had become mini escarpments of rock. The place was a hell-hole. He told us to back off the river and ride directly towards Mount Brennan. Every time I looked at the mountain I thought of my cousin Mary Brennan standing on the summit with a schooner in each hand, waving us on. She liked a drop and was still dropping them in her late seventies.

Heather ate very little for dinner and next morning the horses too were showing signs of stress. There was one meal of rice left.

The heat rose rapidly and the footsore horses picked their way over the stone at a tired-man's pace. Creamy favoured his shoeless foot and with a little bit of fractious behaviour One Sock had sent himself lame. Only Dusty, Shorny and Stallion Tom seemed unscathed.

Fanned by a persistent northerly the fire front had crossed the range and it appeared Millie Windie would be burnt out. There was no threat to the mountain horses. In the cool of night they knew to cross back into the burnt country and there was enough feed left along the creeks. Within a fortnight the new shoots from the burnt pasture would sprout. But it was not the Bunuba's wish to have the fire in the first place.

Somewhere ahead was the burnt country. Sometimes we could smell it; a wind shift, a gully with a draft slipping west, and to the south we could see tiny smouldering patches on the range. The only welcome distraction was the black cockatoos. The red plumage under the wings signalled a male and yellow a female.

One of the boab trees we rode under was loaded with fruit. Peter cut one open and passed Sal and me half each. It had a nutty taste and the closest comparison I could make was a bland passionfruit taste. It was filling and I am sure very nutritious. I read later the seeds are not normally eaten. They gave a rich nutty taste, so I am glad we didn't know. At the time the fruit had more appeal than boiled rice.

Two hours out from the camp we rode into burnt country. Grass scorched to black butts did nothing for our spirits. It had been a 'cool' fire. The trees were charred around the base, but the high foliage had escaped destruction. On some of the trees the leaves had curled up from the heat and already showed signs of recovery. It reinforced my view that early corridor burning was a possible solution. The concept gave wildlife an escape, edible grass species would survive, newly shot trees and scrubs had a better chance and the possibility of an explosive spring bushfire was minimal.

An hour past noon the horses at last splashed their way across the Adcock River crossing near old Mornington Camp. The supply truck was there and shouts of welcome floated across the water. The first expedition in fifty-one years, we had crossed the range.

'Got a damper in the coals?' Peter asked, before One Sock had struggled out of the river. They were all standing at the water's edge, waiting for us to cross. There was a fire on the rocks and the smoke drifted through the river bank trees. I couldn't see Peter's face, but I knew he was teasing. Their faces looked guilty. There was another young man with them. The one missing was Robert.

'There's plenty of tucker in the supply dump,' I said, looking at those hangdog expressions as Star stepped out of the water.

'Got some bread and onions,' Buddha said.

The girls laughed as though sensing the implications.

'I told you, Mike,' Peter laughed. 'They'd hit the grog and forget about the food.'

'We catch them fish,' Harold said quietly. He always spoke quietly. 'Don't need Derby tucker. All here.'

'Where's Robert?' Peter asked.

'Robert, he go after horses at Millie Windie,' Harold replied, and added soberly, 'He don't like the country on this side.'

Robert had told me several times it was the dry side. Bush tucker was harder to find and the Adcock River was far inferior to the Lennard. I knew he was right in a pragmatic sense, but gazing across that sheet of water and listening to it murmur across the submerged boulders and stones and seeing patches of white dance in the sun, at that moment the Adcock was home.

CHAPTER 9

The Tenacity of a Woman

'My shout,' Michael Cur announced, after Peter, Heather and I drained a couple of stubbies. 'Not a bad effort on green horses.'

We were seated at the bar of old Mornington Camp, about four o'clock. Sal had stayed behind to wash some clothes. George lay on his swag. I had promised him a couple of stubbies on our return with the supplies from the old engine room. A late lunch had been the bread and onions. In good-humoured disgust Peter confided they had all got so drunk over the weekend the only tucker anybody could remember was bread and onions. We'd all hopped into it. I had tears streaming out of my eyes. We were so hungry and no one gave any thought to the embarrassing consequences.

'If it's okay with you, Michael, we'll camp a couple of nights on the Fitzroy and then head back,' I said, savouring every mouthful of the Emu Bitter. 'I've got inflatable rafts. I want to paddle up the canyon and look for art.'

'That's okay, but I don't think you'll be going back that way. CALM rang me soon after your call to see if I knew where you were. They want to light up. It's late enough as it is. If you don't burn in this country the fuel's life threatening by late October. We had a bad fire last spring. I would have lost the whole camp if I hadn't mown the grass a few days before.'

'Might have to return up through Mount House,' Peter said, taking the news well. It was nearly two hundred kilometres back to Inglis Gap that way.

Before we left I asked Michael if I could hire the canoes at Dimond Gorge for the following day. I wanted to be sure everyone got an opportunity to see this magnificent gorge, even though I was chafing at the bit to paddle up the canyon and look for the gallery. Michael didn't hesitate: the oars were in the pantry and we were to grab them as we walked out. He also gave us a box of meat.

'No charge for anything,' Michael added generously. 'None of them have seen the Dimond. Give them a good day.'

The next morning, leaving the horses to graze, we took the truck over the rough track. When we got to the gorge George and Buddha wouldn't be in the canoe excursion.

'Never rode a canoe,' George said flatly. 'Not learnin now.'

'What about you, Buddha?'

'No – catch him big fish here,' he replied, pointing at the river in front.

I couldn't even get George or Buddha to walk to the launch beach. We left them to it. Harold and Rachelle were willing to give canoeing a go.

Heather's enthusiasm was indomitable. She had thrown the fatigue overnight and she paddled down the gorge with our new addition to the camp, a young Bunuba man whose name was Len. Harold was more reluctant. About two hundred metres from the beach I passed him standing on a rock edge. He told me he was going to walk down. That wasn't possible so Rachelle coaxed him back in and together they paddled and splashed down to the little box canyon with the waterfall.

Peter took Priscilla with him and in big strong strokes he set off for the rapids at the southern end. He knew to be careful and paddle out of the main stream at least fifty metres from the head of the rapids. At the bar Michael had told us about a tourist, a few days before, who had been sucked into the rushing water and overturned, losing all his camera equipment. He had retrieved the canoe and arrived back at camp shaken and bruised.

We all met up for lunch at the box canyon. More than the food, which was bread and two tins of baked beans, the one thing we all wanted was a mug of billy tea and I'd left it behind. I climbed a young snappy gum, broke off a handful of leaves and dropped them into the billy. It aroused both amusement and scepticism, until they tasted it. The tea had a strong, compelling flavour and Bushells had better beware, although admittedly heaps of sugar went into the mugs.

Dimond Gorge was a barramundi hole. It had to be fished early and late – noon fishing yielded little. But the Bunuba men and women were clearly overwhelmed by this massive gorge, the spiritual home of their ancestors. Beyond argument, Dimond was the pearl of the Kimberley gorges.

Back at the launch beach we heard the usual fishing story. Poor George had hooked a barra, only to lose him at that final lift from the water. We didn't have a net, which was essential for barra fishing. Still, they didn't go hungry: Buddha caught a two-kilogram bream.

It had been an inspiring day for everyone. More than ever they realised the devastation the construction of a dam would cause and they intended to tell their extended families and network of friends in Fitzroy Crossing. While the truck lumbered up the gap between the main Leopold Range and Fitzroy Bluff, those of us in the back talked about what we had seen. I'd climbed into a cave to find a colony of rock wallabies, delightful little creatures facing extinction in the eastern states. Rachelle was relating her canoe trip with Harold when we topped a rise at the head of the gap and saw the darkness in disbelief. Away to the north Tableland Station appeared to be well alight. To the west spirals of smoke rose. It seemed all the ranges were alight.

Back at the camp Peter and I had a hasty conference. We had intended to ride east to the Fitzroy and hobble the horses out for about three days. It was an easy stage on level country. I had enough supplies for a fortnight and Michael's pantry was a back-up if necessary, although it wasn't fair to rely on his supplies. Geraldine was driving out from Derby in a hired four-wheel-drive and Heather could have returned with her to start work. Dusty and Trigger would have walked back over the range with the others to be loaded at Inglis Gap. I had been planning a ride on the big buckskin. While the horses were resting along the big river Buddha, Len, George and the girls were planning a raid on the barramundi. It had all been a tight, neat plan, now erased like the strike of a match under a handful of dead leaves.

Taking the horses on to a Fitzroy River camp was out of the question. Peter telephoned Geraldine on the satellite and asked her to try and organise a truck from Derby to meet the horses at old Glenroy Station, now a portion of the 700,000-hectare Mount House Station. Peter would take the horses there tomorrow, load them and return to collect Sal and me from the mouth of the canyon. We could have two days. It wasn't much time, but under the circumstances he urged that should be the limit.

With a forbidding day planned we left at 6.00 a.m. Peter had become increasingly concerned for out safety and had talked Harold into going with us. Sal and I were delighted. The second raft was for gear and supplies and we were going to tow it behind the more durable Sevylor raft. In a narrow canyon the current would be stronger than Dimond Gorge and I had been concerned the struggle would have exhausted us. With Harold we could share the load and paddle together.

The trip to the gorge took nearly two hours. Peter wouldn't arrive back at camp until late morning, but he had left instruc-tions for Buddha and Len to bring in the horses and pop the nosebags on. It was only a three-hour ride to old Glenroy. Just the same Sal and I were eager to launch as quickly as possible so he could head back. He was always such a gentleman. With the rafts pumped up I wanted him to go, but he waited until the first bend in the river took us from his vision. He probably thought this was a dangerous escapade of mine.

Harold struggled from the start. It was the first time he'd been in a boat on his own, and he couldn't coordinate the dual paddles. He held his head in his hands and the raft drifted downstream. I felt very mean, but I decided to let him battle for a while, hoping he might pick it up. He was much stronger than I was and once he got the hang of it he'd drive the raft through the relentless current like an expert on the sculling oars, I thought. After several circle spins he made it to the toe of the first lot of rapids, very frustrated and stressed. I put him in the big raft with Sal and gave them the packsaddle pack with all the food and cooking equipment. Sal kept the camera and the Telstra telephone in her boat. She guarded that telephone as though it were her fifth baby.

The portage around the rapids demanded two trips across the boulders. The big raft was the test. To hop from one boulder to the next Harold and I had to carry it on our heads. I got Harold to lead, because I felt if I had to follow on I'd find some reserves of strength. Harold set a fast pace and the concentration was nothing less than vicious. We danced to the song of the rapids and one week of it and I may have been ready for ballet lessons, if my ankles were not all smashed. It was a relief when we were back on the water.

A kilometre on and we faced another portage. The flow of the river swung towards a rock wall on the far side and we were able to portage across the crest of a narrow peninsula and drop back into the water.

For the next three hours we paddled ceaselessly. The river took us deeper and deeper into a canyon of vertical walls, like a suburban highway ushers in the city skyscrapers. It reminded me of Utah, a very dramatic comparison, where the Green River carves a canyon eight-hundred metres deep through the greatest sandstone block on the planet. But unlike the Green River in Utah, there was the constant sound of birds, which echoed off the cliffs, accentuating their warning calls. It was nature's own auditorium. The kingfishers and the rock-hopping spinifex pigeons I knew, but the vocal birds way up on the cliffs were new to me. I felt frustrated knowing I was so out of my depth.

Mostly the current was invisible. It wasn't hard work. The luxury of stopping for a rest, however, was denied. The rock wall would begin to slip away and where rock projections broke the surface the water gurgled quietly, reminding you never to stop paddling. With Sal, Harold developed confidence almost immediately, and Sal's trip up the river was like that of some Victorian English lady being propelled by a zealous suitor. Harold was loving it and Sal sometimes giggled at the speed and ease with which the big raft soared over the water. The water here too was pure. Like the ocean, the colour was more a capture of light. In the shade of the cliffs you stared into a cold shade of green and when the river swung to the north-west the sun lifted a light shade of blue in the distance.

We could hear the water a mile away. At the source of the sound the whole river spilled down a series of narrow cascades, hugging the western precipice in a sweeping arc. It was here the whitewater men roped their rafts and brought them down over unrideable standing waves and treacherous whirlpools. The great volume of water was now far away in King Sound and we looked upon a picturesque spectacle of swiftly flowing water, with the spray catching the light from a high sun.

By the time I paddled into a backwater, Sal and Harold had portaged their gear to the next entry point, which proved to be a magnificent river beach. The Castlereagh River – the river of sand – took some beating when it came to beaches, but here was a beach of pure sand one hundred metres wide. We gazed across a lake of water, like some freak-sized mountain tarn locked up high in the mountains by impervious red cliffs. I didn't think Harold usually had an eye for scenery, but I caught him just standing, looking, soaking up the vision. Fringed along the lake's edge and growing out of the sand, paperbarks cooled the sand with an intricate pattern of shadows. Sal selected a fire site in the shade and collected some driftwood while Harold and I collect the big raft.

Our living items were sparse for this journey. The billy Sal put on to boil was a litre size, and we had a mug each, a plate, knife and fork. Food consisted of two kilogram-packets of flour and a kilogram of rice. Jam, spices, powdered milk and sugar were the only supplements. Harold was clever with a fishing line and I had made sure a piece of old raw fish wrapped in tinfoil was packed for bait. Harold threw a baited hook out into the depths as soon as possible.

My raft had collected a gallon of water in the bottom by the time I'd beached. The dual paddle was too short for the job and with every stroke I had flicked in a dessertspoon of water. I was wet from shoulder to boots so I put my clothes out on the sand to dry, except for my underpants. I glanced over to Harold to see how he was doing. He was pulling in a fish. It was a catfish. Cooked fresh on the coals they're delicious. I pulled the skinning knife from its pouch and went over to cut it off the hook. I thought the blade would be too long for the dorsal venom gland to reach my hand, but I forgot about the lateral venom glands. The catfish jerked high and hard, driving the venom spike two centimetres into the flesh between my thumb and forefinger. The pain was swift and sharp, but awareness of the consequences exceeded the agony. A full dose of poison was potentially serious.

I ran back to the fire and got my Swiss pocket knife. I always kept the small blade razor sharp for splinters and burrs. The pain was so severe I didn't feel the incision. The blood ran and Harold trotted up with the fish. He'd smashed its head with a stick and cut the poison spikes off with the long blade knife.

'Rub along tail,' he said, in his deep, slightly sing-song tone. 'Along tail the juice stops the pain. Hand good again.'

It was a natural antidote known only, I was sure, to the Fitzroy River people. I took the fish and vigorously rubbed the excretion from the fish's slimy tail into the wound. It worked within minutes. The pain subsided and the only persistent symptoms were mild swelling and numbness. Sal gave me a couple of Panadeine and I sat down to enjoy damper and blackberry jam. We didn't cook the fish and Harold rolled up his line, knowing we were eager to get further up the canyon.

A better-known Aboriginal antidote to catfish poisoning was the chewed leaves of the freshwater mangrove, which were common along the big streams in the Kimberleys. Harold told me later there was a mangrove on the upstream end of the beach. The problem was the time gap between sting and application. Over the years I'd been bitten and stung by a number of venomous creatures and insects, and the instant pain of the catfish was more severe than the redback spider. The CALM warning booklet recorded symptoms from the catfish sting as intense pain and shock, causing death on rare occasions. I didn't think for a second that Harold saved my life, but he did save the final leg of the expedition. Being left-handed, temporary incapacity of that hand would have rendered me useless.

Beyond the broad lake-like stretch of water I expected more rapids and more portages. Harold and Sal surged one hundred metres ahead of me and when I saw them both standing on a ledge, making no attempt to carry equipment, I knew something was wrong. The rapids above were too noisy even to shout over. I unloaded my raft, hauled it out and climbed up to where they were looking up the canyon. It was a daunting scene. Rock fall after rock fall, with stretches of water in between about the size of Olympic swimming pools. Past the heap of giant boulders in front of us a flat shelf of rock encased one of the large pools. I decided at once to carry the gear and the rafts there and leave Sal and Harold to fish while I walked on and did some reconnaissance.

For ten minutes I walked along a series of smooth rock ledges. The going was as easy as a city street. But a shoulder of perpendicular rock, almost from the river bed boulders to the skyline two hundred metres above, seemed to throw up a warning of what lay ahead. It was the end of the street-like ledges. Beyond, the cliff plunged vertically to the water, offering nothing but fractures and fine ledges suitable only for birds. Below, a nightmare jumble of boulders filled the canyon to the opposite wall. I couldn't see the water, but I could hear it. It was like listening to a fleet of diesel-engine trucks waiting for the lights to change, a vibrant, sinister sound. I returned to our new base knowing it was madness to attempt the crossing of such a rock fall with only two hours of daylight remaining.

Harold didn't mind. He baited his line, threw it in and a two-kilogram bream pounced on it. I was no seaman, but I knew that when fishermen struck a school it was a matter of how quickly they could haul them in. In river fishing that didn't happen; Harold, Sal and I had never seen anything like this. Sal finally gave it away because she was sick of unhooking and throwing back. Harold loved it.

The fish went out and in like a yo-yo while Sal and I set up camp. On bare rock there was little to do. Sal rolled out the swags, I collected driftwood and then we both went for a swim. Looking down from a rock ledge the current didn't appear to be anything to worry about, but down in the water there was a tow like a savage beach rip.

The night came with the swiftness of a pulled blind on an only window. The campfire flickered eerily on the bare rock and it was dangerous to be close to it. Every now and then an explosion showered us with tiny rock fragments. It was common for old volcanic rock in the Warrumbungles to explode under a campfire, but the same mini explosions on the dolomite were unexpected. The dingos, too, added to the ghostly atmosphere, howling from the canyon rim above. Endowed with a superb sense of smell, they must have picked up the odour of fish cooking on the coals from kilometres away. It was an uneasy feeling in a world where many wild animals had had no contact with man. We were simply another animal, with strong distinct odours.

We retired early. Not since a child had I gone to sleep at seven o'clock. It was a disturbed, long night and I was relieved to see a horizontal flame on the canyon rim, like the tail of a shooting star frozen on a postcard. I got up off the little rubber mattress. There was no dew, and brittle dry, the wood for the fire caught with the lighting of a single piece of paper. Naked on the warm rock, the fire in the dark, the rapids murmuring and bubbling and the red brilliance of the canyon rim, I felt as if I had taken a forty-thousand-year journey back in time. It was a religious experience lasting but a moment, for the light filled the canyon again, as though the window blind had shot upwards, right to the reel.

At 6.30 a.m. we were packed and ready. Sal shouldered the Telstra telephone in her haversack. Harold slung the rope across his shoulders and I took the big haversack with the food and camera bag. The temperature was perfect, probably about twenty-five degrees Celsius, and during our walk along the wide ledges Sal stopped a couple of times, took the camera from my haversack and recorded on film the diffusion of light on the red canyon walls as the sun rose. At the edge of the rock fall the little picnic was over. We were forced to climb as though on the side of a mountain, without the requirement of a rope. It was tedious and, with the weight of the gear on our shoulders, tiring. The flow of the river rumbled, gurgled and growled from hidden cavities, as though we were traversing the back of a living, resentful animal. The only respite was the likelihood that the river flow under the rock fall would reach the western side of the canyon without a difficult rapid traverse. But after twenty minutes of heavy work I saw miniature rock atolls breaking the surface of the water. In the final stage there was more water than rock. The water ran quietly – suspiciously quietly – and from a raised boulder I looked into deep water moving with sinister strength. Downstream, maybe fifty metres, the sun sparkled off white water and the longer I stood there the louder grew the sound.

I got the rope from Harold, tied Sal on as number two and then Harold at the end as number three. Harold didn't look very happy about it. I tried to explain the channels between the boulder outcrops were deep and if one of us were to slip we'd be swept into the white water, but he remained very apprehensive.

I positioned Sal at the lee side of the boulder at the edge of the first channel and showed her how to feed the rope out across her shoulders. From the moment I waded into the water, waist deep, I felt the tug of water like someone pulling on a rope from below. For the first three or four metres I had a rock shelf to stand on. The anxious bit was whether I put my boot on a slippery patch. Near the boulder outcrop the shelf ran out and the water was deep and green. I had to allow myself to topple forward and seize a handhold on the boulder. Once committed a move backwards was impossible. Safely over I took up the rope slack and Sal crossed without mishap. Harold made it look so easy he glanced at me with a look that said, 'What the hell did you put the rope around me for?'

If a strong individual slipped they would have scrambled out, I now felt sure. But, apart from injury, Sal and I had the responsibility of the telephone and the camera. In the camera bag was every photograph from day one. Sal guarded them like the phone. We had the valuable equipment wrapped and tightly sealed in four heavy-duty plastic bags. One of us had to be drowned before anything could be lost.

The next stage looked easy until I moved into the water. It was the central channel and had double the velocity of water. I got over without incident, but I knew Sal would struggle. There was no rock projection from which I could belay a rope. I stood as square as I could, taking in the rope across my shoulders.

'The water's taking me,' Sal called, nervous.

I snapped up a full metre, the rope stretched and her hand reached the safety of the dry boulder. She was over, still dry from the waist up. Harold had untied himself and he followed quickly. I coiled the rope up out of the water and gave it back to Harold. The next two channels we waded across without the rope.

The river altered coarse sharply to the north after we left the rock fall. Walking in wet trousers and boots we were forced to climb a rock-shattered slope covered in rocky spinifex. The slope became a series of ledges, but they were not easy walking like before. If we followed a broken ledge angling upwards across the slope it terminated at the base of the canyon wall, making us climb down again to another ledge. If the ledges angled down we arrived at a vertical drop into the water. We began to tire quickly and I was staggered at the build-up of heat so soon after sunrise. The sting was the river itself, for below a lovely wide ribbon of water stretched to the next bend, at least a kilometre upstream.

An hour went by slowly, as we slogged through the spinifex and constantly searched for ledges. Harold seemed to be having second thoughts. On one occasion Sal and I waited for several minutes for him to catch up. I went back and tried to explain we had little time. He was barefoot and I wondered whether the spinifex spikes were getting into his feet. The vicious plant clawed at our trousers and to touch it was like bumping a barbwire fence.

Aboriginal people were often so shy communication was as much eyes and body language as it was language. I realised it was the rope. Fifty metres long and bulky, it would be very uncomfortable to the uninitiated. Like an old harness horse, I usually carried it almost oblivious to the impediment.

The higher ledges had a bit more soil on them and provided a better habitat for the rocky spinifex. Climbing around big clumps of the tussock and sometimes jumping from one boulder to another was taking its toll. I knew Sal was stressed, but she wouldn't admit it. My knee ached from the jarring and the weight and I began to follow the lower ledges. They were better defined and reasonably free of spinifex. The trap was the long bands of cliff which formed overhead as you walked lower down near the water. They were, in fact, a gamble for time and at about 10.30 a.m. my luck run out. The ledge I had been following petered out into a cliff face. To retreat and work through the broken rock and spinifex high up meant the loss of an hour and would nearly exhaust us. There was no other option but the one confronting us – the cliff. I felt so uncomfortable about the decision I could barely look at Sal.

'I'll pull you up if necessary,' I said to her quickly, undoing the rope. Then I glanced at Harold and told him a big fib. 'Big fishing hole the other side. We'll boil the billy and fish.'

Harold smiled. He was awake to it, of course, but he'd climb to hell and back to toss in a line all the same.

The first pitch was easy enough with ample holds. It led onto a ledge with an overhang half a metre above. It reminded me of a horizontal chimney. Very tight, it demanded a full-length body wriggle to get through to a comfortable pocket in the rock face. From here it was only eight metres to the top. Eight metres of smooth, holdless rock. The only chink in the canyon's armour was a perpendicular crack from top to bottom. In rock climbing language it was a 'layback' possibility. You jammed your hand into the crack, planted one boot hard and flat against the surface and by alternate hand jamming worked your way up. At my age and fitness eight metres was too far. In the Warrumbungles, scrambling around the crags on a day off from the farm, I wouldn't have done it in a fit.

In the heat of the moment I was one for working fast, while the body was hot and your mind was riveted to the job. As soon as I reached the top I took in the slack and Sal started up to the ledge. She moved quickly and in no time she was in the cleft. To secure her safely I dropped onto my backside, planted my feet hard against a projection of rock and took the tension on the rope.

'Just grab what you can in the crack,' I yelled. 'Just a little help and I can pull you.' I am quite small for a man, but years of holding racehorses on the training track had put a bit of size into the biceps.

Sal was courageous, as the pitch was an intermediate grade. When I pulled her over the rim I thought she might berate me for exposing her to such an ordeal. Instead, she was elated and so flushed were her cheeks I was tempted to look for another pitch. We stood on a wide terrace that sloped gradually down again for about three hundred metres to the next lot of rapids.

Getting Harold up was a bit more difficult. He weighed about seventy-five kilograms. He seemed to almost leap to the ledge, he came so fast. In preparation for the second pitch I applied every trick I knew for dispersing the weight across my body. Sal held my shoulders from behind. She wanted to pull up front with me, but that was too dangerous. When Harold went for the crack there was a lot of vibration on the rope. My climbing rope was made of the same material as bungee-jump ropes. It stretched and absorbed like a shock absorber in a vehicle. Harold came up rapidly and the weight wasn't as bad as I'd expected. At the top the whites of his eyes had Sal and I laughing, and when Harold smiled the immediate problems dissolved, even if only for a few minutes.

'Big fish along there,' he said in his deep husky voice. He had me backed up to the wall on my promise.

'I think we've earned a billy boil, anyway,' Sal said with a smile. Let's head for the spot.'

The cliff top we left was less than one-third of the way to the canyon rim, but it was high enough for a good view of the river. Ahead was the horseshoe bend where I hoped to find the gallery. The cliffs rose vertically out of the water on the western side of the bend, which meant we had to cross somewhere in the next four hundred metres. From a middle distance perspective it was impossible to gauge the rapids and we trekked on.

Halfway along the terrace I didn't like the sound. The low-pitched rumble consumed the canyon, and indicated deep water flowing down through corridors of rock. The canyon had narrowed slightly, creating a bottleneck effect.

The terrace terminated at a wide shelf on the edge of the water. I gave Harold the fishing line and the bait he had saved. Sal and I picked up a few sticks and lit a fire.

'I'll make the tea and mix a damper,' Sal said calmly. 'You better go and take a close look at the rapids.'

The rock shelf overlooked a backwater. There was no movement in the water. I had to climb over boulders as high as a house to reach the channels. For twenty metres I waded into water with no pull, which I knew was a bad sign. I reached a big boulder island and climbed over it to the other side. The first channel was ten metres wide and deep. The next channel was wider still. I stared down the river, beyond the last boulders jutting from the water to the unbroken, tranquil expanse of water. With a haversack and rope on my back I'd get twenty-five metres in a straight swim, maybe – seventy-five metres I had no chance. I couldn't go without the rope. If I blundered onto a vertical drop I could abseil down Swiss style. If I had to drop into the river for a short stage to get back I could double the rope and belay myself in the gravity-driven current. The rope was my security against perilous situations. I went back to the lunch camp to tell Sal I'd go alone.

'I know I can't do it,' she said quietly, looking very disappointed. 'The rope in deep water worries me too. What if you couldn't pull me in against the current and I couldn't release myself from the rope?'

I had to agree there was potential for great danger. In white water only a metre deep the rope was a safety aid. In deep water there was an element of risk if things went wrong.

'What about Harold?' she asked. He was fishing and didn't appear to have any interest in our conversation.

'He'll stay here with you.'

'You mean he'll stay in case you don't come back.'

'It's not dangerous,' I countered, but she knew me too well. 'If anything goes wrong in the water I'll discard the lot.'

'What about cliffs?'

'It's good clean rock. The only fall I've ever had was on bad rock.'

'I'll give you three hours,' Sal said finally. 'I hate it. God, I hate this sort of situation.' She paused, gazing past me to the bend in the river three hundred metres upstream. 'But you've got to go. We've come too far to turn back now.'

I didn't wait for my mug of tea and damper. I had a dread that the final obstacle could cause the whole expedition to fail. Time, too, had slipped away. At 2.30 p.m. Sal would use the satellite phone to report me missing. It wasn't much time. It was a reminder I had a responsibility not only to Sal and Harold, but also to the others waiting for us at the mouth of the canyon. I thought I could do it in two hours.

Fear of turbulent water has a sharp edge when the water's cold. The Fitzroy water in autumn bordered on tepid. It was a relief not to have that breathless, tortuous sensation as cold water spread through your wetsuit. Most of Australia's river-rapid locations are high in the continent's south-east ranges where the water is numbingly cold for most of the year. Sometimes my spear fishing excursions on the New South Wales south coast were spoiled by cold water. If fish didn't appear soon after entry, focusing me on the hunt, I began to look behind for sharks. It could get so bad I would visualise a white pointer beyond the entrance of every deep channel. Cold water and negative thinking are close allies.

I was sorry I didn't bring my wetsuit. The rubber gave extra buoyancy and protected the body when thrown against rock. Knowing the coast off Broome was shark infested, I had left all my gear at home to avoid the temptation of a quick dive to get a fish for the barbecue.

Moving out from the boulder outcrop I had my boots on the bottom. I was in water waist deep and could stand against the current. When I took a tentative step to go another metre there was no more rock, and I had to swim for it hard and fast to reach the next clump of boulders emerging out of the water. My initial fear was more the weight of the gear than the current. Never before had I attempted to swim with so much encumbrance. To my delight the haversack had lifted in the water like a life jacket. It filled me with instant confidence.

In the flurry through the water the current took me down no more than a metre. I had my eye on a sharp rock, missed it and the current washed me against the flat side of a boulder where I clung like a spider with nothing more than a shallow groove to press my left hand into. On the downstream side, my right hand was useless. Stabbing around with my left boot I found a shelf of rock, stepped onto it and eased myself out of the water. I sat on the warm surface of the boulder for a couple of minutes, breathless. I couldn't believe a struggle that must have lasted only seconds could force me gasping like a sprinter at the end of a 100-metre dash. Sal and Harold had walked along the rock platform to get a clear view of the rapids. Across the water they were little figures, forlorn almost, because if I made a mess of the crossing they were helpless to do anything. I raised my hand and gave the victory sign. There was no response. From their perspective there was nothing to feel but apprehension and dread.

The next channel was wider. If there hadn't been two boulder outcrops it would have been impossible to breach the gap. The water would carry me this time and if I missed the upstream outcrop I had another chance. With no sub-merged shelf to walk out on I entered the water low down, like a shallow dive. To stand a chance I had to get the first five metres with a vigorous thrust from my thighs. The instant I felt the dive slowing I flew into the overarm action. The rope was around my neck, with the coils on top of the haversack. But arm movement was restricted and the current snatched me away from the upstream boulders. It took a desperate effort to make the lower outcrop where I fumbled for a secure hold. Alarmed, I realised the current was like a running tide in the centre of the river and my body lifted away, like a sheet on a clothesline caught in a gale. I felt the nails in my left fingers pushing into the quicks and knew I had about ten seconds to find a hold for the other hand. On the surface there was nothing. I went below and felt a narrow groove. Another climb-ing trick – bunch the fist and drive down hard. It took and I drew myself into the eddy between the outcrops. Adrenaline surging, I brought the free hand up and slapped the dry rock hard with open palm, pushing upwards at the same instant.

Highly skilled rock climbers applied fluid, coordinated movement where the rock was stable but holds were scarce. It required nerves of steel and I never made that grade.

There was another channel to cross and I remembered nothing about it. I didn't think it was too bad. On the eastern bank at last I checked the camera. Not a drop had worked its way through the string bindings that closed the plastic bags. I shouldered the haversack and the rope and raised both arms with the victory sign. This time Sal acknowledged it with a single wave.

10 Willa Cather's Inspiration

There are times when logic, clearly defined and predictable as a supermarket, will fail. Discovery and exposure of the ancient art was to attach such great value to the canyon in its pristine state no government or consortium would ever obtain the sanction to flood it. That was the purpose, but the trauma of danger and early symptoms of exhaustion will douse the spirit of the uninspired like a bucket of cold water taken full on the chest. For me, the motivation to capture photographs of the mysterious paintings had dwindled in the fight to cross the river. I began to roll over the names of people, living or dead, who had influenced me in the past. Anyone who could inspire me to go on, for I was weary and consumed with the harrowing thought of recrossing the river. With men it was usually a woman who kindled that inspiration. For me at that moment it was the famous author Willa Cather. I knew about her visit to the Anasazi ruins at Mesa Verde in the United States in 1915.

Searching for inspiration to commence a writing career at the age of nearly forty, Willa Cather arrived at Colorado's Mesa Verde in a horse-drawn wagon. A frontier national park at the time, it was dangerous to go off alone and look for the little-known cliff ruins. It was still dangerous – in 1997 a ten-year-old French boy wandered away from a group and was taken by a mountain lion. In almost one hundred years nothing had changed much at Mesa Verde, except the roads and the vehicles, and that was an astounding achievement on the part of the Colorado authorities.

In 1915 Willa would have faced the same peril as the French boy when she separated from her guide. Climbing up trails in the moonlight it appeared she was spiritually moved by the sight of the full moon lighting up the cliff ruins now known as Swallows Nest. It didn't appear that Willa was lost, or several coo-ees would have disclosed her position in the canyon. She went out on her own in the moonlight to look for something and she found it. Following the experiences of that night Willa Cather was inspired to write two novels, both of which touched on the mystery and sacred nature of the ancient Indian ruins. Further inspired with religious fervour she went on to write the highly acclaimed *Death Comes for the Archbishop*.

To the horseshoe bend in the river I made easy progress along the edges. With two hundred metres to go I could see the eastern wall was going to throw up a formidable barrier from the water's edge and I began to follow the ascending ledges. From the top of a cliff I expected to be able to view the river's new course, but the real bend was further upstream. An experienced climber, I had coped countless times with this sort of frustration. In Colorado once I climbed for hours towards a lofty crag, thinking it was the summit, only to find the highest point had been hidden.

It took twenty minutes to reach the next corner in the rock wall. I found myself on a terrace, locked in between the precipice entering the water and the one towering above me to the canyon rim. The time began to worry me. Forty minutes gone already and I hadn't even reached the broken cliff full of rock shelters. That was the second clue Sam had given me. All he'd heard from the since-deceased Elder was a horseshoe bend and a broken cliff face. When I discovered the terrace petered out into narrow exposed ledges I felt a sense of panic. There was no time to look for climbing routes. I undid the rope and coil-split it to the middle marker, attached one end around a stunted turkey bush and pulled half the rope through. With the rope safely anchored at centre I threw the rest of it down the cliff, where the rope ends reached a ledge near the water.

Modern-day abseiling is executed from a harness or a separate rope and snaplink gathered around the waist and groin. Beyond argument it's easier, but old habits die hard. I still used the old Swiss style – rope between the legs to begin with, then lifted around the right thigh, across the chest to the left shoulder and collected by the right hand from behind. The right hand controls the rate of descent. It's fast and it's easy. The disadvantage is the risk of rope burn. Ever since I taught myself forty years ago I had carried a glove for the right hand.

I went down with ease and pulled the rope through. While I looped it up I looked ahead, almost praying for a better passage. The water was only a few metres below, rumbling over a very jagged riverbed. I tried to imagine what it must have looked like under full flood. The rope back across my shoulders I followed a ledge under an overhang, climbed up again another ten metres and there before me was the river on its new course. A wide rock shelf lay between the river and another rock fall, which lay at the base of a full-length cliff. The rock face itself was a pockmarked tangle of rock shelters, caves, bulging overhangs and scrubby ledges. Medium-sized plum trees grew near the mouth of one of the caves. I elected to inspect it first and found nothing. In the next half hour I climbed and scrambled up to three other rock shelters, all of which were nothing more than low ceiling caves, smelly from the droppings of rock wallabies and bats.

The face on the watch began to glare back at me. Minutes were ticking by, the heat was sapping my strength and my weak knee was cracking up. It always did where jarring was unavoidable. First it would begin to ache, then the strength would disappear. I could run two more ledges. Climbing back down for a drink also used up precious energy. To save weight, I hadn't brought a water bottle.

The next ledge, further upstream, gave me great encouragement the moment I climbed onto it above the rock fall. In front was a shallow rock shelter with the painting of a human male on the wall. It was not life-size and the powerful arms appeared disproportionately long. Rust-coloured weathering of the rock obscured the head, which more than any other part of the human body helped identify style, which, in turn, may have given a clue to the period. I photographed the painting, but it had little significance.

The ledge ran out and I scrambled over boulders to a ledge lower down. There was no warning. I stepped around the boulder the size of a room and stared into the most perfectly shaped rock shelter I had ever seen. It ran along the base of the cliff for about thirty metres, its square and sharply defined shape reminding me of a cinema entrance on the street. Almost level with my eyes were the paintings. The art was displayed on the rear wall in a form of order and clarity equal to a city gallery. As though the architect was nature herself, the viewing shelf ran straight and flat for the entire length of the gallery. Considering the incidence of weather exposure I concluded only wild, wind-driven gales would blow any moisture onto the paintings.

My sensitivities sharpened by the ordeal in the river and the preoccupation of likely failure, I found it an overwhelming experience to stand at the entrance and look upon such ancient art. The antiquity of the paintings needed no confirmation by qualified people. It was sobering and almost beyond comprehension, but someone standing on the same platform six thousand years before the birth of Christ may have seen at least two of the paintings I was looking at. It made me feel very insignificant and I hesitated before taking a step inside, under a ceiling of rock half a metre above my head.

Magdalena's warning echoed from somewhere far away and I took the cross from the little pouch, conscious that I was responding to a spiritualism far outside my childhood religious initiation, that I believed in the devil spirits and the power of the cross to dispel them. After very early intense religious training I had been taught to think like a soldier and to rarely show emotion, so it was difficult to come to terms with this new fear.

Still, I had no compunction whatever about what I had to do, because I had defied all reasonable odds of getting here. The paintings, exposed to the sun for one or two hours every cloudless day and occasionally lashed by fierce storms, should have disappeared before the earliest recordings of history. We knew as much about our place in the universe as white Australians knew about prehistory in Australia. I put the cross in the sun on a boulder and got the camera out of the haversack, briefly wondering whether William Henry Jackson had taken a few moments to reflect before he took the first-ever photographs of the ancient Indian ruins at Chaco Canyon in New Mexico. It was 1877, at the height of the Geronimo campaigns, and Jackson was close to the heart of the war chief's territory.

Jackson was a legend in the American west for his early photography. When he took a packmule expedition over hundreds of miles he was very experienced and well equipped. Not a single photo came out. It was as though the Ancient Anasazi had never sanctioned it.

The first painting I photographed made me think of Captain Joe Bradshaw's initial reaction in 1891 – Egyptian! In 1890 Bradshaw had sailed around the coast from Wyndham and claimed the Prince Regent River region for a sheep station, a prospect that would amuse the most humourless sheepman today, as the place is so wild the crocodiles and dingoes still have it to themselves. But before the Aborigines had burnt every stick of this fragile outpost Bradshaw discovered some rock art that set his imagination alight. His theories have long since been discredited and some archaeologists hate the term 'Bradshaw', and have adopted the term 'Kimberley dynamic figures'. What has not been appreciated is that Joe Bradshaw was in this country during the period of first contact with the Aborigines. Through interpreters there may have been stories regarding some of the paintings, which at the time was of only passing interest. But what Bradshaw saw and what I was photographing now was ironically not Bradshaw art. Archaeologists today describe the style as consisting of curvaceous, floating forms of humans, heavily decorated with feathers about head, ankles and wrists and often a boomerang attached to a hand.

This painting was clearly not Bradshaw. It was crude, limbs out of proportion and no decorations or weapons. There were no Aboriginal characteristics. The face was aquiline and the hair style reminded me more of old Phoenician art than the art displayed inside the Egyptian tombs. Geographically speaking, the link stretched beyond reasonable credibility.

It was a tantalising mystery, deepened by the obvious antiquity. One figure with boots or feathers attached to the legs had been damaged by an oxidisation stain across the upper right arm. Oxidisation on hard quartz rock is a time process measured more in geological time rather than human time. The paintings were very old. Much older than the Bradshaw art a little further along the wall. Standing there, looking at these figures, I had a gut feeling we would never solve the riddle.

The second figure I photographed appeared to have been painted by the same artist, but was better executed. The figure had a slightly more natural form and it possibly was wearing ankle-high boots. The material flared away from the legs above the ankles and would either have to be attached to a boot or a leg garment.

The next group of paintings I focused on were splendid examples of Bradshaw art. For my own identification purposes

I named them, from left to right, 'the mounted warrior', 'the medicine man', 'the dancing girls' and 'the kangaroo man'. There were no theories or any evidence from palaeontologists that horses or camels existed in Australia before first contact with Europeans, so 'the mounted warrior' had to be one painting superimposed on another. Luckily the camel-like figure didn't clearly show four legs and a small tail or there would be real confusion, because the Bradshaw style has been dated from 1500 years B.P. to the lower Pleistocene (beyond 10,000 years).

The 'medicine man' dominated the scene, suggesting a very important occasion; the 'dancing girls', which were fluid and feminine, may in fact have been boys; and 'the kangaroo man' appeared to be swinging, as though dancing as well. The whole scene struck me as ceremonial with a powerful hint of spiritual transformation from boyhood to man – an initiation ceremony.

The photography took about ten minutes and sealing the camera another five. The clock against me, it was an effort not to hurry when it came to binding the open ends of the plastic bags. But Sal was not a time watcher – she would have extended the deadline. Still, you made a time, you kept to it, no matter what. It was one of several survival disciplines I'd learnt that had saved my life on more than one occasion.

Packed up again I put the cross back in the pouch, feeling self-conscious, as though a thousand people were watching and rolling their eyes. Magdalena's voice was again echoing in my head and I stepped out of the rock shelter without looking back.

My knee was no good. The inflammation was at the front, around the cartilage area. I had to avoid the stress of a rock climb and search for ledges. After two dead-ends I found a ledge that went right through to the vertical cliff above the bend. Looking for easy walking I opted to walk along the cliff line, hoping I might come upon a ledge angling downward to the water. I was out of luck and had to abseil down, but that didn't place any stress on the knee. The two figures across the river were tiny, but they had heard my coo-ees above the sound of the rapids. Both were standing on a high boulder so I stood up on a boulder and raised both arms.

On the way down, walking along the side of the rapids, I kept looking for a safer crossing. Everywhere else was far worse. There were whirlpools and low-standing waves, and in tight narrow channels the water rushed through at a frightening pace. It had to be the same spot. I didn't feel very confident.

In the first channel the water picked me up, gave me a ducking and swirled me into the boulder outcrop. Two left to go! I looked up and saw Sal and Harold standing on top of the rock fall opposite. Below me was the centre channel – the heart of the flow. Whether it was a state of mind, or a different angle, didn't know, but the river took on a malevolent swirling shade of green, like the shadow of a cloud across the green lawn of a cemetery. I didn't want to go in. My legs seemed to be obeying a command from somewhere else. Near level with the water, I sprang outwards with the same desperate need a mountain lion has when it springs for an elk deer. The mistake was allowing myself to go under. The water had me, it was giving me a ride and I had no control over whether I went feet or head first. At least the buoyancy of the haversack had not been an illusion. The pace verged on a thrill ride. Into a whirl-pool, found ground with my feet, kicked clear, swept down a corridor between boulders and my feet hit the bottom again. Driving my legs like pistons I worked for the western bank and struggled through the final stretch of shallow water on all fours. It was probably all over in thirty seconds. I was alive and I had the film. For me it was the moment of triumph. Sal ran from nowhere and was pulling the gear off me.

'Before we jump around like kids after a minty hunt let's inspect the camera,' she exploded breathlessly, undoing the haversack straps. I stood with both hands on a boulder, trying to catch my breath. 'You've done it. The camera bag's dry.' Then she paused, staring at me anxiously. 'You did find it?'

I hadn't uttered a word. 'I thought you knew,' I gasped. 'I found it. I signalled from the other side.'

Sal laughed. 'Here I am alive! That's all I read out of that. No – we knew. I just wanted to hear you say it.'

She gave me a big hug, wetting all her own clothes, and together we climbed over the boulders to join Harold, who was waiting at the top of the rock fall.

'Harold's got a big fish for you,' Sal said brightly.' He's been keeping it warm by the coals for an hour. He's been so anxious. For nearly an hour he's been looking for you through the telescope.'

Instead of binoculars I carried an old rifle telescope, which weighed only two hundred and fifty grams. It was one of the items I had offloaded from my haversack before crossing the rapids.

I stripped to my underpants and Sal squeezed the water out of my clothes and spread them across the warm rock. It was a large bream Harold had for me and I ate it quickly, washed down with tea. Even with a good run through the rapids, it would be after dark when we met up with Peter. We had to get moving. We packed up. Still wet, my clothes were warm on the skin. Harold took the lead for which I was very thankful.

'Don't think he wants to be lowered over your lay back cliff,' Sal said jokingly.

Harold stayed high up in the broken rock, laced with spinifex. He got us through to the rapids without any need to rope up. At the rapids he waded through and waited patiently. Tired and battling exhaustion, the last thing Sal and I felt like was roping up again. She belayed me across and when it was Sal's turn I wedged myself into the rock and passed the rope across my shoulders. I had a gut feeling the final channel would sweep her off her feet and it did. The rope shot out of the water like a big barramundi taking the fly. With no slack Sal may have drifted a metre before I had her weight securely held on my shoulders. Now a seasoned climber and a wild rapid traverser, she unroped with a relaxed smile and we stumbled on towards the rock fall.

The next half hour was as rigorous and painful as anything I had ever done. I was very lame and every step was concentrated effort. Overloaded herself, Sal took the rope which was wet and therefore much heavier. Harold had gone on to the camp, unaware of the problem we had with gear. It was about 4 p.m. by the time we reached the camp. Sal immediately organised Harold with the portaging and insisted I lie down while she packed and Harold carried. When it was time for the big raft she woke me up. Harold in the lead, she and I stumbled along behind. We couldn't wait to get in the rafts and drift along with the current.

It took only minutes to glide across the lake. We took the rafts close to the throat of the cascade rapids and the portage took less than ten minutes. Into the river for the long float down the canyon I soon went to sleep. I woke to the sound of rapids in the distance and was surprised at the heavy pall of smoke. The sun had already sunk below the canyon rim and I looked at the sky like a farmer. Fully awake, I scanned the water downstream for Sal and Harold. They were a speck in the distance, waiting for me in a backwater.

'You go first,' Sal said laughing. 'If we see you flip we know to portage around it.'

The light was beginning to fade. I was very uncertain about the decision to go for the easy ride, but provided there were no water drops I didn't think the water was turbulent enough to tip me. Getting drawn into rapids was like going into the barrier for a race start. Once the gates flew open nervousness vanished and you became focused on the job. I loved the thrill of the fast water, the vigorous paddling, and it would have been quite a tame run if it were not for a hole where the fast water tumbled into the big stream. If the raft plunged in sideways it would definitely flip. I straightened in the nick of time, down the funnel, water over the sides and out. Like all holes, whirlpools or standing waves, it was about three seconds from entry to exit.

I had to warn Sal. An upset in my raft wasn't that serious, but Sal had the camera and the telephone. It was madness. We should have carried everything over the point. I paddled strongly out of the flow and scrambled onto a rock, pulling the raft out of the water. She and Harold were halfway down and their expressions were wild with delight. When they shot out of a channel the hole was only twenty metres below and I bellowed, 'Straighten up!' Sal had great hearing. She heard me and ploughed into the water with her paddle. Harold was no help at all. He looked like a rabbit in a squat as the current propelled them towards the hole. The water broke over them, the raft bounced hard on the baby standing wave and they were through. Next time Harold and his mates hit the Emu Bitter I wanted to be there to hear his account.

The next lot of rapids we portaged around. It was nearly dark, our wet clothes felt cold and we still had a long paddle ahead. The thought of a big fire on the river-bank, freshly caught fish and a billy of hot tea kept our spirits up.

In the final stage I knew something was wrong. No fire, no sound – Peter wasn't there. Only when I heard Sal speak did I now someone was there. She and Harold were a few strokes ahead of me. The first person to emerge when my raft brushed against a rock shelf was Heather. She held the raft steady while I got out.

'The truck didn't come,' she told me. 'The fire wasn't far away, so Peter rode through the night towards Mount House.

He took Len with him and they took all the horses, including mine.'

'Did he pack one of them?' I asked.

'No – all they have is a water bottle each and one torch. That's why George is so anxious. We've been here since three o'clock, hoping you might be back early.'

'Where's the fire front now?'

'One front has stopped at the Mount House road. Somewhere west of Tableland the country's well alight and the heaviest smoke of all seems to be on the ranges we rode over. Peter said if he could get to Stumpy Creek the horses would have plenty of feed and he thought the grass along the flats would be too green, stopping the fire.'

All the gear and the deflated rafts were carried to the truck in one go. George was in control. Sal and Heather went into the front with him. I got into the back with the girls, Harold and Buddha. I did some simple arithmetic and resigned myself to one hundred and twenty kilometres of bounce and bump to a creek somewhere east of Mount House homestead.

The cool evening air on my wet clothes quickly chilled me to the bone and thinking the dark gave me privacy I stripped off. Even my wet underpants were intolerable. There were plenty of swags in the back of the truck and I intended to get under one. At the critical moment George hit a bad bump, throwing me forward naked, right up towards the front. A recurring nightmare for nearly forty years had finally come true. The dream was always the same. I'd lost my clothes, I was in a city street and everyone was looking. There was an outburst of laughter from the girls and Harold exploded too. It was the only time I had ever heard him laugh out loud, so something had been achieved. When I buried myself into the swags it was from more than the cold, but the embarrassment soon faded and I fell into a heavy sleep.

When I woke it was to the smell of smoke. I sat up to see the flames only metres from the south side of the road, so close the firelight lit up the back of the truck. To my relief I saw everyone else had decided to sleep away the trip as well. George had the job on his own. I didn't offer to drive, because that meant him getting in the back and me getting into the cabin naked. I had no idea where my wet clothes were in what had become a mountain of gear and I didn't feel like looking for them either.

It was about 1 a.m. when we stopped. The headlights lit up stone-covered ground and a small creek. George got out and walked into the dark. Stiffly and slowly, Sal and Heather got out.

'George says Peter's camped somewhere near,' Sal said to me. 'He wants to camp here.'

'How does he know Peter's camped here?'

'I don't know. Maybe he saw tracks.'

The bush skills of Aboriginal people were unfathomable sometimes. George didn't know this country.

'You cold?' I asked.

'Freezing – I'm still in damp clothes.'

I didn't like to say I was naked. The girls were sitting up and I knew the word would prompt laughter all over again.

'I'll feel around for my backpack and get the torch,' I said, feeling guilty she had suffered the dampness of her clothes for nearly five hours while I was in the back, snug and warm.

'While you do that I'll look around for some firewood,' Sal said, wandering into the scrub by the road, faintly lit by the reflection from the headlights.

George's shadow moved out of the dark and he walked down to the creek in the headlights. 'Four-wheel-drive tracks here, Mike,' he called. 'Geraldine pick Peter up. Horses hobbled out behind us. Peter get em to a big creek with green feed.' He came back from the creek. 'Horses safe now. Mount House under good management and all the grass out here needed for the cattle.'

It would come as a shock to some environmentalists, but if there was any alternative to the Kimberley fire culture it was the big introduced herbivore – cattle. Under modern procedures corridor burning would probably have been impossible in mountainous terrain. If an ecological balance was ever to be reintroduced it had to be without fire, which destroyed micro-organisms, insects and vulnerable plant life and ruined the habitat for native wildlife. Although still in the initial stages, the Kimberley was inexorably sliding towards semi-desert. As the old trees died off and fire destroyed the juveniles, the rainfall would diminish. Vegetation removal in central Queensland followed by altered rainfall patterns were a scientific fact. In the Sahara there had been no archaeological evidence unearthed to provide proof, but the rapid ecological collapse from lush grasslands, full-flowing rivers and lakes to desert suggested humans began to live above nature there about seven thousand years ago. The Tassili rock art paintings in Algeria documented four distinct cultures – Round Head (hunter–gatherers) commenced before 8000 years B.P; Pastoral commenced about 7000 years B.P; Horse from 3200 years B.P. and Camel from 2100 years B.P. Given that the North African latitudes were within the savanna cycle – dry and wet seasons – it was reasonable to assume that the cattle herders from the Pastoral rock art period were locked into the fire culture, which may have ultimately resulted in the world's largest desert.

Advocates of the Australian fire culture persistently sought to quell opposition by citing Aboriginal burning practices. There was no argument about Aboriginal management of the eco-systems prior to 1788, but their knowledge of exactly when to light up and how to effectively back-burn was handed down over millennia. They burned the way a farmer ploughed a field – total control over area. European settlers had never acquired that skill and never would. Anyone who thought pre-contact Aborigines lit up and let the fire go had no knowledge of the Aboriginal nomadic cycle.

In the softwood region of central Queensland cattlemen used to lament every winter over the nutritionless dry grass from the summer wet. Unlike the Kimberley, burning didn't result in automatic reshooting of green grassland. Until the arrival of the widely adopted perennial buffel grass, a large portion of Queensland's cattle country had a low carrying capacity. The problem with buffel grass was the ruthless deforestation necessary for establishment. The cost was enormous, often beyond many cattlemen, and some turned to the discovery of another solution – urea. If a small quantity of urea was introduced into the diet, cattle would eat the dry grass and do well on it. The combination of the urea and old dry matter in the rumen produced digestive protein. Like the fires of old, the cattle cleaned up the dead material, their droppings providing life to micro-organisms, and insects thrived. The management of cattle on urea was also very simple. Half-starved on nutritionless old grass, cattle would instantly home in on urea blocks or molasses roller drums containing urea. With no fires a good percentage of seed reached the ground ready to explode into life on the first monsoonal storm. In my hands-on experience the soft edible grasses competed better than the coarse grasses under the cattle-urea system.

Some environmentalists argued that cattle and wildlife didn't integrate. They advocated a pure native ecology. I believed this was an area where we had to compromise to achieve the best result possible under the circumstances. The vulnerable species were disappearing rapidly and only specialised exclusion from the many adverse impacts would save them from extinction. What could be done in the Kimberley was the re-establishment of the hardy species. On my farm of twelve hundred hectares

I had eighty permanent grey-forest kangaroos and twenty wallaroos. Birds of prey would bounce back quickly if other farmers didn't poison carcasses to kill crows. The cost to me of the marsupial animals in reduced carrying capacity was about four thousand dollars. Some farmers would not tolerate any reduced carrying capacity for native animals. I argued they were very privileged to own land in the first place and had an obligation to preserve it, which included wildlife.

Rachelle tapped me on the shoulder. I knew she had been fossicking through the gear, trying to find something. 'Dry pants, shirt and your old riding boots,' she whispered.

I was so grateful I nearly kissed her. 'I don't know how you found them.'

'You get around blackfella dress without them,' she giggled, and away they both went again. I was touched by Rachelle's thoughtfulness.

I dressed quickly and went to help Sal look for firewood. She had a few small pieces and I suggested she light up so George could turn the headlights off and save the battery. There was so little wood I had to shine the torch into old trees and break off deadwood low down. Rachelle had given me the only torch she could find. In the dark no one else could search for firewood and the headlights only picked up the track down to the creek. Sal fanned her few pieces into life and when I added a couple of old branches from a box tree a soft glow at last broke the darkness. George switched the lights off. Next was the search for food. There was so much gear in the truck the whole tray must have been half the length of an arm deep. Lifting, pulling and sometimes kicking, I found a packet of rice, a tin of peas, salt and from my haversack the tea. I passed the items on to Heather and went to search for the cutlery bag.

From a near hopeless prospect of any warmth or food Sal and I had produced a blazing fire and a tasty meal, provided you were liberal with the salt. George was smiling again and if he was reluctant before I didn't blame him. None of us wanted to leave the fire but when the embers began to die for lack of wood we all dispersed before the cold air from the creek could chill our bodies and send us cold to our beds. Harold, Buddha and the girls slept in the back of the truck. George and Heather rolled out swags near the hot ash and Sal and I found a tarpaulin in the truck and spread it out on the track.

It's not often you feel thankful for exhaustion. When we lay down rocks seemed to collide with bone. Roll away or shift, another rock was waiting. But it was more than exhaustion that let us sleep. It was over. The horses were safe, everybody had benefited enormously from the expedition, I had photographs of the rock art and, very significant for the future, the Bunuba people attached to Millie Windie had a blueprint for packhorse tourism. The Bunuba people had an opportunity to operate one of the most unique forms of eco-tourism anywhere in the world.

Early next morning I had to gently move around the sleeping bodies in the back of the truck and find my medical kit. My knee was very painful and I knew from past experience tight bandaging and Panadeine was the only relief. Otherwise I would be useless and so much more would fall upon Sal. I didn't disturb her. I tried not to disturb anyone. It was a cold hole of a place and if it were not for the pain I would have stayed in our stone bed for another hour.

I got a fire going, put the billies on and turned around to see Peter walking up from the creek.

'I am sorry you had such a doing,' I said quickly. I did feel responsible for what Peter had been forced to do.

'Would have been easy if the truck had turned up,' he replied in his easy manner. 'I'll walk mine to Millie Windie. Problem now is Heather's two. We got to get them back to Derby.'

'I'll pay the transport,' I said. 'I want to make it as easy as possible.'

'I think I can borrow a float,' Peter said thoughtfully.

When there was a hiccup Kimberley distances were forbidding. The two-horse float Peter intended to borrow was one hundred kilometres east of Derby. The whole exercise tallied up to about 1100 kilometres over three days. He needed the hired four-wheel-drive to tow the trailer. In Derby I had given him money to cover the extra costs and on the whole I had come out very well. Whether it was an expedition or a wheat harvest, hidden costs never failed to emerge. This one was no fault of anyone – simply fate.

I made the tea and we both just sat on the ground. It was the last billy of tea he and I would share for a year. After breakfast we would all head for Derby. I wondered how to begin. 'The art's very important, Peter,' I said at last. 'It doesn't matter who the custodians are. They're probably dead, anyway. What does matter is that all of you are aware of it. It's your spiritual connection.'

Life had forced Peter to become a gentle pragmatic. He had dreams and hope still lay there in his soul, like a flower bud under too much shade. Around him, everywhere, was unresolved grief and despair. He had more than felt the chill winds that descended from modern bureaucracies, like a southerly off the snowfields. He'd been to hell and back and wondered whether the scars would ever heal. 'How do you go back?' he asked simply.

'Inspiration – men have turned the tide of human culture before.'

He stared into the flames for a while before he spoke. 'Yeah – it would be good. It would be good to get back to the bush with the horses.'

The task ahead was daunting. The photographs would determine whether there was an unquestionable case to preserve the upper Fitzroy River and the northern tributaries. It would not be up to me to value the significance of the rock art. The great riddle for archaeologists would be to determine the nature of the culture of these ancient people and why it had disappeared. But like the ancient cultures of the Sahara, rock art may provide the only archaeological clues. For the Bunuba people, their homeland hung in the balance. If they didn't return home I believed it was only a matter of time before the King Leopold Ranges and the major offshoot ranges became a national park. The resources would be insufficient to manage such a volatile ecology and the current regime of management would become endemic.

Some would argue that encouraging the Kimberley tribes back to their traditional lands was not an environmental solution. I refuted that bias, based on my observation of Navajo reservations in Arizona and New Mexico. Despite tens of thousands of tourists entering Canyon De Chelly each year, there was no evidence of environmental degradation caused by the tourists, which reflected very positively on Navajo management. There was a spiritual connection to tribal lands and the visitors respected this.

I left Peter on a positive note. I said I would be back to help him start packhorse tourism at Millie Windie.

'You come back next year, Mike?' George said, with that wide smile.

'He'll be back all right,' Peter cut in, suddenly laughing, as he often did. 'He drank the water of the Fitzroy. He'll be back.'

To establish a unique form of tourism demanded inspiration and ideas. I knew the Navajos in New Mexico and Arizona operated horse tourism, very successfully. The horse culture had survived there, which helped people to maintain a bond with the natural world. When Sal and I flew out of Broome I was dreaming again, of another land of great eroded plateaus and indigenous people who worshipped the earth. I had visions of Frederick Remmington's famous graphic paintings of the American west between 1880 and 1910; of the mountain lion at sunset against the red rock and the Navajos on their multi-coloured horses. We had decided that our next trip, after a sojourn on the farm, would be to America, and to the land that had inspired Willa Cather.

CHAPTER 11 Desert Time Bomb

September 1999

When I woke I realised the sun had already lifted above the eaves of the old building, one of the few historic hotels in Albuquerque, now converted into Hostel 66. The air was warm and through an open window I could hear the Saturday morning traffic in Central Avenue. For the first time since leaving home I felt excited. I hated airports. They were alien places for me. I was not used to reading signs, finding queues and making efforts to look inconspicuous. If I had packed my hat it would have been ruined in the suitcase squash. The carry-bags were all full, so I had carried it in my hand. My knife had to go into the luggage or I would have been taken aside at security. Odd as it may seem, without a multi-purpose knife bushmen felt almost as undressed as when they were without their trousers. The next item of concern had been my climbing rope. I never went anywhere without it and I refused to part with it and consign it to luggage. Sal had taken the eccentric behaviour very well and said the positive aspect was that no matter how crowded the American airports were she would always be able to find me at a single glance.

But now the trauma was all over and I ran downstairs in my pyjamas, said good morning to the bemused manager in the office and went out onto the front lawn. I wanted to see them immediately – the Sandia Mountains. We had arrived from the airport about two hours before midnight in a taxi and at that hour Albuquerque was a dark and complicated city like any other. In the sunlight it was the hub of New Mexico and the Sandias loomed above the city to 3400 metres. The largest tram-skyway in the world was hauled by cable to the summit and when I ran back up the stairs I couldn't wait for Sal and Tom to wake up.

Tom had arrived from London about midnight. We hadn't seen him for a year but clearly his sense of humour hadn't changed. 'Oh no,' he cried when he woke up and eyed me sitting at the table orientating a map of the city with a compass. 'Not even Crocodile Dundee did that. You can't use a compass to get around in strange cities.'

'I don't know where north is,' I said laughing. 'My instincts tell me the Sandias are south-west from here. The compass says they're east by north.'

Tom was persistent. 'You won't attempt to navigate around the city with a compass, will you?'

To Tom's chagrin he had forgotten to extend his international driver's licence in London. That meant I would be driving in the city and he knew that the compass would occasionally be used. Compasses were actually very helpful. You could quickly locate the general direction and pinpoint the street you want.

Sal had a long bath then we all headed down to the Oldtown plaza in our Rent-a-wreck for a late breakfast. In the Oldtown there was two-hour parking and I found a spot by the little central park in the plaza, opposite the San Felipe de Mari Catholic church, built in 1706. In a narrow street behind the church we found the Church Street Cafe. There was a courtyard at the rear of the historic building with tables and umbrellas. Seated at one table was a lone Navajo man. In traditional style he had his long black hair tied back. I observed a colourful object made from fabric around his wrist and I thought his belt was snakeskin. He looked the part, and as soon as the waitress took our orders I went over and introduced myself.

'I know it well,' he said, when I told him we were heading west to Canyon De Chelly. 'It's the heart of my homeland.'

I asked him to come over and join us and have a cup of coffee. His name was Clarence Clearwater and he was a traditional singer and guitarist. He said he moved around a lot, but when he was in Albuquerque he entertained at the Church Street Cafe from 6 p.m. till eight. I began to draw him out on Native American culture.

'We're all Americans now,' he said sadly. 'Many of us are trying to salvage the traditional values and in pockets it's working, but the young generation are educated and want a share of the modern affluence.'

Although a Navajo, Clarence saw all the various tribes included in a single nation trying to come to terms with a rapidly changing economic environment. Thankfully land degradation was not the cause of that change. New Mexico's Elephant Butte Dam was the largest in the state but a mere sixty square miles in area. Water for irrigation was very limited. The changing economic climate for native Americans was their place in an urban society. Clarence said the combination of Catholicism and traditional spiritual beliefs inspired a powerful sense of spirit along much of the Rio Grande and adjacent reservations. Ironically, the Spanish had wreaked havoc on the pueblo people in the sixteenth and seventeenth centuries in the name of the cross, but now this cultural group had combined the two religions into a formidable force and with their indomitable spirit, modern America would never quite smother them.

'You've come to the wrong place,' he said gently when I explained I was looking for inspiration on how to encourage indigenous people to go back to their tribal lands before it was too late. 'In the Chiapas region of far southern Mexico the people are mounting stiff resistance. They don't want change and they're resisting it by force. They view the modern world as another form of enslavement. Only a privileged few are free. They liken it to a life in hell.' He stopped and looked directly at me. 'Down there is your inspiration.'

'What about their religious beliefs?' In my own mind I still couldn't clarify what I was searching for. Something held these people together in the face of voracious change, in a world that no longer cared whether they survived or disappeared.

'It has been said the soul of the cross and mountain ran together,' he replied, smiling broadly. 'In some churches you will see the pale faces of the saints and a sign of the sun god. The sign may be a mirror attached to each of the saints. Some have broken away and become evangelists. Others are warriors whose only religion is freedom from Mexico.'

'I thought the whole of Mexico was Catholic,' I remarked.

'Beliefs are complex in Mexico. Many resent the notion that the Spanish brought the cross.' Clarence's eyes twinkled. He was a teacher of tolerance. Religion was the driving force in his life, but he was still Navajo, with a defiant spirit inherited along bloodlines. 'The way of the cross has been in the central Americas for a long time. Sometimes absorbed and altered to Indian tradition, but there are regions in Mexico where legends handed down claim the cross was pre-Columbian.'

Nothing ignited my curiosity more than a prehistory mystery, but Clarence had finished his coffee and I didn't think it was fair to ask any more questions. Besides, the three of us were jet-lagged and we needed a ride on the tramway to make it through the day without a flop on the bed.

Three months had elapsed since we left the west Kimberley. The photographs of the rock art were developed in Sydney and the result was rewarding. The Konica films had captured the paintings with the exact shade of light I saw with the naked eye. Thanks to the quality of the film a mug photographer could produce perfect photographs. I had shown them to Doctor Paul Tacon, a senior research scientist in the division of Anthropology at the Australian Museum. Paul had recently published an article in *Australia Nature* magazine on the mystery surrounding rock art in the Kimberley. For fourteen years he had been active in recording and researching rock art over much of northern Australia and he was also head of the museum's People and Place Research Centre. So impressed was he with the mystery and prehistorical implications of the photographs, that for a little while we talked about another expedition in July next year. At the heat of the moment I had been keen, but I was quite ill at the time. Medical specialists had examined me and found nothing. It was superstitious non-sense, I suppose, but Magdalena's warning hung in my mind like valley fog refusing to lift: 'People get sick. Sometimes they die.' I also couldn't forget the look on Sam's face when he said, 'Don't go there.' I didn't want to go back. I had come back to earth. The gallery had a powerful significance when it came to stopping a dam and that was not romantic nonsense. The Portugal decision had proved it, but I knew from rumours there were galleries towards the Kimberley west coast that prob-ably provided more information than this one. One rumour was about an archaic, ocean-going vessel, painted thousands of years ago. Archaeologists were merely chipping away at an iceberg. Would we ever solve the enigma surrounding those Phoenician- or Egyptian-looking figures? I doubted it. The more conservative-thinking archaeologists contended that they simply reflected a phase of culture that came and went. I believed that theory contradicted human evolution. So the mystery remained!

America has been accused of extreme materialism, racism and having bizarre gun laws, but one thing was certain, the

Ancient Anasazi ruins in New Mexico, Arizona, Utah and Colorado would never be flooded to make dams for cotton growing. In the fifties they had flooded thousands of archaeological sites in Glen Canyon, Arizona. They never would again: they had taken a cultural stride Australia seemed incapable of taking in the near future. When Sal, Tom and I mounted our horses, ready to ride into Canyon De Chelly, we knew we were about to see one of the world's most beautiful canyons and it was under no threat.

It was a monotonous, semi-arid landscape of juniper and pinon pine. The soil looked acidy and infertile. Somewhere to the north a canyon carved a trench into the mile-high plateau, slicing westwards from the Chuska Mountains.

Justin Tso had just unloaded the three of us and one of his guides from a horse trailer. He managed and owned Justin Tso's Horseback Tours. A Navajo man with direct generational links to the earliest occupation of Canyon De Chelly, Justin seemed like the 'horse whisperer' man for the canyon area. Justin would send the horses out for as long as you wanted and the more days you wanted the better the rate. There weren't many horseback tour operators anywhere these days because operators could never charge a fee that was anywhere near relative to the time factor. Horses required twenty-four-hour care once engaged in the tourist industry. Quiet horses, known as 'bomb proof' in the industry, were not easy to acquire because everybody from the schoolgirl with a backyard to aged graziers wanted one. Insurance premiums to cover tourists were absurd and reflected a total misunderstanding of the risks. But if you wanted to see the real Australia or the old America, horseback had no equal.

The pick-up and trailer gone, the wilderness closed around us. For my own interest I had a compass hung from my neck, as I always loved to know direction. There was no need for it, though. Percy, our Navajo guide, was reared in the canyon country. Like many Navajos of his generation he had left his homeland to find work, and disillusioned he had returned with a new passion and a determination to make a contribution to the preservation of traditional lands. He had brought his own horse, a buckskin like Heather's Dusty, with strong shoulders and hindquarters and the fleet legs of a quarter horse. Hair tied back in the old warrior fashion and coiled lasso hanging from the saddlehorn, Percy only needed a gun to be a replica of one of Chief Manuelito's warriors. Manuelito was instrumental in securing the release of some 6000 Navajos from a concentration camp in eastern New Mexico in 1868. He negotiated the peace terms with Washington. The Navajos suffered terrible losses in the final wars against the invaders, but they were never defeated. They remained today very proud people and the most striking thing about the Navajos I met was their intelligence.

Navajo people didn't warm quickly to strangers. Centuries of conflict had made them wary and you had to earn their confidence. The signal to kick-off was Percy heading north along a horse trail that joined a vehicle track. I urged Mohawk into a trot, but he was an aged horse and was in no mood to travel. I broke off a small pinon branch and had to wave it like a jockey on a horse at the end of its run to get any response. Sal's Blackie, on the other hand, responded generously and tacked on behind. Further back Tom was hard at work on Cookie. It seemed Mohawk and Cookie knew what lay ahead.

The horses weren't walkers. We moved along at a jog. It was the best way to cover ground if you knew how to deal with it, because it was the natural gait of horses. The rider simply transfered weight into the stirrup irons and sat straight in the saddle.

Rainy Night was a free mover and Percy frequently reined in to wait for us. While he waited he picked a few pinon pine seeds to eat. You bit on the soft shell and spat it out. The seed had a nutty flavour. The juniper seeds were also edible, but the flavour of the seeds was more widely known among gin connoisseurs. You would never starve here, despite the bleak aridness of the high plateau country. It was scarcity of water that would claim the life of anyone lost in the pinon and juniper country. Percy told us, too, about the sap on the trunks of the pinon. It would eradicate the infection in a wound.

The featureless country gave the horses a chance to warm up before the descent. There was no warning. Suddenly we were on the rim and before us was a hole so deep the autumn-turning cottonwoods on the canyon floor were like wind blown leaves seen from a raised verandah. Entry was down the Bat trail, the same trail used by American militias in the Navajo–American wars.

Tom had a fear of height and went as white as a sheet. I told him the horses were bred in the canyon, were footsure, and all he had to do was focus his eyes over the horse's ears. Cookie's reluctance to go down didn't help Tom's confidence. Percy was still getting a long way ahead of us at times and when I caught up, only a quarter of the way down, he remarked that the occasional lion wandered into the side canyon, coming down from the Chuska Mountains. I passed the message on and it took Tom's mind off the height. With a stick he got Cookie going. In reality lions were rarely seen by anyone and human encounters were only marginally more than shark attacks in Australia.

The horses took the descent in their stride and adroitly stepped over and around boulders. The secret was to let them be boss and pick their own little routes on the steep sections. At the bottom we rode into a dry wash, which threaded through a corridor only one hundred metres wide. The reddish-brown De Chelly sandstone walls permitted a strip of blue sky no wider than the canyon floor. The big old cottonwoods had stood since the first clan of Navajos had entered the canyon three centuries ago and down in the dry wash bed Mohawk walked into a clump of Russian olives and tore off a mouthful of the silver-grey leaves. Rainy Night loved them too and thanks to these trees, weighed down with foliage, we at last caught up to Percy. He told us the trees had been introduced some decades ago to stem the erosion of the alluvial soil. When the U.S. Cavalry and some Mexican militia units commanded by Kit Carson invaded the canyon in 1864 they torched the flood plains bare of all vegetation. Only some of the big cottonwoods withstood the fire. Erosion began to eat out the flood plains from that year on and today wide silt plains devoid of any vegetation scarred the canyon floor. Where once 1000 people had grown corn and lived a rich cultural life, not a single family remained. It had been far more than soil erosion, though, that had caused the depopulation of the canyon. Decades before a reservoir had been built at the head of Canyon Del Muerto, and in the event of a dam bust anyone living below would be trapped. Consequently the canyons had no sealed roads or power facilities, which was a blessing.

The horses fell into a group on the canyon floor and at the first flowing wash they drank until I thought Mohawk might burst. Percy deciphered to us the tracks of the animals that had foraged or hunted the night before. A lone black bear had wandered along the edge of the water, two badgers had been scampering around the sand and a coyote had disturbed them. In Navajo myth a coyote had power of indiscriminate use and could use its power to perform good deeds.

We pushed on into a landscape of almost unbelievable colour. The rabbit brush provided a carpet of yellow on the narrow flats, the wash was lined with the soft green of the cottonwoods, thick copses of Russian olives intermingled and either side the sun fired a redness into rock walls that rose abruptly like skyscrapers from the street. Around a shoulder of rock and there before us towered Spider Rock, a vertical pillar of rock from canyon floor to rim. According to Navajo legend Spider Rock was the home of Spider Woman. White veins of conglomerate formed intricate patterns at the summit and in the legend they were interpreted as the bones of naughty children captured and eaten by Spider Woman.

Ten miles into the canyon we stopped for lunch and Cookie developed a colic spasm. His reluctance to travel from the start may have been mild colic. It was not uncommon with stabled trail horses. They ate a big breakfast, got thirsty from a long dry stretch and drank copious amounts of water. When the pain hit, horses always went down and rolled, instinct telling them to try and release trapped gasses in the intestines. When Cookie went down Percy spoke softly into his ear and the horse lay still.

'How does it work?' I asked Percy, after the horse had regained his feet.

'You must talk to horses like we talk to one another,' Percy said, very serious. 'I tell him it's okay and he relaxes. They listen to us and if we stay alert they make us safe. In the old days my people always relied on their horses to signal danger. They know long before we see it.'

Cookie jogged along freely after lunch and for the first time Tom was able to enjoy the ride. Sal's Blackie was a lovely horse. He was a shade bigger than Blackjack but the hair colour was all those two horses had in common. Sal deserved a break with horses and Justin had provided her with one of his best. I had the key to Mohawk at this stage and we got along well, so long as I let him regularly chew on the Russian olives.

Every time Percy reined in I scanned the cliffs for signs of Anasazi ruins. The little corn storage caches were hard to see. The 'ancient ones' as Percy called them, built the corn boxes with the same coloured mud as the sandstone in the cliff. The ancient ones had lived in the canyon from approximately 200 A.D. to 1300 A.D., when the canyon was suddenly and mysteriously abandoned. Percy said they had lived a peaceful existence and stored their corn high in the cliffs away from rodents and bears.

The intriguing mystery surrounding the quite sudden abandonment of the canyon between 1276 and 1299 A.D. may have been related to the cultivation of cotton. On a hypothesis basis, the speculation was as sound as any other. And it was worth careful consideration, because cotton would always be grown. I couldn't wear any other fibre against my skin and there would be millions of people in the same skin-sensitive situation. To ensure the survival of the industry governments would have to lay down strict environmental guidelines, which would include the banning of growing the fibre in highly volatile climate zones where the leaching of herbicide and pesticide residues were impossible to control. Unfortunately, greed could never be eliminated on a voluntary basis and legislative controls would prove to become necessary, no matter how repugnant some would find that concept.

The Anasazi had been initially hunter–gatherers, with a culture known as the 'early basket makers'. From about 450 A.D. they began a more sedentary way of life, growing corn. Through trading networks with southern civilisations like those in Mexico, cotton arrived some time after 700 A.D. The great heat inside the canyon during summer made it possible for cotton to be grown at altitudes normally well outside the plant's environmental range. Archaeologists had discovered cotton seed was a major source of food and great quantities of fragments of cotton-woven fabric had been unearthed at excavations in Canyon Del Muerto. Whether it was unrelated socio-economic factors or the result of extended trade has not been determined by archaeologists, but the Anasazi moved into an advanced stage of communal living about the same time that cotton appeared on the archaeological record. In anthropological language they became a chiefdom society – a hierarchy. Archaeologists call it the Classic Pueblo Period. But suddenly the civilisation crashed and the cause still baffled scientists to this day. Tree-ring studies supported the severe drought theory while more recent studies favoured the theory of chronic stress on arable land.

The modern farmer today knew that cotton placed huge demands on soil, and crops could not be grown profitably without heavy applications of fertiliser. The argument against my hypothesis is that it appears the Anasazi grew cotton for a long time in the canyon and so something more drastic than soil degradation must have caused the exodus out of the canyon. Other theories included inter-tribal warfare, disease and even earthquake. Still another theory was that the kiva communities amounted to several families living together in a circular structure constructed from clay like mud. Some researchers claimed male and female partnerships were forever under threat and the friction was too destructive. I favoured the theory of human greed . and soil depletion, compounded by drought, which led to a micro-economic collapse. The sudden collapse of the Classic Pueblo Period was a warning for our own time.

Our horseback journey down the canyon was an opportunity to observe the cultural changes over the centuries, from the earliest Anasazi cliff dwellings to the little subsistence farms of the present. No one lived permanently in the canyon anymore, but in the summer some families in Chinle grew vegetables. We often saw a few sheep, a pair of donkeys and lots of horses. If it were not for the presence of Percy the archaeological sites would have been a mere addition to the scenery. It made me feel very envious of the south-west, for the Anglo-Americans had drawn back from total annihilation in their fight to take the Navajo lands. They won the wars, but they did not ruthlessly pursue all the roaming clans of the Navajo, and in the long run that enabled the establishment of the Navajo Nation. It appeared that, while the Navajo had been dreadfully oppressed, there had been an element of compassion in

Washington that had never existed in Perth during the white settlement of Western Australia. Today America benefited enormously from that moment of compassion when the Navajos at Fort Summer were allowed to return to their homeland. In the Kimberley it was a race against time to save the little remnant of Aboriginal culture left and the homelands with which it was inextricably linked. As I gazed across the Canyon De Chelly and searched for ruins of Anasazi corn boxes I tried to be optimistic. It struck me more forcefully than ever how vital it was to save the Fitzroy River. If the Leopold heartland was flooded a whole new culture would emerge in this region. It would be strictly hard-core commercial, because the traditional culture and the magic of the Kimberleys would be lost forever, and due to the isolation, it would be unlikely that the tourist industry would expand. The modern adventure tourist wanted to see wild, unspoiled landscapes, and if they could be in the company of indigenous people that was a tremendous bonus. Having a white man or woman explain points of interest about an old culture site or a prehistory site could be a bit like a geography lesson from school days, but when the indigenous people talked to you they sparked life into the whole scene. Their passion came through, their perceptions were different and, most important of all, their values came from the heart. This was how we felt about Percy.

We were driving north through the rock desert where the summer heat could claim the unwary and in the winter the high plateau lay covered in snow and was equally dangerous. In Moab in eastern Utah we selected a camp ground in the cottonwoods. There was hot water in the office for our coffee, and seated under a cottonwood we watched the valley shadows creep up the canyon walls until only the barren summit skyline was ablaze with light.

Moab seethed with life. People from every corner of the

planet walked the shopping blocks until ten at night. A second-hand saddle, dark from wear and grease, sat on a wooden stand in the street and enticed me to walk into an antique saddle and harness shop. It was a nostalgic concept and I bought a lasso to carry on my saddle. It would probably hang in my office. If anyone had reservations about the power of the wild to attract the tourist dollars they only had to travel to this town of just ten thousand permanent residents. Everywhere you sensed passion for the wilderness. I loved the Americans for their passion for their country. The concept of colonial exploitation here had died a long time ago.

The following day we headed north for Vernal on the upper reaches of the Green River for the beginning of a whitewater adventure. The Green–Colorado river system is one of the most dammed in the world. The stored water had contributed to the establishment of more than three million people in a landscape that was once arid waste, home to just a few nomadic Apaches. The hydro-power plants provided a significant proportion of the energy for the arid south-west and irrigation had created a huge agricultural infrastructure. Completed in 1963, the same year as the comparably sized Lake Argyle in Western Australia was completed, Lake Powell on the Colorado River had to date been a spectacular success. Thirty-six years later the Lake Argyle town of Kununurra had a population of just 4900.

In the late afternoon we arrived at Vernal and found the raft depot. It looked very shut. I peered through a window and saw the chairs up on a table.

'I think they're all gone,' I said when I went back to the car.

'They've gone to do the shopping,' Sal said, always positive. 'I think you've forgotten. We used to shop the afternoon before an expedition.'

Sure enough, not long after Nick Berich, boatman and expedition leader, returned from a trip to town. A young man in his late twenties, Nick was a very fit Texan with a charming disposition. We drove away and made camp feeling greatly relieved. Nick and the supply raft oarsman Tom Beckett were organised to leave early next morning. At 7 a.m. we would load the rafts onto a trailer and drive right up through south-west Wyoming to rendezvous with the Green below Flaming Gorge Dam, just south of the border back in Utah.

'We'll have our first stubbie in Colorado,' Nick laughed, after explaining the map ordinance.

We didn't meet Tom senior until next morning. An ex-boatman, Tom was now an attorney, living near Salt Lake City. The season was over and with only the three of us booked in if Tom hadn't wanted to escape his office for a few days there may have been a manning problem. Tom was tall, strong and fit. He relished the thought of battling the rapids for four days, through the Canyons of Lodore, where no man had navigated the fifty miles of cataracts until 1938, when whitewater adventurer Buz Holmstrom had ridden the rapids all the way to the river plains near Vernal.

The best documented exploration of the Colorado River system is from John Wesley Powell in 1869 and 1871. Because many of the early trappers were not recorded in history it's possible no one knows who first ran the Green–Colorado system. Maybe Powell was the first – certainly history has bestowed that honour upon the explorer. In 1825 a General Ashley attempted to open up a fur-trading route on the river and was wrecked in the vicinity of Hell's Half Mile. It appears he and his men managed to walk out through a side canyon. The next attempt to be recorded was that of an ox-driver in 1849 or 1850. William Manly was desperate to get to the Californian goldfields and signed on as an ox-driver to cross the Sierras before winter. Arriving at the upper reaches of the Green in late autumn, word came through that the high passes were already under snow. Manly and his fellow ox-drivers anticipated hostility from the Mormons if they dug in for the winter, as some of them were from Missouri where the Mormons had recently been expelled. Finding an old ferry boat abandoned and half-filled with sand, the ox-drivers repaired it and attempted to run the river, which at that time was thought to flow directly to the Pacific in southern California.

The greatest threat to life on rivers running through perpendicular canyons was the impossibility of a retreat if the exploring rafts or the boats were wrecked. Manly's ferry got snagged in Flaming Gorge, so, retrieving their supplies, Manly and his men shaped the trunks of some big ponderosa pines into dugout canoes. Lashing the canoes together in pairs they continued on into the canyons of Lodore and, rope-lined through Disaster Falls unscathed. However, when the river narrowed, they shot into the white water of Hell's Half Mile where one outfit was swamped and all the equipment on board lost. Manly and his team managed to salvage the dugout and their wild ride, with much disembarking and rope-lining of the dugouts, continued to the eastern Uinta Basin which is now Vernal and the surrounding districts. They were the first to run the river through the Uinta mountains and if the story didn't have a humorous twist it would have been relatively uneventful. In the Uinta Basin Manly was signalled by an armed Ute warrior to pull over. Having lost their guns at Hell's Half Mile they were in no position to ignore the order and it quickly became apparent that the Utes in this region and the Mormons were friends. To survive, Manly and his companions had to declare themselves Mormons. According to some historians the Mormons supplied the Utes with produce and guns to achieve a secret agenda. Some argue it was to lull them into a false sense of security while the Mormons established an increasing hold on the territory, with a covetous desire to usurp all the Ute lands. Others saw it as a sign of encouraging Ute raids on Californian ranches, which stalled eastward expansion towards

Mormon territory. Whatever the reason, Chief Wakara of the Eastern Uinta Basin conducted raids which sometimes netted up to one thousand head of cattle and horses, which he and his warriors drove along the Old Spanish Trail to Santa Fe for sale. The 'Wild Bunch' I encountered in Queensland a few years ago would moan with envy if they could hear all the tales about Chief Wakara.

The ox-drivers had enough of the river and believed the chief when he told them there was far worse downstream. It appears they had a wonderful time – buffalo hunts, dancing with squaws to the drums and the flute by campfire and plenty of good tucker. However, still impatient for the goldfields they left with horses and packs given to them by Chief Wakara. Unwittingly they rode into hell itself on the way to California– Death Valley. Some of the ox-drivers perished. The record doesn't disclose what happened to Manly. The Utes have long gone and their demise had little to do with the Mormons, who appear to have been genuine in their desire to live in peace with Indians. It was the US cavalry who finally drove the Utes out.

The raft company was called Holiday River Expeditions. Despite the best equipment available, running the wilderness rivers in America still demanded the scale of an expedition. Food supplies, tents and clothes had to be meticulously planned for. The second raft was more than a supply raft. If someone became ill or was injured they would be taken as quickly as possible to the nearest access point. Before embarking a Park Ranger inspected the rafts and systematically ticked off a safety list. On this occasion it was a young woman. She was an oarsman, herself, and in good shape. Nick suggested he could do with some relief on the oars and if she hadn't been duty bound she would have come too.

The river run we were about to undertake was called the Lodore Canyon. Entry into the mountains was through the

Gates of Lodore, aptly named as the river appeared to almost disappear into a gap in the mountains, which looked more like a groper's mouth than ancient water erosion, through very hard quartzite sandstone one billion years old.

An hour after leaving the boat ramp the river twisted deep into the range until the walls on either side were so high we could only make vague guesses about the height above the water. Dead trees up to forty metres long washed up on river islands and high banks revealed the high water mark during the thaw. At Disaster Falls it was easy to see how perilous the cataract was with a big flow. There was no waterfall. What made the water boil white were some big boulders in the wrong place.

When Nick oared the raft into the correct channel, there was an unnerving scraping sound as we brushed the side of one of these boulders and then we plunged into a hole below another. The raft reared high and hit the water with a loud smack. A spray of water lashed the bows, landing in our laps like a bucket of ice cubes, but we were through.

Initially I thought running the rapids entailed brute strength on the part of the oarsman. On the contrary, it was very technical and proof of skill over strength was the number of boatwomen appearing on the rivers. It was all a matter of anticipation, reading the current and knowing how to execute the most spontaneous response from the big seventeen-footers with the stroke or push from an oar.

Two hours above Hell's Half Mile we pulled over at the end of the first day's run to make camp. The rafts were secured by a big steel spike driven into the ground for the ropes. We grabbed our camping gear and headed for the shady box elders growing on the narrow strip of alluvial soil between the river and the cliffs. We were about six throusand feet above sea level, but the canyons retained the warmth of the midday sun.

While we set up camp Nick and Tom erected a kitchen with

as much work space and gadgets as a modern home. Connected to a portagas cylinder was a hot plate for cooking, a warming plate and even a burner to keep the coffee pot hot. The meal prepared and ready to cook, Nick made some savouries and our Tom extracted some beer and wine from the esky.

'Have we crossed the border yet?' I yelled out to Nick, holding up a stubbie. Alcohol was not encouraged in Utah.

'Oh yes,' Nick replied. 'We always row for Colorado to make first camp. I'll come and join you.'

Something in the light caused a golden iridescence across one side of the river downstream. From our log seats we all watched in awe. Not much appeared to have changed here since the first expedition had set off down the river one hundred and thirty years before. But Tom said Flaming Gorge Dam had made the water too cold and many of the micro-organisms had vanished, depriving the water of the organic life essential for healthy, fully oxygenated water. Although clear and clean in appearance, in fact the pale green wasn't natural. The Tamarisk trees had been introduced to hold the silt on the banks and stop deposits being swept downstream in the spring flows, but they made the alluvial soil too acidic for the seedlings of native vegetation. The native fish too were becoming increasingly rare. The magnificent pike minnow, which grew up to two metres, had all but disappeared. It was the Colorado's equivalent of the Murray cod, which was disappearing from the inland river systems of New South Wales and southern Queensland.

Pitted against one of the world's fastest-growing desert population growths the micro environmental problems seemed almost pathetically insignificant. If you could drink the water with no ill effects and irrigate crops, who cared if the oxygen and hydrogen components were out of balance? How many people would lose any sleep if the pike minnow became extinct? Environmental watchdogs were a minute voice among millions of people commuting nearly every day to work, struggling with mortgages and trying to maintain happy relationships under the unforgiving regime of new modern societies. Should someone who wanted to save a river and the whole ecology of the region dependent on that river waste time on water quality, invasion of alien species and extinction? Most people were so run off their feet they didn't have time to think about it. The only thing busy people were interested in was what the future held for them.

The world was yet to witness the dire consequences of watering the desert and encouraging massive population growth. America had the resources to overcome most problems. The reality was, however, that a water crisis in the major southwestern cities was far more likely to occur than earthquakes. Los Angeles obtained a significant proportion of its water requirements from the Colorado system, Phoenix drew from natural underground aquifers which were replenished by Colorado water and San Diego drew sixty per cent of its total requirement from the river. To varying degrees fifteen million people were now partly dependent on Lake Powell and the smaller reservoirs downstream. In addition, hundreds of thousands of hectares were irrigated. If the cap could be put on growth, the looming crisis would be solved, but economic growth fed on development and expansion. There was no more water and there never will be. In fact, on a per capita basis, the availability of water was diminishing annually – Lake Powell was silting up. In 1983 the spring thaw was so huge the water in Lake Powell went within a foot of spilling over the canyon wall. Since then the silt level at the bottom had increased three per cent and engineers had been forced to carry out extensive repairs to stabilise the sandstone on both sides of the dam wall.

The long-running debates about the future of Lake Powell would have nothing to do with the ecology. It would be about the plight of civilisation in the desert. How would you dismantle the infrastructure? How does a politician tell 2.5 million people in Phoenix their economy must stagnate because there was insufficient water to satisfy demand? Politically nothing could be done and people would have to exist on less and less water and pay higher and higher water rates. It was a sobering thought. Gazing into the unnaturally green water of the river it occurred to me that if the Western Australian government ever gave the green light for a dam on the Fitzroy it would be flying in the face of incontrovertible evidence that watering the desert was unsustainable.

After a beer at our log bar Nick lit the gas to cook dinner. In the King Leopolds Sal and I had been responsible for the meals and to sit back and smell the cooking, listen to the river, watch the canyon descend into soft shades of light and hear the final call of the ravens before dark was a moment poets dream about. When Nick called we moved down to the beach to eat. Tom senior had lit a campfire from wood that we carried on board. The campfires were lit on a grill with a pan underneath to catch the ashes. Every ounce of rubbish was bagged and taken on board so that the next group of river adventurers would find the beaches as unspoilt as we had. It was a very tasty vegetable lasagne Nick served, and a pudding followed.

A storm blew up overnight and the tent flies had to be secured with rocks at the corners. We woke to dripping dew, wet soil and sunshine. Nick said it was the 'sleep-in' day and we would only run the river for seven miles, but it was to be a full-on whitewater day. Tom junior rode up the front, Nick in the centre and Sal and I in the rear. Tom senior had to pilot the supply raft alone, under safety regulations. It was sunny and warm on the river when we set off and during the drift to Hell's Half Mile the river became even more tranquil.

Rapids were caused by rock debris falling from the cliffs above or a steep descent on a rock-strewn surface. These rapids appeared to be caused by a sudden fall in the river. Nick explained the route we would take. We would enter on the east side, pull fast across the current to avoid a boiling plunge of white water and swing the seventeen footer between two boulders, where the water looked to be surging at a hundred kilometres an hour.

'What if you don't pull across fast enough?' I asked.

'We'll flip,' he said, but unable to maintain a sober face he added, 'I won't miss though. We'll just get wet from spray.'

Drifting towards the wild water seemed to happen in slow motion. The sound was everywhere, the raft buckled and bent and the oarsman was seized with a new expression. He was in another world.

Then the waiting was over. The seventeen footer bucked like a wild horse, someone was throwing buckets of freezing water across the raft, Sal was shrieking in delight and at the front Tom was as rigid as a stockyard post. I was loving it so much I was searching through the spray for more. None of us thought about the oarsman, for he was invincible.

Perhaps it lasted three minutes. It was all too short and we shot back into the wide river, once again deep and peaceful as though it were all a dream. Nick pulled to the side while we watched Tom. He had complained of a pulled muscle in his back and Nick was a little worried, but the veteran rode the white water without a single technical error.

'Forget about a race ride,' I said to Nick as the current picked us up and we swung back into mid-stream. 'Nothing will unleash a bigger adrenaline rush than white water.' Nick had never met anyone before that had ridden racehorses. Like my own boys he felt he might have missed something.

'You've been wanting to have a go,' Nick said. 'Have a crack at this big horse for a couple of miles.' Nick, of course, knew the rapids below were only ripplers.

I jumped straight into it. I had no control. We went down

sideways and backwards, but little by little I began to read the river and anticipate what strokes scored a response and which were dead in the water. When the river began to roar again I had to hand over.

At camp two we were on a thin strip between the river and the cliffs. Nick offered to take us to a waterfall if we felt like the climb. There wouldn't be much water, he explained, but he would play the flute in the cavern, under the overhang where the water tumbled down in the thaw.

High above the camp in the cavern Nick took a Navajo flute from its case. Above, the mountains speared into the blue for yet another span of space. Coming from a flat land the spell of the scale of great uplifts could last for days. It was more than rock in the sun. Long before Europeans kept records, the mountains inspired the great cultures of the spirit. The flute was a living, vibrant object in the mountain cultures of the south-west. Melancholy, soft, it drove all from the mind that was doubtful, and as the notes floated skyward to the firs and the autumn turning aspens, before the blue of space, I felt that heaven did exist after all.

The next day at camp three we went on another canyon excursion. This time Tom senior was the pathfinder. He wanted to show me the Fremont art, named after one of America's famous western explorers. Fremont rock art had provided archaeological evidence of an ancient culture in Utah and Colorado. The ancient people were known as 'the early basket-makers'. Carbon dating of organic material from rockshelters indicated people had first settled this high, cold land about 100 A.D., following a period of severe drought. The rock art was possibly the most distinctive in North America. They painted the animals they hunted and the medicine man, known as shamans, always seemed to feature in the principal galleries. The petroglyph figures had horns on the head, and to people of British origin they looked like paintings of kings.

The most famous gallery of Fremont art was called the Three Kings. Some of the rockshelters in the Uinta Mountains had been described by archaeologists as the best rock art in North America. But the drawing skills here were disappointing. Some animals were not clearly identified and the human form was executed in abstract style. The straight-line figures may not have been humans at all – they may have been gods. The square-shaped heads had what appeared to be dual, pointed horns. The paintings were in red ochre and the artists must have known to mix protein with the ochre for rock penetration. It was soft sandstone, though, and in a few centuries or a far less period of time, only a trace of the art would remain.

Towards the upper end of the rock shelter there was a moose's head and antlers skilfully painted. Then, a metre further was a cross, drawn and painted in such perfect balance the artist must have used something for measurement. It was not a cross of the Crucifixion, and more puzzling than its perfection was its genuine antiquity. Paintings on rock walls were not always genuinely old, but this one was definitely ancient. The sun had bleached it over the centuries and the original ochre had penetrated deep into the sandstone. Furthermore, on the cross arm painted upwards dual horns had been painted, attached to the cross and forming part of the whole painting. Mysteriously, the Fremonts knew of the existence of a culture symbolised by the mark of a cross. Perhaps to some degree they absorbed the cultural contact into their traditional beliefs and that may have led to the stylistic, abstract human forms the Fremont culture was famous for. Unfortunately, it was all conjecture until science could date fragments from any given painting.

Before arriving in the south-west I had never heard of the pre-Columbian cross. Now, ten days after Clarence, the Navajo man in Albuquerque, had told me about it, I was looking at what I believed to be a painting of the pre-Columbian cross.

For one that had struggled with belief and disbelief since the days with the nuns, it sent a tingle to the nape of my neck. No Spanish friar had run the whitewater and ordered a Ute to paint a cross. Other than maybe a few wandering bands of Utes, no one had entered these mountains for more than five hundred years.

One of the best-known Native American writers was Joe S. Sando. He was a member of the Sun clan at Jemez Pueblo in New Mexico and wrote the book *Pueblo Nations*, 'I believe that,' he wrote, 'the indigenous people of this hemisphere migrated thousands of years ago from the Old World, so long ago that the memory of it has been lost through the ages. I also believe that people from the Near East came across the Mediterranean, at a later date, before the Pillars of Hercules [Gibraltar] were closed by the Romans when they became the most powerful nation of the world at that time. It is said that the warning to people crossing read: 'Ne plus ultra' – No more beyond.

I left the fragile sandstone gallery, more convinced than ever about the significance of ancient rock art to our own time. The very existence of the art made archaeologists aware of an ancient culture. Who were they? they then asked. How did they survive? Why did they disappear? Those questions then led to scientific research, and in this case it had been discovered that the south-west of America had entered a severe dry period about 1275 A.D., and by 1300 A.D. the population had abandoned the upland regions. In the terms of climate change it was not long ago. What would be the impact on such great cities as Los Angeles and Phoenix if it happened again?

Clearly rock art in its various forms was the most significant of all archaeological evidence. In Algeria, the Tassili galleries had documented climate and cultural change in the Sahara over 10,000 years. The secrets of the past would have remained locked in the desert sands if it were not for the existence of those galleries. In Australia we were yet to untap the mysteries which surrounded ancient cultures.

Next day we floated out of the mountains into the undulating terrain of the upper Uinta Basin. It was a desert under stunted juniper, but everywhere we looked there was evidence of native animals and birds undisturbed for centuries. Sal's quick eye saw the beavers on the bank. She had an uncanny eye for detail. But like Australia's, a lot of America's wildlife was nocturnal and it was the birdlife that captured our attention. Blue herons glided down the river and on one occasion a bald eagle rose from the river sand to glare down at us from a dead tree. Overhead, golden eagles circled. We watched as one did a full dive to the ground. Folding its wings, it fell like a stone until, with a split second to spare, it spread its wings and presumably caught its quarry, because we didn't see the eagle fly up again.

In the Kimberley, an area large enough to blanket New Mexico and Arizona combined, and with less than ten thousand people if Broome was removed from the map, an encore to the eagle dive we witnessed may not have been possible. I found this disturbing and a reflection on Australia's political inability to manage a fragile environment.

We were sorry to be coming to the end of our river expedition. Nick and Tom senior had been wonderful company. Nick had put me in the saddle a few more times, and thanks to him I was becoming a boatman. Tom junior had inflated the rubber kayak and demonstrated some considerable skill in the rapids. We took bets between ourselves, but he never got thrown. When the rapids called Schoolboy drew close Nick had to call Tom junior in. It was as though the river would have one last lash at us. Lifejackets clipped tight and knuckles white, we shot into the last compulsory bath. We were soaked to the skin. No one knew why those rapids were named Schoolboy. I had a fair idea.

'Plenty of life left in this river,' I remarked to Nick, removing wet clothing to let the sun on my skin. Not even the rain suits helped.

'The river's a desert time bomb,' he replied with a stern sort of grin.

To see something wild, beautiful and truly magnificent in the creation of things took passion. Sometimes that passion over-rode credibility and defeated the original purpose. Advocating and urging defiance in the face of progress was like walking a tightrope with no end in sight.

What I feared most for the Australian interior – the river-lands and the great plains – was sterility of soul. Much of the interior was fast becoming a culture devoid of laughter, fun and the simple things. It has become a place where the middle-aged and the old move as though lost on a landscape with no signs. The horizon is dotted with sprayriggs, utes on tractor wheels and four-wheel-drives bristling with antennas. The dance halls have fallen down or been dismantled and the churches are a lonely refuge for the few. It has become a land of gamblers, and when the old seasons return it will be a land of the skeletons.

It was a sad moment saying goodbye to Nick and Tom. We had become good friends and our worlds were so far apart there was a possibility we would not meet again. Their love of this great river left a lasting impression and when we drove away, heading for Albuquerque, my thoughts were with the Fitzroy.

Next day, at the crack of dawn as we boarded a plane in Albuquerque the light was gathering on the Sandias. As we taxied out for take-off I thought of Willa Cather and her travels around New Mexico on horseback. It took a long time to go home in those days. She was lucky.

What happens to beasts will happen to man. All things are connected.

If the great beasts are gone, man will surely die of a great loneliness of spirit.

Chief Seattle

Epilogue

May 2000

Not much changes dramatically in a year, except through war or natural catastrophe. Cyclone Rosetta had ripped through Broome in April. Fortunately the pearling town had escaped serious damage but when I arrived early in May there were few tourists. Everyone was talking about the cyclone and no one was talking about the Fitzroy. The dam issue was off everyone's agenda. Had the opponents of the dam succeeded or was the issue like warm ash on the Pindan: asleep, innocuous – until a sudden Willie Willie sends a spark into the dry grass? Time would tell.

Up in the King Leopold Ranges the packhorse safari were about to start. Following the wettest monsoon on record it was an extraordinary feat of resourcefulness on Peter Brooking's part that we were ready to run. Blocked by scores of creeks running like rivers Peter had been unable to reach his horses on Millie Windie, where he'd left them to graze along the Leonard River for the duration of the wet. Instead he'd assembled another team in Derby and in round trips of 400 kilometres floated them back three or four at a time in a four-wheel-drive truck. Two young horsemen, Ralph and

Francis, stayed with the horses on the Lennard River until Peter arrived with the final load just ahead of his guests. I went along as chief storyteller and damper cook. With the dampers I experimented and they varied from cinnamon-fragrant cakes to flour omelettes you could bounce like a tennis ball.

From the Lennard the five-day horseback safari covered fifteen to twenty kilometres each day. We loaded one pack-horse with some basic tucker and the light mosquito-netted tents in case the two supply vehicles became hopelessly bogged. They did bog often. When one went down a snig chain was hooked on and the other pulled it out. Then the boys would go looking for a drier patch across the narrow floodplains. For the riders the mud was no more than a squelching sound under hooves, and crossing the creeks was fun. The packhorse frequently wanted to have a bath and we had to chase him out when he started to paw the water. The filly foal Bossyboots had a roll and swim in every creek and if I reined in her mother for just a second, Bossyboots fastened onto a teat. For all my years of riding it was a new experience to have a big foal draw alongside and leave me no room to dismount. Mulehead was always thirsty too. This colt's mother was the spare packhorse, broken in a few days before. So on the horse side of things it was a family affair. On the human side we had David White, a solicitor from New South Wales, and his daughter Edwina; a very modest man from Wyndham who I think was a carpenter and the artist Judy Prosser from Broome. Judy loved horses and was looking for artistic inspiration in the Leopolds.

When the horses were unsaddled and hobbled out it was an opportunity to go swimming in what might be the most pristine water on the planet with the choice of deep, shaded pools or swift-flowing currents. Then it was billy tea and damper fol-lowed by a bushwalk to a nearby waterfall. I pushed through the deep, newly green grass in leather leggings and urged everyone to walk in my tracks. Only two snakes were seen and one was a Kimberley tiger snake, a magnificent specimen a metre and a half long and displaying black bands on a light brown to orange skin.

Near the river camp we called 'the Rocks', where our 1999 expedition had left the Lennard to cross the Lady Forrest Range, the valley opened out into a plain more than a kilometre wide. In the distance with the ragged range behind them we saw Peter's horses. They were already aware of us and seemed to be waiting for some sign that we knew they were there, for seconds after the excited talk began we observed a moving scene.

It was Creamy who provided the show. 'Cut proud' as the saying goes, which means he still had the instincts of a stallion, he exploded across the plain towards us at full gallop. The next act was a pantomime of high leg-kicking, half-rears, bottom-smelling and intense nostril contact with our horses. My Bunuba friends closed in and from Peter's hand a lasso curled high, opened and fell neatly over Creamy's head. Creamy stood still – perhaps he knew struggle was fruitless, or maybe he craved that human smell again. At any rate Peter had a saddle on quicker than a human can set a campfire and Ralph sprang into the saddle. Creamy tossed in a couple of vigorous pigroots then Ralph gave him full rein across the plain and with big bold strides they reached the other horses. Far out on the plain the cream-coloured horse looked like a toy and the rider a stick on his back. Suddenly the horses glided through the tall green grass and formed a pack. Maybe it was a signal from Creamy, maybe mere instinct, but when Ralph turned and headed towards us the little herd followed him in.

Apart from Heather Campbell's two horses and George's Stallion Tom all the old crew were present. One Sock had grown a little, Johnny was fat, Star in his sleek coat looked like he'd be harder to mount than ever and I felt there would be no catching Blackjack until he was run into a yard. The old chestnut gelding had come down from the pass and the only sign of the bullet wound was small lump on his nose.

Peter didn't need Creamy so Ralph let him go. There seemed to be horses all around us and I wondered what would happen overnight. We talked about a gorge no one had been near for many years. Peter wanted to go in on horseback next morning. I thought the horses would scatter and there would be a big delay while we caught them. Looking up at this great gash in the range it was certain the last few hundred metres would have to be on foot and on the rock the heat can be like noon by mid-morning so we'd have to leave early. Sure enough, in the morning the horses had vanished, so at daylight I left with the guests on foot and Peter and the boys went horse-tracking.

The gorge proved to be another Kimberley jewel. In these merciless, arid ranges you simply can't believe nature to be capable of such paradoxes. Damp with sweat and a little breathless we struggled out of the cane grass to find ourselves beside a river that tumbled through the magnificent gap in the range. I waded out into the water for a better view of the deep pools locked between vertical cliffs and there between my legs was a little freshwater crocodile. It had no fear: I was simply another creature.

We would all have loved to have taken a whitewater roller-coaster ride through the gorge to the other side of the range. It looked safe enough, but there was no possibility of a return without ropes and sundry mountaineering equipment. The heart of the gorge would keep its secrets for the time being.

Peter's first packhorse run with the tourists was a great success. We were privileged to see the King Leopolds in the lushness following the heaviest wet known since white occupation. Other packhorse trips were planned for the future.

While the dam is off the agenda, the Kimberley will in time be developed. There are already plans to seal the Gibb River road between Derby and Kununurra. In my view, development doesn't have to be anti-environment. Creative, eco-friendly tourism could save the Kimberleys and the Pindan region around Broome. An unpolluted coastline is also essential for Broome's key industry: pearling.

There are people who want Broome and the Kimberleys left alone, but this is unrealistic. Australians are waking up to the unique beauty of the Kimberleys, and if increased airline competition reduces fares, the tourists will come in droves. Such natural beauty is becoming rare on the planet and the more people who see the Kimberleys the better, for they will return home and spread the word it must be saved.

When I drank the water from the Fitzroy I didn't think much about the melodramatic comment: 'you will come back and here you will die one day' but the Kimberleys and Broome had thrown out the lasso and it was tightening around me. Already Sal and I had plans to go back. Sal loved the region, a photographer's dream, and I had promised to help Peter flush out the feral bulls for the bull catcher. Brian Shadforth, who acted as camp cook on the safari, had offered to take me mangrove fishing: a fishing line in one hand and a .308 in the other to stop yourself becoming a crock meal! I would have plenty to write about.

Author's Notes

1. Some Notes on Geographic Names in *Wild Horses Don't Swim*
The traditional owners of the Precipice Range area were
invited by the Western Australian Geographic Names Committee to submit Aboriginal names for the features referred to in
this book as 'the Galleon' and 'the Mule Range'. The committee was advised that 'the Galleon' is known to the traditional
owners as Mount Banggalarowi – the Bat Dreaming: 'This hill
he nearly collapsed and bats pushed it back.' This name is now
officially gazetted for all new maps.

No name for what I call 'the Mule Range' has been forth-
coming from the traditional owners. The maps on page xiii use
Mule Range as a temporary name.

In May 2000 it was discovered that one of the most impressive
and deep gorges in the west Kimberley does not appear on any
map. The traditional owners are the Bunuba people, and their
name for the gorge is Winjuwiy. The location of the gorge and
this name has been submitted to the W.A. Geographic Names
Committee.

Love and respect for any land is demonstrated in names.
A region of no geographic names is neglected, shunned,

forgotten. The traditional Aboriginal place names should be revived wherever possible.

2. Sanctuary Planned for the Kimberleys

Hailed as the world's first conservation company, Earth Sanctuaries Limited is a public company formed to secure twenty-five native animal and bird sanctuaries across Australia within twenty-five years. Earth Sanctuaries Foundation is the company's 'not for profit' arm. It seeks membership and financial support to tackle the most pressing environmental problems.

Earth Sanctuaries Limited plans to acquire 250 000 hectares of the Kimberleys as an endangered species reserve. Species at risk in the area include the orange leaf-nosed bat, pygmy long-eared bat, yellow-lipped bat, Carpentarian dunnart, monjon, Lakeland Downs mouse, narbalek, scaly-tailed possum and golden-backed tree rat.

To save these native animals is a huge job, as it entails erecting a feral-proof fence and eradication of all feral animals within the reserve.

3. The Role of Fire in the Kimberleys

A quote from Greg Martin, project supervisor for Earth Sanctuaries Limited, aptly applies to the King Leopold Ranges. I have reproduced it with his kind permission. (Note however, that instead of ten-year fire cycles, the Kimberleys are faced with big fires every dry season.)

In many areas of Australia, such as the Blue Mountains, the Adelaide Hills and Mount Macedon in Victoria, periodic large bushfires occur. These fires usually happen around every ten years or so and are horrific in their intensity and destruction. One of the major causes of these destructive fires is the absence now of the small native mammals. It was their niche in nature to clean up the bush understorey. Without these animals, huge fuel loads build up which lead to extremely hot and intense fires. When the animals were present, fuel loads were minimised and any fires that did occur were slower, cooler and less intense. Secondly, once this cycle of hot intense fires had started, it favoured vegetation and animals that could survive it, further strengthening the cycle. This is not a normal occurrence, as can be seen in the Yarra valley in the Healesville area of Victoria. The skeletons of the massive mountain ash killed in the 1930 fire can be easily seen. Mountain ash are killed by relatively small fires. This was the first fire this forest had seen for a thousand years.

Also available from Bantam

THE HORSES TOO ARE GONE
Michael Keenan

The drought had reached crisis point. Cattle farmer Mike Keenan decided there was only one solution: he would have to get his starving cattle – and his beloved horses – to greener pastures north of the border. But when he finally got there he found his troubles had only just begun. South-west Queensland seemed like a modern-day Wild West, and as Keenan moved his cattle along the traditional droving routes in search of long-term pasture, he had to match wits with a host of characters – as well as Nature herself.

The Horses Too Are Gone is the true story of Keenan's struggle to survive against mounting odds, and it's an action-packed adventure that rivals any fiction. A fresh voice from the Bush, Mike Keenan writes with a deep passion and knowledge of Australian life on the land, tinged with a sadness and nostalgia for a way of life that is under threat. *The Horses Too Are Gone* will strike a chord with all Australians.

Bantam Books
ISBN 0 73380 167 6